Doing the *Work* of Equity Leadership for Justice and Systems Change

Doing the *Work* of Equity Leadership for Justice and Systems Change

Edited by
Decoteau J. Irby
and Ann M. Ishimaru

Afterword by Keisha Scarlett

Teachers College Press
Teachers College, Columbia University

Published by Teachers College Press,® 1234 Amsterdam Avenue, New York, NY 10027

Chapter 4 was originally published as Ishimaru, Ann M., Irby, Decoteau J., and Green, Terrance. The Paradox of Organizational Double Jeopardy: PK–12 Equity Directors in Radicalized and Gendered Educational Systems, *The Urban Review,* Vol. 55, 364–392, 2023, Springer Nature.

Front cover photos: Sun by Ravi Sharma, Clouds by Sam Schooler; both via Unsplash.

Library of Congress Cataloging-in-Publication Data is available at loc.gov

ISBN 978-0-8077-8748-9 (paper)
ISBN 978-0-8077-8749-6 (hardcover)
ISBN 978-0-8077-8329-0 (ebook)

Printed on acid-free paper
Manufactured in the United States of America

Contents

Acknowledgments

The research that informs this book was made possible in part through the generous support of a Spencer Foundation Large Grant award for our study, "Leadership Activity in the Era of the Equity Director: Racial-Historical Contexts, Proliferation, and District Organizational Change."

We deeply appreciate our colleague Muhammad Khalifa for bringing us to Minnesota for the conference, where we had the first lunchtime conversation that birthed this research project; Ben Herold for helping us connect our work to a broader audience; and Jay Braunstein for the editorial support that helped us finish this book under a tight timeline. Thank you to the individuals who contributed to the book. We thank our research team members Brian Colar, Shannon Paige Clark, Ahreum Han, Jeremy Horne, Fannie Martinez, and Taylor Smith for supporting various stages of our project design, data collection, and analysis.

Thank you, Terrance Green, for your thoughtful partnership, collaboration, and friendship over the years. This project would not be possible without your contributions. Finally, we extend our sincere thanks and love to our families and friends.

Doing the *Work* of Equity Leadership for Justice and Systems Change

Introduction

Wake Up

Decoteau J. Irby and Ann M. Ishimaru

Doing the Work *of Equity Leadership for Justice and Systems Change* is a story of district-level education leadership within and across school systems. The leadership pursuits of educational equity and justice that we explore grew in prominence after George Zimmerman shot and killed a 16-year-old unarmed Black boy named Trayvon Martin in 2012. After six weeks and in response to growing protests and calls for justice, Florida police arrested Zimmerman on charges of second-degree murder, only for him to be acquitted a year and some months later. He was free. It hurt. Infuriated, we marched, as people had done in years past. This time, people marched with hoodies—we'd like to think a million hoodies. It was not the first—or sadly, the last—time a Black youth would be killed, but this particular incident seeded the Black Lives Matter movement and catalyzed presidential action to address racism.

On July 19, 2013, President Barack Obama addressed America from the White House. In a rare moment of racial candor, he shared, "When Trayvon Martin was first shot, I said that this could have been my son. Another way of saying that is Trayvon Martin could have been me 35 years ago. And when you think about why, in the African American community at least, there's a lot of pain around what happened here, I think it's important to recognize that the African American community is looking at this issue through a *set of experiences and a history that doesn't go away*" (2013). In 2014, Obama instructed the Department of Education to distribute a Dear Colleague letter addressed directly to school districts about their responsibilities for addressing racism, specifically the need to redress racial disparities in school discipline. We claim this convergence of events compelled school districts throughout the United States to invest in activities that educators across the country refer to as "doing the work" of equity leadership.

The fight for justice in education is not new. Educators and communities have led struggles to realize education as a form of liberation and self-determination amid colonization, enslavement, Indian boarding schools, and deeply segregated systems. In the past decades, court battles and protests aimed at school desegregation characterized the 1950s and 1960s, followed by the emergence of Black independent schools and reforms focused on community control of schools. Prior to the Obama years, the standards and accountability movement purported to leave no child behind, even as high-stakes testing and neoliberal policies often deepened racialized academic disparities (Au, 2022) and organizers built a national movement to dismantle the school-to-prison pipeline (Warren et al., 2022). Leadership for educational equity and justice has followed neither a steady linear progression nor a one-size-fits-all approach. And because U.S. public schools serve multiracial, multilingual, and transnational student populations across a broad geography and communities, the fight for justice, democracy, and human rights varies by era and region.

As with past pursuits, educational leaders have taken up various approaches to fight for educational justice from within formal systems, each best understood alongside the sociopolitical and racial-historical contexts in which they occur. Many accounts of educational leadership are snapshots in time or memoir-like individual narratives. In this book, we open up the "black box" of equity and justice-focused systems change to examine leadership activities across a particular era in U.S. public education. The era is characterized by polarizing cultural politics, a seemingly endless tug of war between different racial-ideological factions, and technologies and social media that bring injustices to our fingertips in real time at a dizzying pace. The practices and approaches we highlight offer crucial learnings to continue the "work," even as dark falls—bringing harm to vulnerable communities, power to oppressive ideologies, and autocratic mandates to undermine democracy in public education.

UNDERSTANDING EQUITY LEADERSHIP

We started this project wanting to understand how efforts to make schools more just and equitable changed and proliferated across space and time—as well as the resistance and pushback that entrenched the status quo. We use the terms "equity" and "justice" to recognize the ways that concepts and language have evolved across time, from a focus on meeting every student's needs and leveling opportunities to dismantling oppressive policies and practices and providing the conditions for all young people's thriving and dignity in a pluralistic society (Irby, Anderson, et al., 2022). We do take these terms to signal different, albeit consonant, motives.

We define "equity" not merely as equal opportunity, but as fairness in processes and outcomes within the context of historical, economic, social, and institutional forces that have resulted in an uneven playing field, particularly for students marginalized by formal educational systems due to minoritized identities (race, gender/gender identity, sexual orientation, disability, citizenship, language, religion, etc.). Our use of "justice," meanwhile, gestures toward broader aims to redress past wrongs, reclaim silenced knowledges and practices, transform oppressive power and systems, and realize self-determined and liberatory futures. Although equity leadership in this book is largely situated within formal systems, we see its aims as part of broader efforts to realize justice both within and beyond schools. Likewise, "systems change" refers not only to school districts but, as we signal in the conclusion, to the need to transform the broader systems that consequentially shape the lives of young people and communities.

We argue that the work of equity leadership for justice and systems change must be understood in the context of the 2008 election of Barack Obama, where districts were compelled—through a confluence of federal guidance, social media–fueled moments, and mass protests—to professionalize and resource equity leadership and advocacy from within school systems. The work of equity leadership must also be examined in relation to the enduring and entrenched legacy of school-based racism that has been bolstered by the re-emergence of far-right conservatism in the forms of anti-intellectual Tea Party politics, the xenophobic birtherism movement, and virulent backlash against anything associated with "diversity, equity, and inclusion" efforts to level the playing field.

These rising conservative sentiments reached a fever pitch in the form of the Make America Great Again (MAGA) movement. Its proponents, their autocratic politicians, and their neoconservative ideologues have worked as hard to dismantle historical and recent advances as educators have worked to realize justice in education (Siegel-Hawley et al., 2023). Amid the current firestorm, the efforts of the past near-decade risk being burned away like the books ultraconservative forces are so eager to ban, but the experiences captured in this book are a testament to a longer arc of change.

Throughout this time, leaders have adopted practices to alter the fabric of districts and schools in ways that are often overlooked or unrecognized. Across time, the educator workforce has begun to better reflect the racial demographics of students (Ingersoll et al., 2021). Students have more access to reading materials and curricula that more accurately reflect the racial, ethnic, and cultural diversity of the United States (Sleeter & Zavala, 2020). In many districts, schools, and youth-serving organizations, gender-nonconforming students have restroom options that affirm their identities. Students of all races and ethnicities have opportunities to organize affinity and coalition spaces as well as celebrate and learn from heritage months, national holidays (like Juneteenth), and Black Lives Matter weeks (Au & Hagopian, 2017). Zero tolerance and its overreliance on school-based suspensions and expulsions have decreased, with many schools attempting to adopt restorative approaches as alternatives to punishment (Lodi et al.,

2021). More teachers and leaders understand the language and practice of culturally responsive teaching, trauma-informed approaches, and socioemotional learning. Gathering and listening to student voices has become a central strategy for motivating change in many districts (Zion, 2020). Districts have increasingly taken up more robust forms of family and community collaboration (Ishimaru, 2020). And the routine use of data beyond conventional test score metrics—especially in the form of surveys and qualitative data—to identify and address inequities has proliferated in schools and districts across the country (Takahashi et al., 2025).

Yet even amidst such changes, by conventional standards, the prospect that U.S. education systems will ever enable the thriving of marginalized students remains as bleak today as it was in generations past. By most indicators—discipline, pushout, attendance, test scores, graduation rates, socioemotional wellness, sense of belonging, and more—the education debt remains unpaid, particularly to Black, Indigenous, and intersectionally minoritized students (Ladson-Billings, 2006). For us, such sobering statistics say more about the entrenched oppressive systems that leaders work against, the subtle and overt resistance they face in their everyday work, and the broader societal inequities that are mirrored in schools than they do about any particular group of leaders' commitments and efforts in the distant, near past, or today.

So what, then, can we make of equity and justice work in these recent times? *These times* when school districts hired cultural proficiency and inclusiveness directors, executive directors of equity, and deputy chiefs of equity, to name a few. *These times* when districts asked equity leaders to draw on their lived experiences and expertise to design and implement districtwide strategies to improve the social, emotional, and academic experiences and outcomes of students who districts traditionally underserved (Irby, Green, et al., 2022). When leaders, mostly people of color and women, wrote and implemented policies and plans, formed cross-departmental teams to lead change, and leveraged data to foster adult learning about inequities. *These times* when leaders influenced policies to account for minoritized student concerns, experiences, voices, and outcomes in district deliberations. *These times* of perils and possibilities.

LIFE CYCLES OF LEADERSHIP WORK: MORNINGS, MIDDAYS, AND EVENINGS

In this book, we account for the emergence and waning of systems-based education justice efforts through a theme of daily cycles—mornings, middays, and evenings—to acknowledge the lessons of days past; remember the ancestral knowledge, cultural practices, and resistance strategies that have long sustained Black, Indigenous, Asian, Pasifika, and Latinx communities;

and consider the perils and possibilities that exist for the future. *Wake-ups* reflect events that bring attention to a long-standing problem: in our case, the school-based educational injustices. *Mornings* are the periods when leaders engage in activities (policy development, framing issues, etc.) that set the stage for more outward-facing *midday* work to institutionalize equity processes and expand activity and capacities. *Evenings* are periods where highly visible justice and equity leadership become more constrained. *Nights* are times when leaders rest, plan, regroup, and resist, knowing that a new morning will require renewed, and perhaps different, approaches to the fight for justice.

The leadership practices we explore in this book grew from several wake-ups, such as the 2012 killing of Black teenager Trayvon Martin by vigilante George Zimmerman (who was acquitted of murder in 2013), the emergence of the Black Lives Matter movement in education (Dixson, 2018), and the Obama administrations' civil rights in education agenda (Siegel-Hawley et al., 2023). And then, Ferguson uprisings and continued resistance against the war on society's most vulnerable populations (Hill, 2016). These events and more were springboards into the "morning" work of creating new formal equity leadership roles in U.S. districts. These leaders did the work of writing and implementing policies; established equity goals, missions, and visions; and fought for organizational resources that ushered in a brief midday of equity leadership, when national and state conditions provided more conducive sociopolitical conditions than was the case in years past.

In 2020, the COVID-19 global health pandemic and national outcry against Minneapolis police officer Derek Chauvin and his fellow officers' extrajudicial murder of George Floyd catalyzed a racial reckoning that gave district equity leadership more momentum. The events triggered sociopolitical conditions and just enough national consciousness-raising about matters of anti-Black racism and settler colonialism to enable leaders to institutionalize equity processes, goals, and plans to fight against the damaging impact of conservative ideologies (Lewis-Durham, 2020) and MAGA-inspired and -coordinated political attacks. Neoconservatives used the Biden administration's tenure to organize their resurgence and codify their political agenda in Project 2025. These attacks ushered in death threats against equity leaders and book bans and culminated with the Trump administration's coordinated attacks on diversity, equity, and inclusion; LGBTQ+ and immigrant rights; freedom of speech; and, ultimately, public education.

BOOK ORGANIZATION

The book is organized into three sections that map onto our morning, midday, and evening framework. Each section begins with Black women narrating the strategies they employed within school systems and concludes with research chapters that offer a bird's-eye perspective on the work in each respective period. The morning work section presents the early "behind the scenes/getting ready" equity leadership work that laid the initial foundation for the work that came later. In Chapters 1 and 2, authors Latish Reed and Shannon Paige Clark offer readers insights into the experiences of Black women who were the first to step into the precarious work of equity leadership. Next, in Chapter 3, Decoteau Irby, Ann Ishimaru, and Terrance Green present the various ways that districts organized and resourced these leadership roles and conclude Part I by detailing the ways leaders reconfigured the roles, pushed their organizations to more adequately resource their efforts, and influenced the approaches and frameworks that came to define the field.

Part II, "Midday Work," consists of three chapters that offer insights into highly visible and formal equity leadership activities aimed at impacting entire school districts. By midday, leaders usually had adequate resources and enough formal authority to do their work. Yet challenges remained. In Chapter 5, readers learn about the work Teresa Lance led as her district's second formal equity leader and the racial battle fatigue that she didn't expect to encounter. In Chapter 6, we learn about how Maurice Swinney confronted the organizational urge to put out fires and create equity programs and initiatives by thinking like a designer to introduce innovative equity routines and tools that would sustain his district's work. Finally, Andrew Matschiner and Ishmael Miller pan out to explore a 2022 national survey of equity leaders that revealed that what leaders were actually doing differed from what they thought they should be doing.

Part III, "Evening Work," explores what happens when people doing the work of equity leadership rightfully grow tired of waiting on their organizations to do better. In Chapter 8, Constance Daw, Fannie Martinez, and Ann Ishimaru explain how a group of Black women principals took a district's equity activities into their own hands after years of witnessing the district leadership struggle to enact wide-scale changes. While Daw and colleagues show how leaders look within their district for solidarity and support, author Dayna Muñiz follows up in Chapter 9 with an exploration of how leaders seek support outside of their districts in regional and national equity leader networks. In Chapter 10 Ahreum Han and Decoteau Irby conclude Part III by acknowledging the reality of leadership turnover, which they argue is likely a defining feature of this stressful, dangerous, and underappreciated leadership work.

Although mornings, middays, and evenings mark distinct periods of the evolution of equity leadership work, they share the constancy of oppression, resistance, pushback, and institutional violence. Colleagues, community members, and strangers sent nasty emails, showed up to board meetings to berate leaders, and made vitriolic social media posts. Employers attempted to silence and dismiss the work. Parents questioned their qualifications for the job. Indeed, if there is one shortcoming of this book, it is that we understate the level and frequency of vitriolic resistance, threats to physical and psychological safety, and day-to-day microaggressions that people doing the work of equity leadership experience. But the ceaseless and escalating pushback were not the only constants. We hope the chapters in this book also illuminate the creativity, strategy, fortitude, conviction, and power of equity leaders changing institutions and the educational experiences of young people in schools.

EVIDENCE BASE

We compiled this book by drawing on nearly a decade of primary research and partnership work with leaders in U.S. school districts. In 2017, we and our colleague Terrance Green were having lunch at a conference at the University of Minnesota and struck up a conversation about our friends and colleagues who had stepped into newly created district equity leadership roles. We knew little about what our friends and colleagues were up to and decided that we should design a study to learn about their new roles and experiences. That conversation set us on a journey that grew from an initial in-depth interview study of 13 equity leaders to a multiyear, multidistrict case study; a small-scale national survey; and over 9 years of direct engagement with equity leaders across the United States to understand, support, and advocate for their work. This book's contributing authors include researchers and practitioners who have influenced our own thinking about this work. But our insights and perspectives reflect particular contexts.

The leadership insights contained in the book are about districts, schools, and leaders who let us researchers into their business. Most of the research represents district leadership in Democratic-leaning or purple battleground states. All of the stories told in this book stem from liberal- and progressive-minded school districts that were open to equity and, furthermore, approved their employees' participation in our research projects and professional learning opportunities. Over the years, we made site visits; sat in on Zoom meetings; conducted observations, focus groups, and interviews; and dug into district data dashboards in an effort to understand what it means to do *the work*, the colloquialism people used most often to name their leadership. We have also conducted professional learning sessions and presented together at research and practitioner conferences; these activities helped coalesce and evolve our thinking while providing feedback and validation from the broader field. As much as possible, we have masked participants by using pseudonyms for their districts and schools and changing exact details throughout the book.

As thoughtful as we tried to be in exploring the work of equity leadership, this book tells a partial story that is skewed toward positive stories of people who were able to keep showing up to workplaces that often impeded their work and threatened their well-being. The leadership stories that are not accounted for in the book are more dire. They often play out in the South and Southeast and in conservative states and districts that refused our request for research participation. In sharing our work with the field, we recognize that there are other stories of suppression, toxicity, and pushout, as well as hidden efforts that need to remain hidden. While we understand what happens to leaders who are silenced, those voices and stories are not presented here in keeping with the ethical standards that guide our approach to social science research as well as our desire to be in solidarity with those whose work better serves children when not made visible. We understand why they couldn't be included. Leading for equity and justice in certain geographic and political contexts is more precarious than in those covered in this book—their days are shorter and their nights are longer.

WHY THIS BOOK

When we set out to write this book, we did so for leaders, educators, and advocates who wake up each day, get dressed, and go to work to undo the small and large injustices that children experience in U.S. school systems. They experience these injustices because they happen to be Black, Indigenous, racially minoritized, immigrant, gender nonconforming, low income, housing or caretaker insecure, neurodiverse, disabled, undocumented, or do not speak English as their first language in their home and community. We wrote this book to shed light on the work that has been underway in U.S. schools, led disproportionately by Black women, to help people appreciate the struggle for equity within school systems. We wanted to accomplish three interlocking goals.

First, we want readers to understand the contours of K–12 equity leadership, not solely as ethical commitments or ideals that guide leaders but as specific practices and forms of activity that seek to change the interactions, processes, structures, and functioning of schools and educational systems. We want to convey what the work is and what it is not. We want to be forthright about what the work of equity leadership can reasonably accomplish and, in doing so, position district and school-based equity leadership in relation to other strategies for working toward educational equity and justice, such as legal cases, community or union organizing, and federal or state policy reform. We argue that the courts, policy, and organizing may be crucial levers for realizing educational justice, but change in education ultimately relies on *people* within schools and districts to implement actions in the course of their everyday activity across time. Despite the relatively recent emergence of formal roles charged with leading equity work, educators have long led equity-focused change in districts and schools. We want to make their approaches and complex theories of change visible. And we want to invite you to attend not only to superintendents or equity directors but to the multiple people and roles in schools, districts, and communities who shape equity work in small and substantial ways.

Second, we want readers to develop a strategy orientation. Since beginning this research project in 2016, district, school, community, and parent-leader groups from across the country have asked us for a "playbook" that can guide their work. We observed people grappling with how to assess the progress and lack thereof. While we do not offer a playbook or suggest specific progress indicators, we do offer readers insights into what organizing, strategy, developing processes, and planning and laying the groundwork for subsequent action and progress entail.

Third, and most importantly, we want equity leaders to apply the lessons and insights shared in this book to their own work. The work of equity leadership looks different in different places and times. Although the chapters are each situated in particular contexts and moments, we believe that critically applying insights from these pages will strengthen equity leaders' capacities to achieve deep, long-lasting changes that improve learning, opportunities and well-being for children, young people, and communities. We hope it reminds educators to be adaptive and to lean on critical reflection, collective care, and holistic well-being to sustain and build on the work that leaders have done in this most recent cycle. Today's *night* offers the time to rest, dream, and prepare for tomorrow. We also recognize that it was under the cover of dark that the underground railroad happened. The *work* must change, but it continues on.

As we wrapped up the book project in early 2025, this book took on expanded significance. In February, Trump's Department of Education issued a Dear Colleague letter that initiated an attempt to erase over a decade of educational efforts to mitigate the enduring racism of U.S. schools. This book works against this attempted erasure. It is for a broad array of people interested in education and beyond—not only educators and administrators but also elected officials; families; community leaders; those curious about systems-based "diversity, equity, and inclusion"; and anyone who seeks to lead deep justice-centered change in education. Now more than ever, we hope this book helps you appreciate the necessity of equity leadership as an essential aspect of creating a more just society.

REFERENCES

Au, W. (2022). *Unequal by design: High-stakes testing and the standardization of inequality*. Routledge.

Au, W., & Hagopian, J. (2017). How one elementary school sparked a citywide movement to make Black students' lives matter. *Rethinking Schools, 32*(1), 11–18.

Dixson, A. D. (2018). "What's going on?": A critical race theory perspective on Black Lives Matter and activism in education. *Urban Education, 53*(2), 231–247.

Hill, M. L. (2016). *Nobody: Casualties of America's war on the vulnerable, from Ferguson to Flint and beyond.* Simon & Schuster.

Ingersoll, R., Merrill, E., Stuckey, D., Collins, G., & Harrison, B. (2021). The demographic transformation of the teaching force in the United States. *Education Sciences, 11*(5), 234. https://doi.org/10.3390/educsci11050234

Irby, D. J., Green, T., & Ishimaru, A. M. (2022). PK–12 district leadership for equity: An exploration of director role configurations and vulnerabilities. *American Journal of Education, 128*(3), 417–453.

Irby, D., Anderson, C., & Payne, C. (Eds.) (2022). *Dignity-affirming education: Cultivating the somebodiness of students and educators.* Teachers College Press.

Ishimaru, A. M. (2020). *Just schools: Building equitable collaborations with families and communities.* Teachers College Press.

Ladson-Billings, G. (2006). From the achievement gap to the education debt: Understanding achievement in US schools. *Educational Researcher, 35*(7), 3–12.

Lewis-Durham, T. (2020). "All lives matter": How districts co-opt equity language and maintain the status quo. *Education Policy Analysis Archives, 28*, 141–141.

Lodi, E., Perrella, L., Lepri, G. L., Scarpa, M. L., & Patrizi, P. (2021). Use of restorative justice and restorative practices at school: A systematic literature review. *International Journal of Environmental Research and Public Health, 19*(1), 96.

Obama, B. (2013). *Remarks by the president on Trayvon Martin. James S. Brady Press Briefing Room.* White House Office of Press Secretary. https://obama whitehouse.archives.gov/the-press-office/2013/07/19/remarks-PRESIDENT -TRAYVON-MARTIN

Siegel-Hawley, G., Frankenberg, E., McDermott, K., McCollum, S., Scott, J., & DeBray, E. (2023). Small advances and swift retreat: Race-conscious educational policy in the Obama and Trump administrations. *Education Policy Analysis Archives, 31*(28).

Sleeter, C. E., & Zavala, M. (2020). *Transformative ethnic studies in schools: Curriculum, pedagogy, and research.* Teachers College Press.

Takahashi, S., Sandoval, C., Jackson, B., Cunningham, J., & Taylor, C. (2025). Practical measurement for equity and justice. *Frontiers in Education, 9.* http://dx .doi.org/10.3389/feduc.2024.1442505

Warren, M. R. (2022). *Willful defiance: The movement to dismantle the school-to-prison pipeline.* Oxford University Press.

Zion, S. (2020). Transformative student voice: Extending the role of youth in addressing systemic marginalization in US schools. *Multiple Voices for Ethnically Diverse Exceptional Learners, 20*(1), 32–43.

Part I

MORNING WORK

CHAPTER 1

Beyond Visions and Missions

Navigating Resistance to LGBTQIA+ Protections in Schools

Latish Reed

I sat in my office, waiting. Sure enough, the call came from the administrative assistant, summoning me to my boss's office. When I arrived at the office, Shari, my boss, was there with Tim, the head of human resources, and Alice, my human resources equity counterpart. I wasn't shaken—I knew this was coming.

Today, Lakeside City Public Schools' (LCPS) nondiscrimination policy reads, "Discrimination, bullying, and/or harassment on the basis of gender identity, gender expression, or gender nonconformity are prohibited within LPSD." The policy exists in large part because of the equity leadership work I, a Black cisgender woman, led when the district hired me as the first equity administrator. LCPS, the state's largest district, educates about 70,000 students with over 10,000 staff members. The district serves over 90% students of color, which include Black, Hispanic/Latino, Asian, and Native American. Eighty-five percent of students receive free or reduced lunch, and 20% require special education services. Over time, LCPS's struggle with equity has yielded inequitable academic outcomes, particularly for students of color. Although challenging, LCPS continues the work to address longstanding obstacles by focusing on equity, access, and culturally responsive practices. A significant part of my charge was protecting and supporting LGBTQIA+ students.

The district's vision and mission boldly professed to ensure the right of all students to access a quality education. But as I learned during my time serving as the first equity specialist, all does not always mean *all.* LGBTQIA+ youth often deal with unwelcoming, unsafe, and unsupportive environments. Students are experiencing verbal and physical harassment and assault based on their sexual and gender identities. Kosciw et al. (2016) note that LGBTQIA+ students often have lower academic achievement and higher rates of absenteeism. They suffer more from depression, anxiety, and lower self-esteem than their peers. They are at greater risk of dropping out of school and have a lower probability of postsecondary education. The results of the Youth Risk Behavior Survey (YRBS) indicate that the experiences of LCPS students who identified as LGBTQIA+ are similar.

When I took on the equity leadership role, I felt more than ready to help the district create inclusive policies to address the needs of all students, regardless of their identities. I earned my PhD in educational leadership and policy analysis from the University of Wisconsin–Madison, where I studied with experts who researched and developed best practices to support LGBTQIA+ students. Under the guidance of Dr. Colleen Capper, I learned about the many challenges LGBTQIA+ students face in navigating school environments. As an assistant professor, I researched and published an empirical case study on a school leader who successfully supported LGBTQIA+ students (Reed & Johnson, 2010). I had the necessary academic preparation. I was equipped with the knowledge. I also appreciated the opportunity to work under the leadership of a Black woman superintendent, a Black woman director, and a direct report who was also a Black woman. My closest colleague, Alice, whose work to create LGBTQIA+ protections for faculty and staff complimented mine, was also a Black woman. Stepping into the role, I felt seen and heard. Thus, I did not anticipate the resistance and challenges that would unfold as I worked to implement protections and resources for LGBTQIA+ students.

In this chapter, I tell the story of revising the district's nondiscrimination policies to integrate gender-inclusive protections for students and staff. I explain how the policy eventually passed by focusing on my sphere of control and, at a point, using my sphere of influence to engage supporters, other networks, and crucial decision-makers. While these efforts were met with resistance, policy creation has laid the groundwork for the equity leadership practices we now see in districts throughout the country. The kinds of largely invisible work I did provided the framework for subsequent leaders to do what they do. Not only do written policies and procedures ensure ongoing accountability for school equity, they promote a deeper understanding of what is required to serve students best. With the current wave of resistance to all things equity, leaders must continue to do the work to ensure policies remain in place and are used to affect change. This is important, not only because of the rights of and benefits to students but because the policies stem from years of significant scaffolding and efforts.

THE FACE OF RESISTANCE IN CENTRAL OFFICE

I was hired to create LGBTQIA+ policy in the district. Many organizations include the word "equity" in their vision and mission, and these statements are essential. However, it is critical to formally commit to equity through policies, procedures, and official practice. Brian Juchems is the senior director of education and policy at GSAFE, which has worked with school districts for over 20 years to adopt inclusive policies and practices. He said, "Adopting policies that explicitly include protections based on gender identity and sexual orientation [sends] clear messages to all students and members of the school community that trans and queer youth belong, have value, and are worthy of dignity and respect" (B. Juchems, personal communication, October 16, 2024).

I knew it was coming. Typically, in a large bureaucratic urban school system, someone with a "specialist" title would never send a direct email to the superintendent. But that day, I did. The ongoing resistance I faced to revise the district's nondiscrimination policy to be more gender inclusive had reached a boiling point. This resistance came from within our own rank of district leaders, most of whom shared my racial identity. It felt imperative to update our superintendent on my work and to inform her of the obstacles I had encountered. In the email, copied to my boss, the deputy superintendent of human resources (a white man), and the senior leadership team, I also shared that while progress had been made in planning, I had not received the necessary approvals from my direct reports to move forward to put the LGBTQIA+ nondiscrimination policy in place.

Up until this point, my efforts to change policies and practices related to LGBTQIA+ students faced significant pushback. Tim, my white male colleague and Alice's boss, was responsible for supporting district staff and had also not been responsive to Alice's requests for approval to implement LGBTQIA+ protections. I alerted Alice about my plan to send the email that morning and asked if she wanted to be included in the email. Her response was an emphatic yes. Alice urged me to reiterate in the email our collaborative efforts to ensure that our district would implement best practices, protections, and policies for both students and staff.

Shortly after being hired, and a few months prior to the infamous email, the superintendent invited me to an impromptu lunch. At lunch, I shared my initial impressions and preliminary plans, and she inquired about any progress made in gender inclusion protections. Reiterating her support, she instructed me to contact her directly if I faced any significant barriers. While I never planned to go over my boss's head, after several months of roadblocks, I recalled the superintendent's open invitation and decided I had nothing to lose. If the work wasn't getting done, a trail of ineptness would ultimately lead back to me, the new equity lady.

In an effort to establish policies and procedures to support LGBTQIA+ students, I held meetings with directors, managers, and department leaders responsible for implementing gender-inclusive best practices within curriculum and student programming. Spanning four months, I met with individuals from communication, curriculum, leadership, psychology, social work, school counseling, and student services to gather input and formulate suggestions for policy updates within LCPS. Prior to these meetings, I was not aware of anyone's personal preferences, biases, or identities as they related to LGBTQIA+ topics. Nor did I see that as relevant. My approach was not considered warm and fuzzy. Instead, I put information before school personnel and inquired how we would implement these best practices to protect the needs and rights of our students. This approach did not garner much leverage or success. Most attendees did not talk in the short meetings, nor did they respond to follow-up communications.

One day, this avoidance culminated in a volatile meeting where Genevieve, my senior director, unloaded on me in front of others. Several managers and directors were there to discuss possible inroads on specific items like curriculum and student service name identification. Like most meetings, I was doing most of the talking. However, about halfway into the meeting, Genevieve completely erupted, voicing her frustration with my persistence on this topic when, in her mind, we should have been focusing solely on Black children. Her attacks became personal. In a yelling voice, she claimed it was outrageous to focus on gender identity instead of race, given that most of our students were Black. While I understood the need to address racial inequities, I also knew that LGBTQIA+ students, many of whom were students of color, faced compounded discrimination due to intersecting identities of race and gender.

I had reached my breaking point. As I began to cry, some colleagues looked shocked and tried to console me. I abruptly ended the meeting and while most people left hurriedly, a few stayed to talk and offer support. Those colleagues who stayed expressed being on board with the work I was doing and discomfort in voicing their opinions due to the leaders' stances and fear of backlash. It was unfortunate that it took me coming to tears for them to come forward and for me to understand the culture and climate related to gender-inclusive student protections. This experience helped me understand the avoidance and resistance I had encountered up to that point.

Shortly after this experience, I wrote the memo to the superintendent. Although I never heard back directly, soon after, my boss Shari gave me directives to move forward with my proposed plans. Shari assured me that she supported me and the work that needed to be done. This felt like a win to me! While feeling slightly bruised by the previous encounters, I was excited to facilitate the plans and looked forward to creating a more inclusive environment for LCPS. I scheduled meetings with the other deputy superintendents to discuss policy drafts and ideas for implementation. Some of these leaders were initially neutral, while others were resistant. However, because the superintendent required them to engage, they interacted professionally and provided the necessary information to move the policy and practices forward. I developed a more empathetic leadership disposition in those meetings by listening to and understanding their expertise.

As I got to know more about the decision-makers and their stances, it became clear that most of them struggled with their dispositions based on their upbringing. Their feelings of unease challenged them to stand by the policy. It became my charge to help facilitate open, honest conversations to support them to move beyond their ideologies and toward serving all students. For example, I listened to one of the deputy superintendents discuss how, when she grew up, anyone associated with being gay was shunned. I was intentional about not shaming her for her upbringing but clarified that it was her responsibility to make better choices for LCPS students. One of the norms I use when facilitating equity discussions is to "get comfortable being uncomfortable." Indeed, when I encountered open resistance and hostility for working to adjust our practices to support LGBTQIA+ students and when I was called to my boss's office for contacting the superintendent, those were two extremely uncomfortable days during my tenure as an equity leader. However, overcoming moments like these ultimately led to productive discussions and planning, resulting in a formal revision of our district's nondiscrimination policy.

CONFRONTING HOSTILE LEGISLATION: THE NEED FOR LGBTQIA+ PROTECTIONS IN SCHOOLS

Since I worked to pass the policy in Lakeside, LGBTQIA+ experiences have been made worse with a wave of recent legislation that, in some ways, legalizes the trauma experienced by students. According to GLSEN, COLAGE & Family Equality (2023), over 550 anti-LGBTQIA+ bills were introduced in the 2022–2023 legislative session targeting schools and transgender individuals. The Anti-Defamation League (2024) describes and outlines the content of these anti-LGBTQIA+ legislations:

- Banning or restricting access to LGBTQIA+ books or curriculum
- Censoring LGBTQIA+ topics in schools
- Forcing school staff to disclose to parents/guardians about student sexual orientation or gender identity
- Denying gender identity pronoun acknowledgment
- Preventing transgender students from using gender-affirming facilities that align with their identity
- Banning transgender students from participating in gender-aligned sports
- Penalizing parents and healthcare providers for providing gender-affirming healthcare

Florida's governor, Ron DeSantis, signed the "Parental Rights in Education" bill (HB 1557) on March 28, 2022. The bill has also been known as the "Don't Say Gay" bill, which prevents any classroom instruction on sexual orientation or gender identity for students from kindergarten through 3rd grade. In a 2023 report, Abbie E. Goldberg of the UCLA Williams Institute highlighted the adverse impact of Florida's HB 1557 on LGBTQIA+ families (Goldberg, 2023). As a result of this legislation, there has been an increase in harassment and bullying for children with LGBTQIA+ parents. The students did not feel comfortable discussing their families or identities. Many parents indicated their fears about staying in the state.

The Williams Institute report indicates that the "Don't Say Gay" law isolates and marginalizes LGBTQIA+ students and families (Goldberg, 2023). As a result, classroom teachers avoid acknowledging LGBTQIA+ topics altogether. The American Psychological Association and the American Academy of Pediatrics, two major health organizations, have condemned the bill due to its harmful impact on students' mental health and well-being and lack of support for LGBTQIA+ families. Finally, these organizations believe this law promotes discrimination.

Given the Williams Institute findings, school districts and schools must have policies in place to support students. It is clear that LGBTQIA+ students are under attack, with similar legislation across the country. Some things are politically and legally outside districts' and schools' spheres of influence. However, we must actively prioritize implementing such policies, practices, and procedures to support students effectively.

MAXIMIZE YOUR SPHERES OF CONTROL AND INFLUENCE

The opening story was a turning point in my equity leadership work. Until then, I had experienced such resistance and pushback about gender inclusion that I could not see a path forward. However, once I notified the superintendent of the challenges, everything changed. I broke the rules. The consequence: Several key stakeholders and decision-makers got on board with my vision and charge to create guidance to support students in ensuring equitable treatment. I used the spheres of control and influence to accomplish part of an equity agenda in a large metropolitan school district. Throughout, I identified four questions that I continually asked myself to gain clarity on what I could and likely could not do and/or accomplish (see Table 1.1).

Maximizing your spheres of control and influence is essential to support your focus on areas where you can directly influence and create substantial change (Reed, 2025). In reflecting on my own time working at Lakeside, as uncomfortable as it was, I've come to appreciate a few important facets of leading for equity. The starting point is to identify that which you have actual control over and what or who you influence. Also, it is critical to

Table 1.1. Guiding Equity Leadership Questions

What Is Within My Control?
How can I maximize what I control to create accountability policies and protections for students?
How can I build relationships to influence decision-makers and those tasked to implement policies and practices to protect students?
What are things outside my control, and how can those things be mitigated?

understand your limitations by identifying that which you are unable to control. Doing so will help avoid burnout, since fatigue from trying to accomplish something you may never be able to impact can only lead to frustration.

WORKING WITHIN MY SPHERE OF CONTROL

With limited decision-making and a lack of control in my role, I made the most of what was within my power. As a mid-level administrator, I was tasked with sharing best practices regarding gender inclusivity with decision-makers. Then, I would support professional learning and development related to their decisions. In order to fulfill my duties, I needed a solid understanding of both best practices and historical context of the district's gender inclusion practices. My deputy superintendent requested that I reach out to other districts in an effort to learn from their policies, successes, and challenges regarding gender inclusivity. I contacted a former mentor who had ascended to superintendent in a neighboring school district during my tenure as equity specialist. He had developed one of the first gender-inclusive policies in the state.

I immediately scheduled an appointment with him to learn about his process and the politics involved in his successful protection of LGBTQIA+ students. Subsequently, I provided a comprehensive brief to my boss, who in turn shared it with the superintendent. When I met with the district attorney to share revisions to our nondiscrimination policy, I was able to provide all of the research and proposed policy amendments.

The second element over which I had control was my own understanding of previous advocacy in the district to promote gender inclusivity. Several teachers had been persistent advocates for protection and support of LGBTQIA+ students, so I sought them out to learn about their dedicated efforts. While significant, their efforts did not advance to the policy level due to a lack of district administrative support. As I examined and worked to shift policies, I grew to understand the process, including progress and barriers, which allowed me to plan a practical course of action.

My goal to understand the work facilitated thus far in the district related to gender inclusivity led me to the physical education curriculum specialist. He had worked with a few local and statewide advocacy organizations and was able to share what had been implemented at the district level. As it turned out, much of the district's efforts to address gender and student and family concerns was neither systemic nor systematic, but dealt with on a case-by-case basis. He also shared the YRBS district data. The Centers for Disease Control and Prevention (2024) provides this nationwide survey to public and private schools to "measure health-related behaviors and experiences that can lead to death and disability among youth and adults." The results from this survey can help us understand emerging trends within our youth population and assist in planning to improve their health outcomes. The district data shared by the physical education curriculum specialist aligned with national trends indicating that students who identified as LGBTQIA+ experienced higher instances of harassment, bullying, and suicidal ideation.

Both the physical education curriculum specialist and one of the teachers suggested that I contact the executive director of GSAFE, a statewide student advocacy organization. The mission's primary goal is to ensure that best practices and gender-inclusive policies are in place in all the schools in the state (GLSEN, 2024a). This organization has helped support students who have experienced bullying and marginalization based on their identities. GSAFE had been instrumental in almost all the school districts that had adopted gender-inclusive student protections. They also supported schools with staff professional development and the creation of gay–straight alliances (GSAs). With allocated funds, I was able to organize professional development for the deputy superintendents and principals to raise their awareness.

I also reached out to Diverse and Resilience (2024), a local organization whose goal is "to achieve health equity and improve the safety and well-being of LGBTQ people and communities" in Lakeside City. This organization had conducted focus groups with students in the district who self-identified as LGBTQIA+. When we presented the findings to the district staff, principals, and teachers, we used actual quotes and experiences of students from our district to illustrate the challenges present in our schools. One student said, "Even though I wanted to be called by a different name, my teacher would harass me by calling me by my born name to embarrass me in front of the class." Another student recounted being taunted by a safety officer, which resulted in a physical altercation. The student was expelled for fighting with the officer despite being provoked by the adult. These compelling data and authentic narratives illuminated the rationale for gender-inclusive protections.

Also, after passing the revision to the nondiscrimination policy, the board wanted to ensure that professional development be mandated for the entire district. The equity intern and I created professional development for every level, from paraprofessionals to teachers, specialists, school leaders, social workers, psychologists, school counselors, and school safety. We facilitated training based on staff responsibility. For example, school counselors, social workers, and psychologists required more detailed training, since many schools identified them as the initial point of contact for students who wanted to facilitate a district-level preferred name change. These staff members also supported challenges with access to bathrooms or locker rooms aligned with students' gender identity. Meanwhile, the teacher training focused on adding gender-inclusive content and language to the curriculum and offered tips for providing more gender equity within the classroom culture. In an effort to elicit comfort levels with ongoing learning, we created FAQs to support staff as they became more familiar with the revision.

MY SPHERE OF INFLUENCE

In addition to working within my spheres of control, I worked to maximize my spheres of influence by relying on the interconnected strategies of building relationships and leveraging political resources in the district, local, and national contexts. Building relationships, sometimes through shared identity, developed trust and mobilized people to action. Leveraging the dynamic assets within LCPS also helped advance change. Also, I made strategic moves at the right time to ensure the maximum impact. Together, I engaged these strategies to develop policies and practices to promote an improved culture and climate for LGTQIA+ students.

Build Relationships

My influence game had to be strong in the face of internal resistance. Building relationships with people was key to getting the job done. As a mid-level manager, I was not what I would call a "shot caller." I did not get to make any final decisions. Much of my role involved disseminating information and convincing "shot callers" to make the right decisions. It was crucial for me to build authentic relationships and provide strategies to support the shot callers' decisions. Having offline conversations with people to help them understand why it was essential to codify protections for LGBTQIA+ students became my driving force.

Relationships are key to successfully adopting controversial policies. You can pass the policy because it is right, but without buy-in, you will be unsuccessful during its implementation phase. Within any organization, regardless of whatever mission draws people together, there is a broad continuum of perspectives. The beliefs and values of the decision-makers directly impact whether the policy will go smoothly or not.

Similarly, if they have buy-in, those who have to implement the policy will do so with fidelity. In other words, they may do the bare minimum to provide a performative response to the policy mandate. Ultimately, no one benefits from the inauthentic implementation of new policies or practices. Therefore, building relationships with the key decision-makers and those required to carry out the essence of the policy is a crucial step.

Certain aspects of my personal identity and experiences were useful in building relationships with others who held similar identities and experiences (Reed, 2025). Identity refers to personal characteristics, such as race, class, gender identity, religion, social interest, and more. For example, I am a Black woman raised in a religiously conservative home where LGBTQIA+ individuals were seen as having an "alternative lifestyle." This enabled me to be relatable to many other Black staff members who grew up with similar backgrounds and expressed apprehension about LGBTQIA+ topics. I helped them understand that despite, and sometimes in honor of, religious conventions, it is crucial to protect all students, regardless of gender identity or expression, as a moral and ethical duty.

Also, I shared with many how my perspective changed once I learned different ways to address LGBTQIA+ advocacy. I became reflective of past incidents where I had not adequately advocated on behalf of students. I recalled reacting with bias to students who came to me with complaints about peers using inappropriate slurs. In hindsight, I should have been educating students as to why those terms were inappropriate to begin with and providing sanctions for the students who engaged in bullying practices. Attending a graduate program with an extensive social justice lens motivated me to shift my perspective into a stance of advocacy. As someone raised in a socially conservative home, I could relate to and understand many of my colleagues' starting points. And once trust was established and connections were made, I was able to share my journey and the best practices for gender inclusivity.

After a day of one-on-one appointments, having shared best practices from other districts, I was in a much better place to implement change. With relationships established, and given their expertise in leadership, they were able to provide clear guidance to move policies forward. Again, relationship building was invaluable in this process. As a follow-up to the meetings, I sent personal thank-you notes to the deputy superintendents and directors for their input and contributions to this work. This proved to be helpful once the policy was passed; since I had fostered direct collegial relationships, they were willing to help me work through challenges with implementation.

Leverage Contexts and Timing

The context involves the environment or setting in which one works, highlighting the importance of understanding the specific dynamics of that space and time. While society has always grappled with the acceptance of LGBTQIA+ individuals, sensitivity to LGBTQIA+ issues in the school context has heightened. Soon after I was hired, in 2016, many equity roles were created in other districts. At that time, educators seemed more open to understanding long-existing issues in schools that had to be addressed. Within my sphere of influence was a progressive school board of directors that wanted to ensure that the district had protections for LGBTQIA+ students. I encountered full support when presenting my findings and plans to the board and was able to reiterate that support while doing the work with the leaders and my colleagues. While I may not have had much influence in the organization, the board of directors certainly did. Thus, the board's endorsement was influential to resistors who may not have fully agreed with our agenda but still complied so as not to be insubordinate. I was able to use both the superintendent's and board's influence to my advantage.

More broadly, I took advantage of LGBTQIA+ guidance measures promoted by the Obama administration. The guidance suggested that transgender students should be able to access bathrooms that match their gender identity (Horsley, 2016). This guidance came after a legal battle with North Carolina over its restrictive "bathroom law." The administration argued that under Title IX, schools must not discriminate based on gender identity, and noncompliance could lead to a loss of federal funding. This guidance also strongly advised schools to keep the confidentiality of trans students and to protect them from harassment.

Finally, timing plays a critical role, as the success of equity initiatives often depends on recognizing the right moment to push for change. As mentioned, while I was working to codify gender inclusivity, the Obama administration released federal guidance recommendations for school gender inclusivity (Horsley, 2016). The timing provided the school board and superintendent with a stronger foundation from which to incorporate district and school policies and to implement changes. While the support of the superintendent and school board was already in place, the timing of the federal guidance was crucial for building relationships and expanding networks to support the changes. The progress made toward gender-inclusive protections in 2017 would have been nearly impossible 10 years earlier, in 2007 when resistance and lack of federal support hindered progress and change at the district and school levels. Now, with the emergence of stronger resistance to LGBTQIA+ supports, equity leaders will need to do the work to ensure LGBTQIA+ protections in education remain solid at the local level. Equity leaders today are right to feel that the current national political context, and many state and local shifts, pose a serious threat to the work.

TIMES CHANGE

The 2024 U.S. presidential election poses a new set of threats to the LGBTQIA+ progress made in the past decade-plus. The U.S. House of Representatives and the Senate also won a conservative majority. A predominantly conservative U.S. Supreme Court was already in place based on Trump's previous Supreme Court justice nominees from his 2016 administration. This overwhelmingly conservative mandate has sparked intense anxiety about potential barriers for LGBTQIA+ people in society and schools based on the anti-LGBTQIA+ rhetoric in advertisements and speech promises (Crary, 2024). Trump and many conservative candidates promised to challenge policies in line with President Joe Biden's administration positions regarding protections for transgender students under Title IX (ACLU, 2024a). This federal civil rights law prohibits sex discrimination in education.

In a 2023 survey, researchers at The Pew Institute found that 50% of surveyed teachers do not believe students should learn about gender identity in school (Lin et al., 2024). A 2022 survey indicated that 37% of parents do not think such topics should be taught in schools (Menasce Horowitz, 2022). Organizations like Moms for Liberty (M4L), founded in January 2021, openly champion parental rights to ban books and censor curriculum and instruction to prevent teaching topics like LGBTQIA+ history (GLAAD, 2024). M4L emerged following the 2020 pandemic shutdown because they felt that the school districts were not listening to their concerns regarding online learning, masking, and other issues. Over 310 chapters are represented in 48 states (Perry, 2024). While M4L presents as a grassroots organization, it has been linked to several high-ranking political officials with significant financial resources from national anti-LGBTQIA+ organizations, such as the Heritage Foundation.

In this current political climate, leaders who are committed to educational equity will encounter opposition from extremely conservative parents, community groups, and political actors. The pushback can create significant obstacles to implementing and sustaining LGBTQIA+ protections. When I implemented changes in the years 2016–2018, I encountered the most pushback from staff. In addition to meetings with central office leaders, I had school leaders, teachers, and other staff openly resist and mock the conversations about implementing LGBTQIA+ protections. I did not face the intense post–Obama administration era resistance from parents that exists today.

SUSTAINING LGBTQIA+ EQUITY GAINS

Progress may seem arduously slow. However, it is important to maintain a student-centered focus when navigating the complexities of actualizing protections; listen to students' lived experiences to foster authentic relationships; and leverage local, regional, and national resources. Change agents can persist in their work, even in the most challenging climates, in order to contribute to a more inclusive and equitable future. For all students. Four equity leadership lessons I gleaned from my experiences and research mitigate misinformation and fear that stands in the way of protecting and affirming LGBTQIA+ students. They include engaging people, developing a deep knowledge of LGBTQIA+ policy, associating with like-minded coalitions, and being creative.

- First maintain open dialogue and engagement with *staff, parents, community, and politically opposed groups*. As evidenced in this chapter, I became more effective in my leadership by developing an understanding of my colleagues' worries, fears, and misconceptions about LGBTQIA+ people. To successfully implement student protections, the community must be heard. Ensure that the meetings include clear guidelines for structure and speaking norms so that everyone is respected and heard. In the meetings, provide accurate information and debunk misinformation. Although challenging, I often conversed and built bridges with opponents who were openly hostile to my efforts. In those conversations, I worked to find common ground that focused on student safety and inclusion. Building relationships helped reduce resistance and tension.

  In the face of resistance, the focus should be on the well-being of all students. In my discussions and professional development sessions, I always focused on how LGBTQIA+ protections benefit all students to address universal values like safety, mental health, and academic success. Politically, I stayed nonpartisan. Although emotions often cloud people's ability to accept data, I consistently used research to amplify my points. I reminded folks about our data: LGBTQIA+ students often have lower academic achievement and higher rates of absenteeism. They suffer more from depression, anxiety, and lower self-esteem than their peers. They are at greater risk of dropping out of school and have a lower probability of postsecondary education. Using data points in conversations keeps the focus on student well-being rather than personal opinions and dispositions.
- Second, develop and maintain a working knowledge of state, federal, and Supreme Court policy and legal decisions that support and challenge LGBTQIA+ student rights. While I did not encounter the legal challenges and political pushback that equity leaders face in many districts, I still worked with groups like GSAFE and Diverse and Resilience to ensure "watchful eyes" paid attention to the work. It is essential to stay informed of the work of national organizations like the Gay, Lesbian & Straight Education Network (GLSEN); the American Civil Liberties Union (ACLU, 2024b); and Lambda Legal (n.d.). These organizations are committed to legally challenging restrictions to local, state, and federal LGBTQIA+

protections. They also advocate for policies to improve the quality of life for LGBTQIA+ individuals. These organizations monitor and provide updates on the legal battles impacting the pursuit of protection in districts, schools, and other organizations. They sponsor awareness initiatives and provide tools and resources to support combating resistance at the local level.

Leaders today can rely on these organizations to remain updated about legal wins they can leverage to advance their work. For example, in *Bostock v. Clayton County, 590 U.S. 644* (2020), the Supreme Court ruled that it was unconstitutional to fire someone based on their sexual orientation and/or identity (Williams, 2020). As a result, several school districts revised their antidiscrimination policies to include LGBTQIA+ protection. Still, several state laws, federal policies, and Supreme Court rulings limit the ability of districts to implement LGBTQIA+ protections. Restrictions on gender-inclusive curricula and gender-affirming care for students limit what is possible in schools. And this is where coalition building becomes an essential part of the work.

- Associate with like-minded coalitions. Equity leaders who join broader coalitions are better able to advance and sustain LGBTQIA+ protections and supports. For example, the national organization GLSEN (2024a) has four major foci to support districts and schools, including programming, advocacy, research, and policy work. Those seeking protection should use the resources provided by such organizations. When describing his work with GSAFE, Juchems said, "Research done by GLSEN and other academics has consistently identified the positive impact LGBTQ-inclusive policies have on trans and queer students as well as school climate for all students" (B. Juchems, personal communication, October 16, 2024). Organizations like GLSEN help districts and schools keep abreast of the fluctuating changes in local, state, and national trends. They also help districts and schools understand how to advocate for stronger protections and how to navigate legal challenges.
- Finally, equity leaders have to be creative. As we face more political and community challenges related to LGBTQIA+ restrictive laws and policies at both the district and state levels, creatively addressing resistance is increasingly important. Districts can still develop policies that protect students and support their well-being while, at the same time, comply with restrictive state laws. For example, GLSEN (2024b) provides examples to expand district antibullying policies to include protecting LGBTQIA+ students. The Family Educational Rights and Privacy Act (FERPA) protects student confidentiality by prohibiting the release of sensitive

information that can harm them (U.S. Department of Education, n.d.). Student groups like GSAs are protected by the Equal Access Act (2010), allowing them to meet outside of instructional time, provided the meetings are student initiated and voluntary.

CONCLUSION

In this chapter, I shared my journey to progress in a large school district. These strategies and tactics will differ depending on your context and timing. Like other diversity, equity, and inclusion (DEI) district and school leaders, the journey to implement protections for LGBTQIA+ students is complex and fluid. The key takeaway is that progress can be made using your spheres of influence to address and combat resistance strategically. Using your spheres of control and influence is critical to the work. Building authentic relationships with individuals responsible for decision-making, as well as those required to implement changes, can also help leverage progress. Understanding the things outside your control can help you face yourself strategically and allow the work to move forward regardless of your limitations.

REFERENCES

American Civil Liberties Union (ACLU). (2024a). *Trump on LGBTQ rights: Rolling back protections and criminalizing gender nonconformity.* https://www.aclu.org/news/lgbtq-rights/trump-on-lgbtq-rights-rolling-back-protections-and-criminalizing-gender-nonconformity

American Civil Liberties Union (ACLU). (2024b). *LGBTQ rights.* https://www.aclu.org/issues/lgbtq-rights

Anti-Defamation League (ADL). (2024). *Anti-LGBTQ+ bills that are impacting children, families, and schools.* https://www.adl.org/resources/tools-and-strategies/anti-lgbtq-bills-are-impacting-children-families-and schools?gad_source=1&gclid=CjwKCAjwx4O4BhAnEiwA42SbVFiRJkP3vPwmsbwed2gFmoOgMPsERHdFZwwx_pf3ZgsTBReoD9Y5BBoCwkEQAvD_BwE&gclsrc=aw.ds

Bostock v. Clayton County, 590 U.S. 644 *(2020).*

Centers for Disease Control and Prevention. (2024). *Youth risk behavior surveillance system (YRBSS).* Retrieved from https://www.cdc.gov/yrbs/about/index.html#:~:text=A%20national%20survey%2C%20called%20the,respective%20public%20high%20school%20students

Crary, D. (2024). *Transgender-rights advocates say the election of Trump and his allies marks a major setback.* Associated Press. https://apnews.com/article/election-2024-transgender-rights-lgbtq-donald-trump-3bb3ace81ff32b6dec382b486ec6a772

Diverse and Resilience. (2024). *Who we are.* https://www.diverseandresilient.org/who-we-are/mission-vision-name/Equal Access Act. 1 20 U.S.C. § 4071(a) (2010).

GLAAD. (2024). *Moms for Liberty (M4L).* https://glaad.org/gap/moms-liberty/

GLSEN. (2024a). *Our work*. https://www.glsen.org/our-work

GLSEN. (2024b). *Model local education agency bullying and harassment prevention policy*. https://www.glsen.org/activity/model-district-anti-bullying-harassment-policy

GLSEN, COLAGE & Family Equality. (2023). *Experiences of students with LGBTQ+ caregivers and their families in K-12 schools*. GLSEN.

Goldberg, A. (2023). *Impact of HB 1557 (Florida's Don't Say Gay bill) on LGBTQ+ parents in Florida*. Williams Institute. https://williamsinstitute.law.ucla.edu/wp-content/uploads/Dont-Say-Gay-Impact-Jan-2023.pdf

Horsley, S. (2016). *White House sends schools guidance on transgender access to bathrooms*. National Public Radio. https://www.npr.org/sections/thetwo-way/2016/05/13/477896804/obama-administration-to-offer-schools-guidance-on-transgender-bathrooms

Kosciw, J. G., Greytak, E. A., Giga, N. M., Villenas, C., & Danischewski, D. J. (2016). *The 2015 National School Climate Survey: The experiences of lesbian, gay, bisexual, transgender, and queer youth in our nation's schools*. GLSEN.

Lambda Legal. (n.d.) *About us*. https://lambdalegal.org/

Lin, L., Menasce Horowitz, J. Hurst, K., & Braga, D. (2024). *Race and LGBTQ issues in K-12 schools: What teachers, teens and the U.S. public say about current curriculum debates*. The Pew Institute. https://www.pewresearch.org/social-trends/2024/02/22/race-and-lgbtq-issues-in-k-12-schools/

Menasce Horowitz, J. (2022). *Parents differ sharply by party over what their K-12 children should learn in school*. The Pew Institute. https://www.pewresearch.org/social-trends/2022/10/26/parents-differ-sharply-by-party-over-what-their-k-12-children-should-learn-in-school/

Perry, M. (2024). *Moms for Liberty now has 310 chapters in 48 states: What will they do now?* Florida Phoenix. https://floridaphoenix.com/2024/02/02/moms-for-liberty-now-has-310-chapters-in-48-states-what-will-they-do-now/

Reed, L. (2025). *The complexities of equity: Navigating the shades of gray in schools and organizations*. Corwin Press.

Reed, L., & Johnson, L. T. (2010). Serving LGBT students: Examining the spiritual, religious, and social justice implications for an African American school administrator. *The Journal of Negro Education*, *79*(3), 390–404.

U.S. Department of Education. (n.d.). *Protecting student privacy*. https://studentprivacy.ed.gov/ferpa

Williams, P. (2020). *Supreme Court rules existing civil rights law protects gay and lesbian workers*. NBC News. https://www.nbcnews.com/politics/supreme-court/supreme-court-rules-existing-civil-rights-law-protects-gay-lesbian-n1231018

CHAPTER 2

Shocking the System

Black Women's Equity Leadership in "Nice" White School Districts

Shannon Paige Clark

Shannon: What should our research team know about this truck with the Confederate flag parked in front of Central Office and the overall racial-historical context of this district?

Dr. Terrell: I don't even know who that truck belongs to. . . . It's a reminder. . . . There are people working with our children who are possibly white supremacists or believe in the premise of the confederacy and they are interacting with our children; they are interacting with Black and brown colleagues, adults and . . . how does that manifest itself in outcomes? Well, for one we know, teachers are leaving, leaders are leaving. As fast as we get a person of color, they're out the door! Um. . . . So yea, I'm sure it plays [pauses to reflect]. This person just so happens to be so BLATANT as to have it on the truck. . . .

Shannon: So you mentioned it to your supervisor; what sort of response did you want and did you get it?

Dr. Terrell: Shannon, I don't know that I was looking for a reaction. I don't even remember her reaction. I am actually shocked that you brought this up. WOW . . . yea. Shannon. It's terrible. It is terrible. . . . It's a BIG RED TRUCK. It's a reminder.

In December 2021, I asked Dr. Brenda Terrell, the chief equity officer of her district, about the big red truck with the Confederate flag that was parked right out front of the district's central office building. With a clenched jaw and raised shoulders, she told me the big red truck with the Confederate flag is a reminder of white supremacy and its enduring presence in U.S. school districts. The driver of this Confederate truck worked in the central office of a nice white school district. Their display of white supremacist pride was so normal, the chief equity officer didn't even expect anyone to do anything about it. These types of overtures were so typical, Dr. Terrell even forgot it was a conversation in an affinity group meeting a few months earlier. The district's white allyship group leader, who professed a commitment to help white people see how their biases marginalize people of color, knew the truck's owner but did not identify or confront them. He was just one of many colleagues who chose "niceness" over confronting the ways the truck and its display of the Confederate flag cause harm.

The routine functioning of nice white school districts perpetuates inequality through silences and actions that reinforce whiteness and white supremacy (Diamond & Gomez, 2023; Diamond & Lewis, 2022). In "nice white school districts" across this country, people look the other way. They choose silence, avoidance, and denial. They claim to be nice and civil. Yet this structural mechanism of niceness functions at both micro and organizational levels to maintain the very injustices and inequalities that have long persisted in schools and that equity leaders work so hard to disrupt.

In this chapter, I describe the predominant organizational culture of *white[nice]ness,* which perpetuates silence, avoidance, and denial regarding racial harm, to shed light on "the work" necessary to sustain equity leadership in U.S. school districts. I draw on data from 10 Black women who lead for equity. Each of them holds a formal position related to pursuing equity in a U.S. school district. I triangulated their interview transcripts with a range of artifacts and observational data gathered over the span of 8 years. I synthesized their stories to form a composite equity leader I call Dr. Brenda Terrell, who is the voice through which I present recurring themes. I integrated the stories of all 10 equity leaders in their own words throughout; however, I intentionally mixed and masked some details to protect each leader given the precarious nature of their positions and careers. After I describe the "nice" white organizational culture of PK–12 U.S. school districts, I detail defining district characteristics that inhibit equity leadership. Then, I describe three ways these equity leaders create a moral imperative to pursue equity in spite of individuals and systems that makes their work feel both futile and dangerous.

Dr. Brenda Terrell is a Black woman in her late 40s with long sisterlocks who greets everyone she encounters with warmth. She was hired in 2020, amidst public outcry over the murder of George Floyd, and she got to work as the chief equity officer of a "nice" white school district. Her first priority was to get to know the people and the politics that could become landmines. Despite more than 2 decades of experience working in U.S. school districts at every level, she was shocked to see just how inequitable things were. Over time, she realized she had joined a district that would undermine her leadership and leave her isolated if she was not unfailingly strategic.

WHAT IS A "NICE" WHITE SCHOOL DISTRICT?

"Nice" white school districts are resilient and flexible racialized organizations that adapt when equity leaders are hired (Ray, 2019; Ray & Purifoy, 2019). In fact, equity leaders detail numerous new mechanisms for racial exclusion when they arrive (Irby et al, 2022; Ishimaru et al, 2023; Ray et al, 2023). While equity leaders are hired to address racial burdens, many, who are Black women, face racialized burdens themselves. When they begin interrogating the "standard" routines, policies, and practices, they are met with resistance in both overt and covert forms. The endogenous shock that districts experience when a new equity leader is hired shows up as denial, avoidance, resistance, and defense. This leaves equity leaders isolated in nice white school districts.

Across districts that varied in location, size, and demographics, equity leaders reflected in this chapter described similar organizational cultures that made it feel nearly impossible to lead for equity. Despite differences between the U.S. school districts represented in this chapter, each was marked by an organizational culture of white[nice]ness, or persistent resistance to equity leadership masked by "niceness" or good intentions (Castagno, 2019; Drake & Rodriguez, 2022; Virella & Liera, 2024). Joffe-Walt (2020) shows "how white parents can shape a school even when they aren't there" in the award-winning podcast, *Nice White Parents*. Whiteness and its organizational manifestations are everywhere, and most of us attended a nice white school district, even if there was not a predominantly white population.

In the "nice" white school districts described by Black women equity leaders, people smile and carry on with little to no reflection on racial inequity. In these districts, curricula are based on dominant worldviews, and policies and practices maintain white-centric norms. The majority of teachers are white women, and it is normal for children to be grouped based on ability and race. In nice white districts, students and families are treated as if they are the problem when grades suggest their needs are not met. Talking about race and racism is taboo. Everyone supposedly has every opportunity to succeed.

Nice white school districts pretend to be neutral organizations, but they are anything but. Instead, these districts are shaped by assumptions of white superiority (Diamond, 2024; Larson & Ovando, 2001; Ray, 2019). They are racialized spaces that embrace social, cultural, political, and moral commitments reflecting whiteness. These commitments are easily perpetuated by individuals who accept that the institution or organization is neutral and inherently good or justified. Yet school districts and the policies that govern them are products of ideology built on the subjugation of all who are not white (ross & Givens, 2023).

The Problem with White[nice]ness

Niceness is a part of "the fabric of educational institutions" that reinforces patterns of inequity (Castagno et al., 2024). Because of the ways U.S. school districts have been legitimized and managed, even people who are not white can uphold a nice white organizational culture. White[nice]ness will look and sound different across contexts, people, and communities, but it takes precedence over addressing racial harm and sustains inequity everywhere. It excuses people from doing the work necessary to pursue equity, and it reprimands and limits those who do. Castagno and colleagues (2024) describe niceness as a mechanism to protect individuals from doing the work of dismantling inequity and as a force that disciplines those who attempt to work toward equity. In nice white school districts, niceness is an institutional norm enacted through policies at the organizational level and by individuals in day-to-day action or inaction (Castagno et al., 2024). For example, nice white school districts reproduce racial inequality by hiring, retaining, and promoting employees and consultants who negate the historical legacy and ongoing impact of white supremacy and racism.

What's "the Work" in Nice White Districts?

Dr. Terrell describes why equity leaders work to redesign systems and routines that perpetuate inequities. She strives to make equity central to everything within the district and to create moral imperatives that compel their colleagues to prioritize equity in ways that restructure systems. Dr. Terrell is rewiring systems to make equity "everyone's work."

> I think equity isn't really a stand alone position. You can have somebody who has that as a part of their title, but if you are really doing equity work it has to be the lens through which you view everything regardless of your role. So there's something to having somebody in the position, it names it. But the work that we've tried to do here is to build it into our systems and structures.
>
> Equity is not a project or a program. It is a system that is laid across the entire district. It is an interrogation of policies and practices. The charge is examining the systems and creating a theory of change around the idea of assuring that our systems are equitable . . . where [equity leaders] are supported by their budget being aligned to every other department, where they'll have the support of other departments, and where every department will have an equity line or a goal around equity.

Dr. Terrell was declarative; changing the systems and structures across the district was *the work*. While equity leaders often commit to professional development and tackling individual biases, they know that sustained change requires new systems or policies and procedures at every level across the district. Dr. Terrell explains that a singular program or project will not amount to any substantive change; instead, the ultimate goal is revamping every single department with equity as the uniting thread.

DISRUPTING WHITE[NICE]NESS TO PURSUE EQUITY

Equity leaders featured in this chapter described their school districts as places with organizational cultures that undermined equity leadership in three defining ways. They also shared the strategies they used to counter these challenges and "do the work" of equity leadership (see Table 2.1).

In what follows, I explore each defining challenge and the approaches the leaders took to disrupt white[nice]ness and change inequitable systems.

The Challenge: Nice White School Districts Overlook Inequity

> My view for equity change is, first of all, acknowledging that it needs to happen because I can't go in and try to change anything if you don't think there needs to be any changes. Equity work is really about pressing up against people's beliefs. And my job is not to change their beliefs. . . . But I do have to talk to you and get you to a place of awareness. So, now . . . if I can get you to a place to go, "Maybe I have done this disproportionately different with these kids." If I can get you to that place, all right. If I can get you in HR to say, "Maybe I have created a barrier to the hiring process. Maybe my teacher pool is not that diverse. Maybe our teachers of color haven't had conversations about promotion" . . . if I can get you to that place, then . . . then we can start the equity work.

Here, Dr. Terrell references people who don't see why change is necessary. She alludes to differential outcomes that are likely linked to individual belief systems, and notes the importance of pointing out patterns that show

Table 2.1. Challenges and Strategies

Challenges: Nice White Districts . . .	The Work: Equity Leaders . . .
Overlook inequity	Talk about race to make inequity visible
Choose silence, avoidance, and denial	Build relationships that compel others to change harmful patterns
Silo equity	Move strategically to embed equity throughout the district

inequity, reflecting how equity leaders repeatedly explained districts' reinforcement of white ways of operating that ignored inequity.

> It's a white dominant viewpoint about how we do things. It's about control. For example, we document kids to death. They don't bring a pencil, they roll their eyes, they lean back in a chair. But a teacher does something to disengage or harm a relationship with a student, and we chalk it up to they [the teacher] had a bad day or that's not what they really meant. We walk into schools and it's clear segregation happening, yet we're not looking at your policy structure about how you're putting kids in the classroom.

Dr. Terrell explains that her district is used to overlooking inequity largely because people exist in a system that is heavily steeped in whiteness, and they are used to doing things in a way that maintains particular power relations; teachers are right and students are wrong; schools are segregated, and it's beyond the district's locus of control. In nice white school districts, it is convenient and easy to overlook inequity.

The Work: Talk About Race to Make Inequity Visible

> If you dig deeper [to understand disparities] it's 15 percent of students who are mostly families of color, immigrant families, or are free and reduced lunch who are not doing really well. And if you look at data by race it's all Black and brown students. Until that changes we're going to lead with race. We can talk about everything else too that intersects. Literally I've been in a meeting and I've had other adults stand up and yell at me and tell me that this is not the work that I should be doing. I've literally had principals get up and walk out of trainings. There were a lot of people who were upset and concerned and who didn't understand and who feel like it's a waste of money to be focusing on race. I'm like, this is the work. There must be introspection . . . equity is about really identifying the most marginalized, right?

Here, Dr. Terrell describes the resistance she faces when she makes race central to conversations about disparities. She told me it's "very tricky to have conversations about race" because district employees will even involve the union and accuse equity leaders of "questioning their intentions." It is not uncommon for other leaders, like principals, to excuse themselves from professional development if they do not value the topic or feel uncomfortable. Still, equity leaders say this is the work.

To address white[nice]ness, equity leaders make conversations about race central to their efforts so that it becomes more obvious how whiteness and inherent perceptions of superiority harm marginalized students, especially those who are Black and Brown. According to Dr. Terrell, people want equity posters and checklists, and while she could easily provide those, she knows they will be ineffective if individuals do not see harm—if they lack awareness. So the work is making sure the racial biases and beliefs that perpetuate inequity are visible. To facilitate this process, she relies on race-specific conversations that make people pause and question their initial assumptions or stereotypes.

> Everything I do is strategic. I made the decision to wear this shirt today. It literally looks like a wheel stuck in a rut. And equity is supposed to be the foundation. Initially, I thought I should wear a [Colin] Kaepernick shirt and then I thought I need to wear the one with all of the people's [victims of police murder] names on it . . . but I decided not yet—too much. I'm going through all this in my head, and I wore this shirt to my first Council meeting and I wore the Kaepernick shirt to the second Council meeting. Strategically. To push them to think differently. And to question, well why would she wear that shirt? What is that shirt, you know? I needed that to be a conversation starter.

Dr. Terrell's energy shifts; she becomes more excitable as she explains why she's wearing a t-shirt that reminds me of a hamster wheel. She describes a schedule of outfits that she intentionally wears to prompt conversations. She starts with a shirt that she believes will be easier to take in and works her way up to a shirt that has the names of Black people who have been murdered by police. The shirts are her opening to taboo topics and conversations on race and justice that rarely happen in open and direct ways in nice white school districts. She continues by explaining how she's working to shift the ways data is analyzed:

> So when we look at data, I tell them to shift the conversation, not to the data, but who are the people looking at the data? If you're sitting around the table with a bunch of like-minded people from like-minded experiences, you're gonna end up with the same results and conversations and it becomes a one-sided approach. We borrowed this equity lens from Portland Public Schools. And we've used these five questions around programs and policies—whether it's business and finance and you're looking at resources, whether it's schools looking at block scheduling, whether it is attendance policies, you can ask yourself these five questions to evaluate whether or not you're being equitable.

Dr. Terrell has intentionally created subgroups within the Race and Equity Council to make sense of data. People who are typically not grouped work together to use an equity lens; individuals are grouped across schools, departments, positions, race, ethnicity, gender, and more to have rich conversations about data. They are required to disaggregate data and consider the role of race, class, ability, and other markers of difference. When council members use proxies or make statements that lack specificity, Dr. Terrell redirects them with probing questions that require them to talk about race.

The Challenge: Nice White School Districts Choose Silence, Avoidance, and Denial

> I cannot tell you how many times the police have been called on kindergarteners. I feel like so many people just have their blinders on. . . . So you want me to calm down to make you feel better. And my anger is not even at full load. We don't know how to have . . . um I shouldn't say . . . I haven't seen evidence of conversations that are challenging where we work on pushing the issue because if you push the issue, I've noticed that people take it personally and it's hard to separate the two. It's a culture of niceness and politeness, but not courage. And that keeps us in a place of being stuck . . . because all the adults are really nice. But we can see the disparities, we can see just plain wrongness happening, and you know, who's the one that's going to say something about it, you know, and if you say something about it, then you just have to watch out for your career.

Here, Dr. Terrell describes a district where silence about racial harm is the norm, just like the murmurs about the Confederate truck parked in front of the central office. She details a school district where it is acceptable to criminalize 5-year-olds, look the other way, and resist conversations that are difficult. In nice white school districts, people defend their harmful action or inaction by proclaiming they are innocent, oblivious, or doing their best. Dr. Terrell describes an organizational culture where it is not okay to offer critical feedback because people take it personally and shut down. She cites people who are "nice" and "polite" but unwilling to confront harm and inequity. While this may seem like an individual phenomenon, silence is an organizational structure that limits and quiets dissent (Valiavska & Meisenbach, 2023). Nice white school districts maintain the inequitable status quo through white[nice]ness practices and routines like silence, avoidance, and denial, which in turn makes it nearly impossible to change inequitable practices.

The Work: Build Relationships that Compel Others to Change Harmful Patterns

> I came in like a tornado. Like . . . okay there's a lot of stuff wrong here, let's fix it people. But that approach didn't necessarily work so taking a step back and thinking about how to build relationships and doing that has been better. I started cohorts, because I felt like I needed a group of people to surround me. So I formed equity cohorts, affinity groups, and a Council on Race and Equity. Now, these groups impact my ability to effect change.

Equity leaders realize they cannot do this work alone and that they must have people willing to work alongside them, so they prioritize relationships. Dr. Terrell formed a series of ongoing groups that met routinely to spread equity efforts across the district. These committees were designed to develop equity champions that would take what they learned and share with colleagues. She explains:

> I've learned I need to get out of this office and go connect with other departments across this site because I'm going to have to have relationships to be able to even have the chance to compel them to think about this work differently. I think the fact that I build bridges with people is a factor that affects my ability to effect change. I figure out how I can help . . . I say things like, "they told me that you have to do x, y & z." So, if I am trying to help them [district personnel] write a SMART goal, we might discuss how they could use an equity lens. As I've gotten to know the principals, when issues come up that are related to educational equity they've started to reach out to me to consult with them and I've also met with a lot of parents . . . parents who have had concerns that they have not really had anyone that they felt comfortable to voice those to, have reached out to me. And I am an unapologetically Black, proud mother. I will use my children in any professional context to help people understand how Black children are marginalized and to give a personal face because they respect me.

Relationships are central to Dr. Terrell's work. She finds ways to connect with people, using her experiences as a Black mother, former principal, and teacher to build "bridges." She takes existing district expectations, like goal setting, and joins work sessions to make herself useful, which enables her to infuse equity or bring an equity lens to the forefront. By making herself relatable and being visible and accessible across the district, she is able to compel others to consider old problems with equity as the guiding orientation.

> I really knew relationships were making a difference when the [Race and Equity] Council presented their action research projects. Like one [person] in particular, they sat so quietly most of the time, and this is somebody with influence at Central Office. And they used the word race in their presentation, and how they wanted to be able to interrupt disparities at the Central Office and they are doing it actively. And the mentor teachers who were a part of the cohort last year . . . they developed their voice to talk about institutional racism, to talk about their whiteness, to call it out and to use it in examples to help principals and teachers understand pedagogy and why they need to do things in a certain way. That's an indicator of change.

Council presentations at the end of the 2021–2022 academic year made it evident that the connections being built through ongoing collective learning like committees, councils, and affinity spaces were effectively compelling others to lead for equity.

The Challenge: Nice White School Districts Marginalize Equity Work

> In [our] district, we have an equity page. We have an equity mission statement separate from the District mission . . . I will say there is a lack of coherence in the district. As an example, like right now, the Chief of Instruction, she is doing her very best to create coherence. But there's a whole other wing of the organization that she doesn't touch, and that's the operations, that's the finances, that's the transportation. And so here's a really plain example. We're talking about children [who] need to have access to after school supports, tutoring, whatever the case is. But transportation is not provided to students across the district after school. So I can say, we need to do this, but operations is saying, well, no, we can't. . . . Equity can't be an afterthought or another add on because we already have so much going on in education from frameworks that you're using to every other aspect of teaching and learning that if equity is just another . . . an afterthought or an add- on, I don't think that it will be successful.

A painstaking lack of continuity across the district troubled Dr. Terrell when we checked in at the end of the 2021–2022 school year. She reflected on what was working and what was not. While she worked with an Equity Council to enact an equity mission statement, their leadership was often limited in scope because these efforts were separate from and in addition to a broader district mission—a mission that had more weight and reached every team member, rather than just those who opted in. Moreover, she described other departments that were not operating with equity as a mandate. In the previous statement, she refers to a stark difference in extracurricular participation that was linked to transportation barriers. While this disparity was an issue the Equity Council aimed to address, the operations team did not have the same priorities. Although Dr. Terrell was hired to focus on equity across the district, the organization was not structured to support her success.

The Work: Move Strategically to Embed Equity Throughout the District

> You will hear people in this District say, *"we all own equity."* I heard that so much, we all own equity. Well, do we really? And who's holding that person accountable? Who is doing that? At my department meetings, my team knew every meeting I was going to ask them, *How did their work explicitly connect to equity?* That was the question they always had to answer because we can get so busy in the day to day, that wasn't happening anywhere else. So you get, you get narrowly focused on, well, this is my job, and your job is still harming people. You don't know it because you're doing your job.

> Equity has to factor into people's evaluations. It has to have some . . . I know I talked a whole lot about hearts and minds, but it also has to have . . . there has to be at some point, *we draw the line here. We've given you support, we've given you time to reflect*, but if there are people who are not coming along, there has to be some sort of way to say, that's not acceptable because in this district, equity is a priority. And so really making it not be optional.

To sustain the work of equity leaders, Dr. Terrell emphasized that equity must not be optional. She worked to shift the district's orientation such that equity is treated as essential work and woven into all aspects of the organization. Earlier, Dr. Terrell suggests that requiring employees to connect their daily work to equity keeps it central. She does this with a simple yet consistent question: How does your work explicitly connect to equity? The question is a starting point. Dr. Terrell ultimately intends to make equity a component of evaluations so that everyone is formally held accountable for equity metrics, which she thinks increases the likelihood people will engage in the ongoing work necessary to cultivate equity. Dr. Terrell was even adamant about developing indicators of success for herself.

> My superintendent said, "we do not really have any outcomes . . . do the best work that you can and we will touch base at the end of the year." I did not feel comfortable with that. I did not like that; there's no accountability to that. So there are no real outcomes honestly, which is why I created my own scope and sequence. It's also why I created a Race and Equity Plan because there has to be something they're looking for. They probably do not know what it looks like. So my scope and sequence starts with outcomes around increasing capacity to understand race and equity, but also to implement policies that are alive and that stay alive in everything we're doing.

Dr. Terrell believed it was integral to have concrete measures of success, so she created her own even in the absence of district-imposed expectations. For example, she established SMART goals related to starting a monthly professional development series for anyone in the district who managed others. Likewise, she prioritized building the capacity of principals because of the power each leader had among their school communities. She also focused on policy creation. Yet she emphasized that the policy must *be and stay alive*; the policies that she worked on creating, modifying, and implementing were all "living documents" that were meant to guide everyday decision-making and action. She leveraged relationships to encourage colleagues to approach their work with equity as a guiding principle. And she used members of the Equity Council to lead Equity Teams at most schools. Now, there are people who champion equity and lead related initiatives in schools and departments across the district. Three years in, she speaks with conviction about the ways equity has been infused throughout the district.

> I'm proud that I elevated the ways in which inequities were operating in the district. I'm proud that we completed that equity audit, which is incredibly robust—300 plus pages of findings and recommendations . . . I'm proud of some of the systems that were put in place. There are seven affinity groups for adults, a revised equity plan—it still needs massaging—but we have a plan that has lofty but important goals, implementation benchmarks that can be monitored along the way, and the right positions to be held accountable. In the first equity plan, it had a litany of positions, but who was responsible? Now we have a guidebook that makes plain what particular disparities each Department must address. I'm proud that we have an equity reporting tool because in the equity audit, people were saying, we're seeing racism [and] discrimination occurring, but we are fearful to report it. So now there will be an equity reporting tool so people have a place they can go to lodge concerns, complaints, whatever the case may be. I'm proud that we have an equity lens that any staff member can use to guide their decision making processes. Our equity policy is alive . . . it's operationalized and people know what they can do to make the policy a reality. I'm relieved the Board has committed to align the new Strategic Plan with the Equity Plan.

Sharing the results of the equity audit widely, creating indicators of success, and developing an equity lens and detailed plan were made possible through a series of strategic moves that Dr. Terrell planned over the span of 3 years. It started with one formal equity leader who compelled a range of people to "do the work" by pushing and prompting others to use an equity lens, finding the roots of inequity, and doing things differently. It was one strategic move after another that expanded district conversations on what it meant to teach and lead with equity as the guiding imperative.

LEADING FOR EQUITY IN "NICE" WHITE SCHOOL DISTRICTS

I have worked in and with public schools for over 15 years, initially as an elementary school teacher, then as an instructional coach, and most recently as an intervention teacher. As a doctoral student, I had the opportunity to document the experiences of formal equity leaders in PK–12 school districts, most of whom were Black women like me. I became increasingly concerned about the weight of leading for equity in systems that consumed people who look like us. I wondered how and why these leaders maintained the will to keep working toward equity in harmful organizations.

I understand now that their presence shocks the system(s), and because of their presence and actions, they face resistance in various forms. Inequity in nice white school districts is maintained through common, taken-for-granted routines or practices that typically go unquestioned until equity leaders arrive (Diamond & Gomez, 2023). To stand a chance of contending with white[nice]ness and districtwide systems and practices that imbue white supremacy, equity leaders have determined the need to create moral imperatives that compel school districts to expand the quest for equity. It cannot be limited to a single person or department. They learn to tell stories and share data that make it morally compelling to change. These leaders understand that the individuals and the systems in nice white school districts must acknowledge, examine, and actively work against the counterproductive presence of "nice" whiteness that undergirds education systems across the United States and maintains injustices and inequities.

The equity leaders described throughout this chapter believe it must become routine for school districts to interrogate issues of power, resource distribution, and student outcomes in race-conscious ways. They sustain equity leadership by making race central to their work; building deep relationships; and planning, speaking, and acting with strategy and caution. When the Black women featured in this chapter utilized these strategies, individuals and departments throughout nice white school districts began to evaluate their beliefs and practices, and in pockets throughout, they began to change both hearts and minds plus practices and policies to work toward more equitable school districts (see Ishimaru & Galloway, 2021).

REFERENCES

Castagno, A. E. (Ed.). (2019). *The price of nice: How good intentions maintain educational inequity*. University of Minnesota Press.

Castagno, A., Contreras, L., & Villarreal, C. (2024). Niceness, leadership, and education: Call to special edition. *Education Sciences, 14*(4).

Diamond, J. B. (2024). Defending the color line: White supremacy and the legacy of Brown. *Educational Researcher*, *53*(3), 135–145.

Diamond, J. B., & Gomez, L. M. (2023). Disrupting white supremacy and anti-Black racism in educational organizations. *Educational Researcher*, 0013189X231161054.

Diamond, J. B., & Lewis, A. E. (2022). Opportunity hoarding and the maintenance of "white" educational space. *American Behavioral Scientist*, *66*(11), 1470–1489.

Drake, R. D., & Rodriguez, G. (2022). Nice to whom?: How Midwestern niceness undermines educational equity. *Berkeley Review of Education*, *12*(1), 5–23.

Irby, D. J., Green, T., & Ishimaru, A. M. (2022). PK–12 district leadership for equity: An exploration of director role configurations and vulnerabilities. *American Journal of Education*, *128*(3), 417–453.

Ishimaru, A. M., & Galloway, M. K. (2021). Hearts and minds first: Institutional logics in pursuit of educational equity. *Educational Administration Quarterly*, *57*(3), 470–502.

Ishimaru, A. M., Irby, D. J., & Green, T. (2023). The paradox of organizational double jeopardy: PK-12 equity directors in racialized and gendered educational systems. *The Urban Review*, *55*(3), 364–392.

Joffe-Walt, C. (2020). *Nice white parents.* Serial Productions and the New York Times. https://www.nytimes.com/2020/07/23/podcasts/nice-white-parents-serial.html

Larson, C., & Ovando, C. (2001). *The color of bureaucracy: The politics of equity in multicultural school communities.* Taylor and Francis Group.

Ray, V. (2019). A theory of racialized organizations. *American Sociological Review, 84*(1), 26–53.

Ray, V., Herd, P., & Moynihan, D. (2023). Racialized burdens: Applying racialized organization theory to the administrative state. *Journal of Public Administration Research and Theory, 33*(1), 1310–152.

Ray, V., & Purifoy, D. (2019). The colorblind organization. In *Race, organizations, and the organizing process* (vol. 60, pp. 131–150). Emerald Publishing Limited.

ross, k. m., & Givens, J. R. (2023). The clearing: On Black education studies and the problem of "antiblackness." *Harvard Educational Review, 93*(2), 1410–172.

Valiavska, A., & Meisenbach, R. (2023). Racialized scripts of silence: How whiteness organizes silence as a response to social protest about racism in the United States. *Journal of Applied Communication Research, 51*(6), 582–601.

Virella, P., & Liera, R. (2024). Nice for what? The contradictions and tensions of an urban district's racial equity transformation. *Education Sciences, 14*(4), 420.

CHAPTER 3

Appreciating the Fruits of "Unsuccessful" Leadership

Looking Back to See(d) Forward

Decoteau J. Irby, Ann M. Ishimaru, and Terrance Green

> I don't care how hard I'm working or if I did this and I did that. I struggle with defining what success is in this role. I have kids from the Performing Arts High School where many don't have binary identities leaving campus to use the bathroom. Students are altering what they eat so they don't have to pee because there's no gender neutral facility in their school. So yeah I did policy, I did training, but that's still happening in schools. So I don't feel successful.
>
> —Lorretta Richards

In 2017, Loretta and the 13 equity leaders we interviewed all described, to varying degrees, the psychological and practical challenge of counting their "wins." They asked themselves questions like: Does the work I'm doing matter? Will it have any sort of impact? Despite the productive ways Loretta pushed her district, she left her role believing the work she accomplished was probably not going to make a difference in students' academic or socio-emotional lives. She perceived that people did not appreciate her efforts and expressed feeling isolated and misunderstood. Time told a different story. As it turns out, her work did have an impact.

Loretta's belief that her work was inconsequential was common among the equity leaders we interviewed in 2017 and the numerous leaders we encountered through professional development, keynotes, conference presentations, and information interactions. As such, we wrote with cautious optimism about the work of equity leadership. We argued it would be "premature to suggest that equity director roles would impact districts' culture, student experiences, or outcomes" (Irby et al., 2022). We had more to say about practice than impact. We maintained that the sheer volume of new leaders and their activities warranted study because of the *potential* to expand the social justice, antiracist, and culturally responsive leadership approaches that aim to confront oppressive education realities and transform schools and districts (Irby et al., 2022). Today, students in the performing arts high school that Loretta referenced no longer leave campus or avoid eating to dodge the forced indignity of using a restroom that denies their gender identities. Paying attention to the proliferation and development of equity leadership over an extended period helped us appreciate the range of activities that characterized the early work.

In this chapter, we revisit what we learned from our earliest interviews with district equity leaders. The leaders whose work we studied early in our 2017 research are summarized in Table 3.1. Nine participants identified as Black or African American, one as Asian American, one as Latino, one as biracial (Pacific Islander and white), and one as white. Eight participants identified as female. Five identified as male. Participants worked in school districts across several regions of the United States, including five from the West, four from the Midwest, two from the Southwest, one from the Southeast, and one from the Northeast. Seven participants worked in suburban districts, and six worked in urban districts. On average, participants had been in their role as equity director for 4 years.

Table 3.1. Participant Profiles

Director Name*	Racial and Ethnic Identification (self-identified)	Sex and Gender Identification	Highest Education Credential	Years in Role	District Name*
Linda Barrera	White (bicultural)	Female; heterosexual	Bachelor's; Current PhD student	5	Valley Farm Area School District
Cole Blassingame	Black	Male; heterosexual	Master's	3	Outer Way School District
Tanya Fisher	Black	Female; cisgender	Doctorate of education	3	Seaway School District
Martin Galloway	African American	Male	Unknown	6	Windsor Community School District
Wesley Gardner	Black	Male	Master's	5	West Mile School District
Lynne Hamilton	African American	Female; lesbian	Doctorate of philosophy	2	City Schools of Division

Table 3.1. (*continued*)

Director Name*	Racial and Ethnic Identification (self-identified)	Sex and Gender Identification	Highest Education Credential	Years in Role	District Name*
Shawn Jackson	Black	Male; cisgender; heterosexual	Bachelor's	4	Broadview School District
Loretta Richards	Black	Female; heterosexual	Doctorate of philosophy	2	Mainline Public Schools
Jesus Salcedo	Latino	Male	Master's	5	Richards County School District
Sara Singleton	Asian American	Female; cisgender; heterosexual	Current PhD student	4	Bearclaw School District
Maria Sturtevant	Biracial (Pacific Islander/ white)	Female; cisgender; heterosexual	Doctorate of education	2	Fireside Public Schools
April Washington	Black	Female	Master's; current PhD candidate	6	Accelera Independent School District
Tracie Yale	Black	Female	Master's	6	Westend County School District

* All individual director and district names are pseudonyms.

Looking back at equity leadership role configurations and activities (Irby et al., 2021), we can appreciate the various forms of invisible, and at the time seemingly inconsequential, labor that laid the groundwork for subsequent waves of leadership. In 2017, when we gathered these leaders' stories, we understandably did not anticipate the impacts their work would have on shaping leadership practices for years to come. The cultural-political challenges they encountered in their respective contexts, presented in Table 3.2, foreshadowed the trends that followed as the momentum of the Black Lives Matter movement gave way to a new wave of conservative nationalism that emerged throughout the Biden administration and into a second Trump presidency.

Table 3.2. Equity Director Contexts

District	Equity Director Title and Year Created	Configuration	District "House"	About the Role	Budget and Resources
Accelera Independent School District	Cultural Proficiency and Inclusiveness Director - 2013	Collaboration	Professional Development	Positioned four people away from superintendent in organizational hierarchy	Very small budget of $50,000; no staff; her position supports 11,000 staff across the district
Bearclaw School District	Administrator for Equity and Inclusion - 2015	Management and Compliance	Department of Teaching and Learning	Single-person role, which has evolved; started working in district in 2007; then became administrator in 2014 for current role	Mid-sized budget of $206,000 + $600,000 for AVID[1]; 8 persons on staff (including 4 TOSAs[2], 2 of whom are in another department)
Broadview School District	Director of Equity and Graduation Success - 2013	Innovation and Development	Student Services	Started as director of graduation success; after 11 months he stepped into the equity director role; reports to the executive director for student services; positioned as the executive of the cabinet as department head	Undisclosed budget information; has a staff of 17 individuals

1. AVID: Advancing Via Individual Determination instructional professional development program

2. "TOSA: Teacher on Special Assignment"

City Schools of Division	Equity Director - 2017	Seeding	Not available	A part of the superintendent's cabinet; directly reports to superintendent; first district-led equity position; created by new superintendent who wanted to close disparities for Black students	Small budget that is still being finalized, nothing permanent currently in place; no staff
Fireside Public Schools	Executive Director of Equity for Scholar and Family Success - 2013	Management and Compliance	Student and Family Services	A part of the superintendent's cabinet	Mid-sized to large budget of \$175,000 + \$500,000 for AVID[1]; mid-sized to large staff of 16 department heads
Mainline Public Schools	Equity Specialist - 2015	Seeding-Collaboration	Professional Development	Reports to director of dept. of organizational development and to chief innovation and information officer; first district-led equity position; created based on Black Lives Matter resolution; position has shifted organizationally at least three times and is four layers removed from the superintendent	Small budget; budget allocated based on district resolution; includes four positions: equity specialist, diversity specialist, student engagement coordinator, and director of business and community partnerships; zero formal; supervises three teachers—ethnic studies and culturally responsive teacher

1. AVID: Advancing Via Individual Determination instructional professional development program

(*continued*)

Table 3.2. Equity Director Context (*continued*)

District	Equity Director Title and Year Created	Configuration	District "House"	About the Role	Budget and Resources
Outer Way School District	Deputy Chief of Equity (Senior Advisor of Equity, Diversity, and Inclusion) - 2016	Innovation and Development	Equity	Directly reports to the superintendent as a cabinet member; only person in role; has been directing African American male achievement for 8 years—shifted to districtwide role 2 years ago	Large budget of $5.7 million (60% foundation funded); large staff—oversees four "targeted strategies"—African American males, African American females, Latinx, API achievement; community engagement for seven networks
Richards County School District	Director of Equity and Diversity—NA	Innovation and Development	Professional Development	Has access to the superintendent as the direct advisor; reports directly to the superintendent	Office has a specific budget; oversees a staffed department with 19 full-time bilingual parent coordinators
Seaway School District	Director of Equity and Family Engagement - 2016	Collaboration	Instruction	Reports to assist superintendent in the instruction department; has "special"/temporary cabinet access; first person in this role	Small budget of $35,000; no staff

West Mile School District	Supervisor of Equity and Student Services—NA	Collaboration	Professional Development	Three positions away from the superintendent in the organizational chart; positioned as a part of the district's instructional framework	No budget but has access to resources if necessary for equity work; does not have staff or oversee a specific department; works with instructional equity coaches across school district
Westend County School District	Equity and Diversity Coordinator - 2013	Management and Compliance	Unknown	Has access to and meets monthly with the superintendent; positioned as the second person down from the superintendent in organizational hierarchy	Midsized staff of 11 people including a secretary, 3 equity and diversity specialists, and 1 Indian education specialist; budget is taken from the district's general fund; budget receives no grant support or title funds
Windsor Community School District	Chief Officer of Human Resources and Equity—NA	Management and Compliance	Human Resources	Role existed for more than 20 years prior to stepping into current equity/ community role; has direct access to the superintendent and reports directly to superintendent; member of the executive cabinet	Budget spent on "equity-related things"; small staff of approximately 7 people

(continued)

Table 3.2. Equity Director Context (*continued*)

District	Equity Director Title and Year Created	Configuration	District "House"	About the Role	Budget and Resources
Valley Farm Area School District	Director of Bilingual Programs and Instructional Equity - 2014	Management and Compliance	Instruction/ Bilingual Ed	A part of the superintendent's cabinet; directly reports to the superintendent; created as a result of growing bilingual population in the district; equity may have been an "attachment"	Small but "adequate" budget; 11 staff: district translators, bilingual staff, family–community liaison, continuous improvement coordinator + paraprofessionals (10–15)

The leaders and the ways their thankless and quiet equity leadership shaped their districts offer blueprints, policies, and core ideas that leaders throughout the United States can draw on to advance their own work. Ultimately, we hope that directors like Loretta, and the people who appreciate her experiences, will see the successes of their work in a renewed light: as creating the tools and laying the groundwork so that those who come behind them might have a light to guide their way in the struggle for more just schools. We hope readers will appreciate the leadership of those who did the work before the positions proliferated throughout the country. Their leadership offers crucial learning about how change unfolds over time and in ways that are often difficult to anticipate. We first discuss the misalignment between the work that equity directors expected to do when they accepted the role and the realities of their everyday activities, then describe four role configurations based on their activities and relation to formal organizational power and authority.

ANTICIPATED WORK

Districts created equity director positions to address the deeply entrenched problems and achieve transformative goals that districts have failed to ameliorate. Typically, districts assigned equity directors day-to-day work that differed from what equity directors expected to do when they accepted the role or in their job descriptions. For example, Lynne Hamilton, who was in her first year serving as equity director for City Schools of Division, explained:

> The job announcement had a full page of things that they were hoping to get from the person who was hired. So I have spent a lot of time doing that, *but* I've also done a lot of other things that district-level administrators are required to do. I participate in a lot of meetings. We have 4-hour cabinet meetings every week. I participate in school board meetings, which are typically 5 to 7 hours long. In my role I'm expected to present to the board every month. They make different requests and ask different questions that I'm expected to answer. I have a standing item on the board agenda which was something that *I didn't know would be required.*

Lynne described her expected work, as reflected in official district documents, as different from her actual work. Her job description, like others in our study, read like a laundry list of tasks. Districts' equity purpose statements also signaled what work districts expected equity directors to carry out. Table 3.3 presents examples of three equity organizational purpose statements. Some statements were far reaching and expansive. Others were rigidly specific. Some offered examples of how the work might be carried out, naming particular frameworks such as cultural responsiveness. Others did not.

Table 3.3. Sample Purpose Statements

Purpose Statement	Ambiguity	Role Configuration	Configuration Affordances	Configuration Constraints
The Department of Equity and Student Support is committed to understanding the root causes of disproportionality; providing input on discipline policies, practices, and culturally relevant pedagogy; engaging faculty and staff in cultural awareness and cultural proficiency professional learning activities; and strengthening family and community partnerships.—*Division*	Low	*Seeding*	Understand disproportionality Provide input on discipline policies and practices Family and community partnerships	Culturally relevant pedagogy Faculty and staff professional development
Support the district in consistent and equitable resource allocation; evaluation; development; and implementation of tools, policies, and practices to achieve racial and social equity for students, teachers, staff, and the community, regardless of race, ability, socioeconomic status, language, religion, sexual orientation, gender identity and expression, and other human differences.—*Accelera*	Low	*Collaboration*	Policy development and implementation	Resource allocation Evaluation
The purpose of the equity department is to create urgency and immediate impact on students of color and culturally and linguistically diverse students using culturally responsive practices and policies, while building racial equity awareness and skills with staff.—*Seaway*	High	*Collaboration*	Create urgency	Culturally responsive policies Build staff racial equity awareness and skills

ASSIGNED WORK

The work that equity directors were assigned, such as Lynne's requirement to "participate in a lot of meetings," is best understood through the configuration of equity director roles, which account for access to power and authority resources. We use the term role configurations to reference (1) the position of the role within the organizational structure and (2) the forms of organizational power and authority equity leaders are afforded to do the work. Four forms of formal organizational power and authority shaped their work and included:

1. Supervisory responsibility and authority
2. Influence on superintendent and board relations
3. Financial resources and budgetary discretion
4. Influence on district professional development related to curricular and instructional matters

Leaders explained the nature of their assigned leadership work and varying abilities to fulfill district expectations, depending on access to institutional power and authority. Table 3.4 provides a summary of the role configurations and associated common leadership activities, forms of power, and formal authority. Role configurations overlapped and diverged in unique ways.

Equity Innovation and Development Configurations and Activities

Equity innovation and development configurations afforded leaders a relatively high level of autonomy and influence on the direction of district equity programs and initiatives. The three directors who worked in roles configured for equity development and innovation experienced higher levels of supervisory authority and responsibility, more frequent interactions with superintendents and board members, more control over financial resources, and more decision-making latitude. Cole, the chief of equity for Outer Way School District, best exemplified the affordances of working in a role configured for innovation and development. He explained:

> You're not going to find me based on a role. But I am a cabinet member. I report directly to the superintendent. I am paid as a founding executive director of my previous position. So the point from which I'm funded has not changed. But when we evolved to the office of equity and I became the deputy chief of equity, I continued that reporting directly to the superintendent. I now supervise a team of directors: African American Male Achievement, Latino Student Achievement, African American Female Excellence, and Asian Pacific Islander Student Achievement.

Table 3.4. Role Configuration Characteristics

Configuration	Role Description (common leadership tasks)	Sources of Formal Power and Authority			
		Supervisory Responsibility and Authority	Superintendent Access and Board Influence	Resource and Budgetary Authority	Curricular and Instructional Influence
Innovation and Development	Creates and develops equity initiatives, programs, and professional learning opportunities. Is a partner with district superintendent, oversees a substantial budget, provides program development and oversight, directly supervises more than 10 district employees (e.g., department heads).	Substantial	Substantial	Substantial	Minimal
Management and Compliance	Manages and improves a portfolio of mostly preexisting district programs and initiatives by creating equity accountability systems, consolidating programs, and creating coherence. Usually reports to a department head but has routine access to the superintendent. Oversees a small staff—usually fewer than 10—and is provided with a modest budget.	Moderate	Substantial	Moderate	Minimal

Collaboration	Collaborates with other district employees to support a wide range of equity initiatives, such as parental engagement, principal and teacher professional development, and special programming. Does not work directly with superintendents, has small or no budget, no program oversight or supervisory responsibilities.	Minimal	Moderate	Minimal	Moderate
Seeding	Writes policies and drafts language; creates equity documents; provides district and community stakeholders with presentations, educational resources, data, and access to student, parent, and community perspectives that make the case for why equity is important. Can be situated in multiple parts of the district but often lacks power or influence to do more than present information.	Minimal	Moderate	Minimal	Minimal

As the deputy chief of equity, Cole was a cabinet member who worked in partnership with the district superintendent and oversaw a nearly 6-million-dollar budget (over half of which he was responsible for fundraising from outside sources). Outer Way Unified School District's position was rare in terms of budget, responsibility, and decision-making latitude. Yet despite the autonomy that role configuration afforded Cole, his directors, and his office, its configuration did *not* afford influence over long-standing organizational units. Cole shared, "We haven't been able to really penetrate teaching and learning, HR, talent investment, research assessment and data," which reveals that all configurations have baked-in constraints that shape equity directors' abilities to do the work they believed would be most impactful.

Equity Management and Compliance Configurations and Activities

Equity directors working in equity management and compliance configurations enjoyed relatively high-level access to superintendents and budgetary discretion. These roles offered more substantive supervisory responsibility than those in equity collaboration configurations. However, their work was overwhelmingly managerial and compliance oriented. We identified four districts with this configuration. For several participants in our study, their authority usually rested in management and improvement of preexisting district programs or initiatives, such as bilingual education or family engagement. Management and compliance role configurations afforded more autonomy and authority than roles configured for equity collaboration. As the name suggests, they primarily required management of programs, logistical maintenance of partnerships, and oversight of initiatives that previously existed. They often did not fit easily into other district units. Defining features of this configuration included responsibility over substantial resources, busy-ness, and an inability to undertake equity work they believed would affect change.

Maria, whose title was Fireside School District's Executive Director of Equity for Scholar and Family Success, worked within a role configuration that was primarily management compliance (but that hybridized with collaboration). As did people working in collaboration configurations, Maria explained her role as the go-to person for equity:

Maria: In a nutshell, my roles and responsibilities are to help teachers and staff, all 11,000, develop an understanding of how their personal background impacts the decisions they make, the interactions they have with students, with families, with other staff, and ultimately how that supports the educational success of the students in our school district.

Interviewer: I just want to be clear. Prior to you receiving this grant, you were tasked with supporting 11,000 teachers and staff by yourself?

Maria: Yes. I still am, technically. It's mostly going to schools to do cultural proficiency trainings. You can take however many staff that are at those ten schools that are now supported by the grant off my plate. The grant-funded people now directly support those ten schools. But, yeah. I am still responsible for the rest of them. By myself.

Her account underscored her busy-ness, which coincided with her inability to undertake the equity work she believed would affect change. She explained the supervisory and district partnership coordination roles that characterize those working in the equity management and compliance configuration:

> I supervise 16 different people and basically 16 different programs. I was charged with launching a national consulting groups' work although it had already been agreed upon what that would look like. They pretty much have a standard model so my role was mostly managing logistics for the consultants. As for the programs, I oversaw all elementary family liaisons. P.B.I.S. implementation Pre K through 12, homelessness, the truancy process, athletics and activities counselors, AVID, all the discipline, and Native education.
>
> I was the lead de-escalator with any very upset person that would come into the district. I would be the one that typically handled the de-escalation. I worked with the Office of Civil Rights and the Ombudsman on a couple of different issues that were brought to the district by parents. Finally, I served on the superintendents' executive board. I was required to attend all the school board meetings. And I was required to provide PowerPoints and all supporting documentation to prepare the superintendent for board meetings.

Maria narrated her work in a discourse of compliance, a key insight into the dynamics of power in role configurations. Similar to others in management and compliance configurations, she talked about what she was "charged, required, and had to do," more so than what she believed would affect change (this was different for innovation and development configurations). The emphasis on management and compliance and the experiences of busy-ness it created persisted regardless of where districts housed management and compliance–configured roles.

Equity Collaboration Configurations and Activities

The equity directors in equity collaboration configurations spent most of their time "supporting" or "implementing" district- or school-based equity initiatives, mostly in the form of sporadic professional development. They supported and worked with a broad range of stakeholders. We categorized four districts as having equity collaboration role configurations. Equity collaboration configurations offered the closest resemblance to Mitchell and colleagues' (2017) concept of role vulnerability, where equity directors encountered flexibility to address everyday demands but with unclear or inconsistent work portfolios. People whose work was configured as such described their work as all encompassing. They experienced lower levels of supervisory authority and responsibility and less frequent interaction with superintendents and board members. They worked with limited or no budgetary authority and had little latitude in decision-making.

Equity Seeding Configurations and Activities

We characterize equity seeding configurations as those suited for leadership activities that planted core equity ideas into the district's guiding documents, policies, and discourses. Common leadership activities included drafting and shaping equity policies, creating and delivering presentations, curating outside resources and supports (e.g., articles, consultations), and gathering and organizing data to make the case for equity to internal and external stakeholders. We categorized Division and Mainline districts' roles as configured for seeding equity. Both districts' equity directors, Lynne Hamilton and Loretta Richards, offered one-on-one thought partnership and equity influence by way of information sharing (e.g., disaggregated district data, latest research on equity). Director roles configured for seeding did not provide leaders with extensive supervisory responsibility, the exception being managing the work of interns and select specialty hires. Although seeding work influenced board decision-making through floating policy ideas, shaping district equity policies and discourses, and generating focused responsiveness to local and national injustices, participants in seeding configurations self-assessed their work as inconsequential absent the approval of more powerful organization members.

STRUCTURES THAT MISALIGN ACTIVITY

Although districts had expectations for equity directors, directors brought a wellspring of ideas, beliefs, theories of change, and priorities to their work. And the role configurations they inherited created affordances and constraints for directors to enact what they believed needed to happen to improve the social, emotional, and academic experiences and outcomes of students. For instance, leaders in management and innovation roles were relatively well resourced and thus assigned more influential equity work but found they still had little direct influence on the instructional culture of schools. Those in collaborator roles were subjected to far-reaching yet ill-defined responsibilities that resulted in them doing "any and everything related to equity" and working at the whim of whoever needed support at a given time. Leaders in seeding configurations developed policies and presented data but had little power to implement policies or influence principals, teachers, or any stakeholder for that matter. In light of these constraints and affordances, all of the leaders engaged in the largely invisible practice of job molding—evolving their roles to be better configured to the work responsibilities and tasks they considered most consequential. In what follows, we explore in more depth the vulnerabilities of the roles while also emphasizing equity leaders' agential actions to reconfigure them for greater influence and impact.

Structural Vulnerabilities

Equity leaders often describe their relationship to their districts as restrictive. They worked amid an unspoken assigned "place" (role configuration, race, gender, etc.) that districts inadequately resourced and/or misaligned with district equity expectations. Scholars define *structural vulnerabilities* as inconsistencies or ambiguities inherent in the structure of a role that minimize a person's ability to carry out the work to accomplish their aims (Mitchell et al., 2017). In the case of equity leadership, the shifting demands and pressures of school districts; unclear, inconsistent, and often unrealistic work portfolios; and roles structured with limited resources and formal authority manifested as equity leaders not being able to carry out expected or prioritized work. Next, Lynne talks about how she found herself hamstrung by her seeding configuration role, which left her unable to carry out the work she believed needed to happen.

> *I am a department of one for right now.* So I have no one else who reports to me. And really no one else on my team. I am a part of the superintendent's cabinet. I'm his direct report . . . *I never know how that works.* I do partner with other people in the superintendent's cabinet, including the Executive Director of Curriculum and Instruction, Special Education, and Student Support. We all sort of work together, but that's where my role fits [emphases added].

Lynne's statement underscores how her being the only person in her department created a sense of vulnerability for her position. She was inadequately resourced. She also reported to a supervisor who she considered incapable of supporting her. Loretta, Shawn, Cole, and Wesley shared the same conundrum: Their supervisors had formal power and authority to shape the district's efforts and the equity director's role and work, but their own roles lacked authority and power. By organizational standards, Lynne held a relatively powerful position. However, the role configuration minimized her ability to affect change. Her influence was primarily lateral. In her role, she did not directly influence principals or teachers (i.e., what actually happens inside of classrooms) as much as she interacted with the school board members. Her job description suggested her work would focus on implementing equity efforts, but the fact that the role was configured as part of the superintendent's cabinet required her to commit substantial time and energy doing, as she stated, "things that district-level administrators are required to do," which was often far from the work of implementation on the ground. In short, the role as it was configured did not allow Lynne to carry out the district's expected work as well as the work she believed was the most important work.

Psychological Vulnerability

If structural vulnerabilities constrain directors by creating unspoken relegations to assigned daily work, psychological vulnerability is its counterpart. Psychological vulnerability emerges as self-doubt and stress that a person experiences as a gap between the work tasks they are actually assigned to carry out and the work that they prefer (or believe is the right work) to undertake (Gronn & Lacey, 2004). For equity leaders, psychological vulnerability revealed a three-fold experiential gap between what the district expected them to do, what they were assigned to carry out by virtue of their role configuration, and what they believed they should be doing to impact change. This multifold gap created stress that was exacerbated by the difficulties equity directors often faced in their efforts to reconfigure their roles for influence and impact.

Loretta Richards, the equity specialist from Mainline Public Schools, explained the chasm she experienced working in a seeding equity configuration for a district that expected her to collaborate. Loretta's early work focused primarily on a nondiscrimination policy that she revived "to include gender identity, gender expression and gender non-conformity, and a comprehensive guidance document to accompany what that actually means in practice." During the time she rewrote the policy, her work was well configured for equity seeding, allowing her to successfully usher the policy through superintendent and board of education approval. After this success, she shifted her focus "to work on implementation of that policy," which was outlined as an expected requirement in the position's job description. However, the district's seeding role configuration did not afford her power to achieve any semblance of implementation. As she worked to implement the newly adopted policy, she found herself facing multiple constraints, including resistance from supervisors who didn't share her priorities.

> Initially I was going to report to the Director of Innovation, who reports to the Chief of Innovation, who reports directly to the superintendent. But nobody really knows what the heck to do with this work. Bless my director. She's sweet as pie but she don't get it [equity leadership]. And so to do the kind of work that I needed to do, I needed to have some of those layers removed.

As noted earlier, Loretta perceived she did not have adequate power or authority to carry out implementation work. She explained how her relatively low position in the organization, the lack of knowledgeable supervisors, and "layers" interlocked to create a set of vulnerabilities that she tried her best to navigate. As we describe next, people within the organization ridiculed her efforts and admonished her for "overstepping" her role when she sought to address the structural vulnerabilities. The compounding experiences manifested as psychological vulnerability, self-doubt, and stress.

EXPANDING THEIR "PLACE" IN THE ORGANIZATION TO ALIGN THE WORK

Despite the structural and psychological vulnerabilities, role configurations are not static. Equity leaders recognized the need to dynamically reshape their roles and activity across time as organizational and sociopolitical conditions shifted. Directors frequently worked outside of their configurations to take on roles they deemed important. For instance, Loretta took it upon herself to fix the structural vulnerabilities of the role:

> I began to just report directly to the Chief of Innovation. I was the only specialist to do so. Since that was "out of order" so to speak, they put me under professional development so I could report to a director. The Director of Professional Development is in the Department of Organizational Development. So I'm in the Office of Innovation, but I report to the Senior Director of Organizational Development, who reports to the Chief of Innovation, who reports to the Superintendent.

Her agential actions, in the form of going around her direct report, expanded the equity specialist role to include limited professional development design and implementation. From there, she designed and implemented district-mandated equity and cultural responsiveness professional development and trainings for principals but noted that "central services units were not mandated to have the trainings." Although the role's configuration with low rank in the organizational hierarchy stifled her progress, she expanded her role to be able to better influence directors of more powerful district units.

Similarly, Tanya took agential action for about 5 years to reduce the vulnerabilities inherent in her role in Seaway School District. When she was hired, Tanya had neither staff nor resources to support students and provide professional development to implement the equity work the district had charged and expected her to complete. Tanya explained, "I don't think there was any expectation about what this work would actually look like. I'm all about strategic moves." She worked strategically across time to leverage grants and shift positions structured under other departments to become her direct reports. Through her agentive moves, she was able to build her department from 2 to 11 staff positions, including equity specialists; specialists for Native American, African American, and Pacific Islander students; and parent engagement specialists and language instructors who worked in the schools.

Although these "seeding" equity leaders restructured their positions to be able to implement programs, even the more powerfully situated configurations experienced structural vulnerabilities due to leadership turnover. For instance, Cole, whose role was originally configured as equity innovation and development, narrated the expansion of his role from overseeing a single specialized program, to overseeing multiple targeted programs with additional staff, to overseeing *all* of the district's equity work. He narrated these shifts as necessary strategic moves to navigate the constant superintendent turnover that might otherwise undermine efforts to sustain equity work in the system:

> Yeah, [I'm on my] fifth superintendent and—you can only imagine—five superintendents, so each time, there's tectonic shifts. So I just say that to say, I've moved all over the place. . . . When the one constant in these institutions is change, and you have superintendents coming and going, when you talk about racial equity work . . . it's really hard to get this innovative prototyping to then grip, to facilitate system change. It's just a constant revolving door. It speaks to the complexity of trying to grow something when you're constantly changing and still trying to calibrate with the traditional structure.

Thus, equity leaders worked to increase their influence and authority in areas they considered important for carrying out their work. In doing so, they reshaped educational systems for future equity leadership efforts.

CONCLUSION

Like Loretta, Tanya, and Cole, almost all of the directors in our study explained that they, themselves, did the politically fraught equity leadership work of job molding and reconfiguring their roles to make them capable of carrying out the work they believed was most important. Ironically, especially in the case of those "seeding" equity work, leaders' own efforts and "successes" in their roles generated the need for new role configurations to carry out new phases of work. Their efforts played a substantial role in expanding equity work from singular positions characterized by structural and psychological vulnerabilities to multiple roles and systemic activity across educational systems. However, their ability to influence systems change varied, not only by district context but also by the race-gender positionality of equity leaders. In Chapter 4 of this book, we examine how Black and other women of color equity leaders exercised their agency to address the compounding "organizational jeopardy" in racialized and gendered educational organizations.

At the time we completed the equity director study, many of the leaders did not define their efforts as "successful." Yet as we look back on their efforts from the distance of time, we can appreciate the fruits of their efforts in now-routine access to restrooms for students with nonbinary identities; racial equity policies, plans, and decision-making procedures; disaggregated data and ongoing educator professional learning about cultural responsiveness; renamed schools; and affinity groups. Their efforts are also reflected in the multiple professional roles and equity activities that have proliferated throughout all corners of districts and schools. Some might even argue that the ferocity of the pushback on DEI work in PK–12 public educational systems can be seen as an indicator of the extent to which this early cadre of equity leaders planted seeds for "the work" to be expanded across systems and taken up by broader teams of educators.

REFERENCES

Gronn, P., & Lacey, K. (2004). Positioning oneself for leadership: Feelings of vulnerability among aspirant school principals. *School Leadership & Management*, *24*(4), 405–424. https://doi.org/10.1080/1363243041000l316516

Irby, D. J., Green, T., & Ishimaru, A. M. (2022). PK–12 district leadership for equity: An exploration of director role configurations and vulnerabilities. *American Journal of Education*, *128*(3), 417–453.

Mitchell, C., Armstrong, D., & Hands, C. (2017). "Oh, is that my job?": Role vulnerability in the vice-principalship. *Journal of the Commonwealth Council for Educational Administration & Management*, *45*(1), 3–18.

CHAPTER 4

Reshaping the System

Paradoxes of Leading From Within Oppressive Organizations

Ann M. Ishimaru, Decoteau J. Irby, and Terrance Green

> "The paradox of education is precisely this—that as one begins to become conscious one begins to examine the society in which he is being educated."
>
> —James Baldwin, 1963 (A Talk to Teachers, n.p.)

Yet again, Kiara found herself at a table of mostly white district leaders. As the equity director for her district, Kiara regularly drew on her professional expertise, formal training, and personal experiences as a Black woman and mother to raise pointed questions, advocate for those not at the table, and flag racial inequities in the system. She knew if she spoke now, though, her insights would be resisted by Janice, the white woman director of student services. Janice had recently complained about Kiara's "aggressive" approach and leadership. And yet Kiara's role required her to raise precisely these concerns. Feeling exhausted, she took a deep breath and spoke in a calm, measured tone.

Versions of Kiara's scenario play out over and over in school systems across the country. Female leaders of color often not only face outright resistance to their equity efforts but must also manage routine racial and gendered microaggressions and stereotyped assessments of their leadership. In this chapter, we shift our gaze to formal educational systems themselves and the paradoxes of leading equity-based change in systems that were never designed to realize the thriving of all children. Across time and context, scenarios like this one illuminate the organizational structures, resources, and power dynamics that constitute what we have come to call an "organizational double jeopardy" for Black and other racially minoritized women "doing the work" of equity leadership within entrenched racialized and gendered organizations.

The leadership of Black and other women and people of color within educational systems often represents a paradox. On the one hand, schools represent institutional aims and structures of settler colonialism (Dunbar-Ortiz, 2014), anti-Blackness, and racism (Woodson, 1933). On the other hand, people within school systems, especially Black women, have long enacted antiracist and even liberatory leadership for all children (Dillard, 2021; Siddle Walker, 2000). Given how many equity leaders identify as Black, Latina, Native, Asian American, and Pacific Islander women, it comes as little surprise that they experience constant limitations and resistance to their leadership as well as racial battle fatigue (Smith et al., 2007). Racially minoritized women are at the vanguard of equity leadership in U.S. schools; while women of color represent 12.9% of superintendents nationally (according to the American Superintendent 2020 Decennial Study), over 54% in our 2022 survey of equity leaders identified as women of color, with 30% identifying as Black women.

In this chapter, we share how the organizational paradox of leading for equity within oppressive educational systems intersects with the organizational change-making of Black and other racially minoritized women. Paradoxically, the very racial-gender positionalities that diminish their change-making influence and exact an undue psychological toll constitute assets and knowledge resources that racially minoritized women leaders draw on to strategically reshape the organizational capacity, structures, resources, and priorities of the system. In the current moment of all-out attacks on efforts to realize educational justice, the strategic knowledge and organization-shaping practices of Black women leaders offer crucial, contextually based approaches for navigating and continuing to "do the work" of equity leadership.

SEEING THE ORGANIZATION IN THE PARADOX OF LEADING FOR EQUITY IN SYSTEMS

Much of the research and media on racially minoritized women leaders emphasize individual strategies for managing the routine racial-gendered microaggressions and negative assessments of their leadership. These are certainly important—and other chapters in this book illuminate strategies that leaders in our research employed to navigate and resist these kinds of interactions—but individuals are not the root of the problem. It's not a random coincidence that so many equity-focused female leaders of color encounter these dynamics. Instead, we must see the organizations that enable these dynamics.

Organizations are what scholars refer to as "racial structures"—a means of linking material and social resources with organizational rules and rewards (Ray, 2019). Organizational paradoxes, then, are contradictory tensions that result from complex, competing demands. These competing elements are not benign or neutral; they are consequential, racialized, and gendered (Lewis & Diamond, 2015). As we discussed in Chapter 3, we also know that instability, uncertainty, and tension are inherent in certain roles like that of the equity director, but structural vulnerability alone fails to account for the institutionalized racial-gender oppression that is a well-documented fact of life in U.S. institutions and society (Crenshaw, 1991).

Kimberlé Crenshaw first coined the term "intersectionality" to recognize the interlocking systems of racial, gender, and class oppression that shape the experiences of Black and other women of color, beyond race or gender alone. Intersectionality highlights how the intersections of racism and sexism (and other powered systems) function to compound oppression in ways that are not simply additive and not fully addressed by single-dimension antiracist or feminist analyses (Crenshaw, 1989, 1991). Although intersectionality explicitly seeks to connect individual experience and identity with broader systems of oppression, Agosto and Roland (2018) reviewed the leadership research and found that most studies using intersectionality reinforced a conception of leadership focused at the individual or interpersonal level alone. Few studies examined intersectional dynamics at an organizational level, such as school districts, in ways that "exposed uneven power relations beyond the leader's identity related to systemic inequities within education" (Agosto & Roland, 2018, p. 276). They argued (and we concur) that this overreliance on individualism in the application of intersectionality theory obscures attention to the organizational aspects of oppression as well as the relational and coalitional leadership practices of leaders. When we instead focus on the interplay between individual leader identity and organizational dynamics, a clearer picture emerges.

Simply put, racially minoritized women leaders face stressors in organizations that their white, cis-male counterparts do not. For example, Rosette and Livingston (2012) concluded that leaders with "dual-subordinate identities" (racially minoritized and female) receive less support, face more pressure, and earn less praise for their organizational performance. In their study, they found that Black women's coworkers were more critical in their assessments of Black women leaders than of any other group. Yet when Black women's leadership efforts yielded favorable results, they were not rewarded or celebrated to any extent higher than male counterparts of any race (Rosette & Livingston, 2012). Thus, the paradoxes and structural vulnerability embedded within organizations are exacerbated for people in minoritized race and gender groups. Our findings suggest that these dynamics are even more pronounced for racially minoritized women who center equity in their leadership. At the same time, to be effective at their job, equity-focused leaders must disrupt the organization itself, which can lead to disproportionately negative consequences for their leadership and professional trajectories. In short, schools rely on Black female leaders while undermining and diminishing them.

What does this all mean for understanding and supporting equity leadership at a systems level? It means that minoritized identities (in systems of oppression) intersect with organizational paradoxes to constitute an organizational problem—not solely an individual one. That may sound abstract, but it has profound implications not only for supporting equity-focused, racially minoritized women leaders but also for transforming educational systems more broadly. To understand the significance of that reconceptualization, we must understand how racial battle fatigue has been studied, understood, and addressed in practice.

Racial battle fatigue describes the "physiological and psychological strain exacted on racially marginalized groups and the amount of energy spent dedicated to coping with racial microaggressions and racism" (Smith et al., 2007, p. 555). In practice, the responses to Black women educators and others who narrate experiences of racial battle fatigue are often about self-care and supports for individual coping. This places the onus on the very individuals charged with changing such dynamics. An individual framing of the problem also obscures the organizational conditions that create racial battle fatigue to begin with. This circular logic situates individuals impacted by racial oppression as both those most affected by the problem and the sole individuals responsible for addressing it.

When instead of individuals, we focus on the organization, we begin not only to address the root causes of experiences but also to better understand the agentic moves equity leaders make to expand their influence and reshape oppressive organizations. Although the findings of this particular study focused originally on those in the equity director role, the organizational dynamics we illuminate here extend to those leading for systems equity regardless of their formal title and role.

NOTICING ORGANIZATIONAL DOUBLE JEOPARDY IN EDUCATIONAL SYSTEMS

As a result of the intersectional racialized and gendered oppression within district organizations, Black and other racially minoritized women equity leaders experienced both structural and interpersonal organizational penalties, a dynamic we refer to as organizational double jeopardy. In other words, the majority of equity leaders who identified as Black (and other racially minoritized) women experienced both racial and gendered oppression—a "penalty" for both race and gender—via organizational dynamics that diminished their agency and professional authority.

This double organizational penalty also manifested in inadequate resources and access to decision-making for their work, conflictual racial-gendered interactions, resistance to, and negative assessments of their leadership. The organizational double jeopardy experienced by Black women equity leaders contrasted with the equity leaders who experienced organizational racism or sexism along only a single axis—that is, racialized dynamics as men of color or gendered experiences as a white woman. These inequities in organizational power exacted a significant emotional, psychological, and physical toll on equity directors, an experience of racial battle fatigue that was particularly acute for those who identified as Black women. Paradoxically, then, Black and other racially minoritized women equity directors charged with disrupting inequities in the district were subject to organizational double jeopardy, undermining their ability to fulfill their charge of leading systems change.

Differential Respect and Legitimacy

First, equity leaders experienced dramatically different organizational and professional returns depending on their racial and gendered positionalities. For instance, within our sample, women directors had higher levels of formal educational attainment than men (see Table 3.1 in Chapter 3). Specifically, seven of eight women participants either already had or were pursuing doctoral-level degrees; of the men in our sample, three had master's degrees, one had a bachelor's degree, and one was unknown (though was not identified in public documents as "Dr."). Although most of the women did not explicitly discuss their academic credentials, Tanya, a Black woman, noted that "I do think for me that we need to be formally educated. Walking into a room where it says doctor versus . . . [Tanya]. I think it carries weight when I'm in front of a room talking about the subject. That can't be easily dismissed in the way I think might be possible . . . in that situation." She named that her perceived expertise on issues of race and equity required additional legitimacy in the form of higher education credentials.

Differential Leadership Assessments

Second, particularly racially minoritized women equity leaders described how racialized and gendered power dynamics negatively impacted perceptions of their leadership and interactions with others in the district. For instance, Tracie highlighted the relatively few Black women in her system, a history of their departures, and the resulting dynamics of power that she perceived as limiting her ability to make change:

> The place I sit [in] the org chart. Our chief officer will say titles don't matter or shouldn't matter but they do. Especially when you are a Black woman. So, being a Black woman in this system who has seen Black women leave in droves and there really weren't a lot of us anyway. Many of the Black women in our system are marginalized to the fullest extent, so that impacts my ability to effect change, because I don't have affinity in the organization.

In this description, Tracie emphasized both the demographic predominance of white bodies that constitutes "white space" in educational systems and the interactional dynamics of power, which tend to diminish the agency and influence of racially minoritized individuals within racialized organizations (Ray, 2019). Tracie's experience resonates with recent scholarship expanding the meaning of "white space" to apply to features of the culture and climate in organizations, such as the norms, expectations, interpretations, and cultural practices that shape everyday interactions (Clark, this book; Lewis & Diamond, 2022).

However, these dynamics were not only racialized but also gendered. The intersecting dynamic of race and gender for these equity leaders highlights what they experienced as a kind of double jeopardy, in which their influence and organizational resources were not only diminished due to their race but their leadership practice was questioned and framed within race-gendered stereotypical tropes, such as the angry Black woman (Doharty, 2020) or the foreign "tiger" Asian mom (Poon, 2011). Building on her description of marginalization, Tracie went on to connect whiteness and maleness with power, alluding to the stereotype of the angry Black woman: "It's a white dominant viewpoint . . . about how we do things. It's about control. So you want me to calm down to make you feel better. And my . . . anger is not even at full load." Similarly, Maria, who identified as a multiracial Pacific Islander, Asian, and white woman, narrated how racialized and gendered dynamics compounded when others react favorably to white male colleagues in leadership but frame her similar approach as problematic and in need of improvement:

> With the men who are white . . . [they] would be like, "oh they're really passionate . . . what a powerful leader." . . . And then I would [say] the same thing, it would be like, "So you really need to tone it down . . . you're too harsh, you're offending the principals, I have had principals complain about you." In my previous district, a white female principal complained to my supervisor because, you know, I was asking things like, "Well you're [a] 70% Latino community—when is the last time you sent something home in Spanish?" You know, anything of that nature. I was perceived just like in this negative tone. But my counterparts? Especially white males . . . are perceived as like, they're passionate, they're just trying to get down to the core problem here.

Thus, educators often perceive equity-related communication differently depending on the deliverer, where a white male leader might be "passionate" or "powerful," but a woman of color would be "harsh" or "angry." In these instances, the white patriarchal space of the educational system focused attention on racially minoritized women leaders' tone and delivery in ways that marginalized their leadership and minimized their influence.

Differential Positioning and Agency

Third, the experience of Black and other racially minoritized women equity leaders contrasted with those who identified as minoritized along only a single axis, such as race or gender. That is, men of color and the one white woman in our sample were positioned more powerfully structurally and did not mention racial and gendered organizational dynamics as constraints on their agency, influence, or access to organizational resources (such as staff, budget, and access to the superintendent and board).

All three male equity leaders experienced racialized dynamics in their roles, but they narrated the affordances of their positions in explicit contrast to the predominant positioning of women (of color) equity directors. For instance, Shawn, an African American male equity director, explained that he had significant resources in his role, a context that he explicitly noted as differing from other equity directors in the region (who, at the time, were all racially minoritized women):

> My position is unique with regard to our regional people, or regional non-profits, or regional school districts that have this role. [Unlike others] I do have an org chart, I do have a staff, I do have a budget. Organizationally, there was a point in time when I first took the role, I reported to the superintendent. I put a squash on that because I was so new in the organization that I needed a good level of support. Because I needed someone to be there, ride or die with me every single day. And when you're reporting to a super[intendent], and you take someone like me who's come from a legacy of non-profit into a public sector role. I just always needed some constant support, like some daily constant support. So my role is under an executive director now, but I have my own sort of vision mission stuff. I have key norms and goals. I'm set up as a department, as an authentic department. And [I'm] one of the 14 people on the executive cabinet. I have a budget, and I have staff. I have a secretary who is pretty much my entire life. I couldn't do my job without her.

Shawn, like all male study participants, talked about possessing the autonomy to craft his own "sort of vision and mission"; he actually changed his role to report to someone a step down from the superintendent so he could have more consistent support as someone coming from outside the educational system. His experience stands in stark contrast with a number of Black women leaders who brought substantially more experience in educational systems (as teachers, counselors, or principals) yet were positioned far from the superintendent. Although gender was likely only one of several important factors (including the background of the leader and context of the district), the other two equity directors who identified as men described their positions as directly reporting to the superintendent, and all three oversaw significant staff and financial resources. For instance, Cole, another Black male equity director, regarded himself as the "architect" of his district's equity efforts. His budget far exceeded any of the others in our sample, and he explicitly differentiated his office and organizational resources from the norm in other school districts across the country:

> It's a very different approach to most offices of equity as when I even did the research before incubating this department in 2000, really it was two years. Most of your offices of equity in school districts are compliance driven, led by women and completely under-resourced and understaffed.

None of the male equity directors characterized their efforts as a struggle to the same extent, or in as fine strategic detail, as did study participants who identified as racially minoritized women.

Similarly, equity leadership in relation to only gender oppression seemed to contrast with the experiences of Black and other racially minoritized women. Linda, the one white woman equity director in our sample, also reported directly to the superintendent and described having "more than enough resources" as well as a significant level of influence on the superintendent and board. In fact, in reflecting on how her racial identity shaped her approach to her work, Linda shared how her awareness of her racialized power in the district necessitated particular care when it came to partnering with communities of color in the work:

> But I do have to really be aware of . . . who I am and how much space I take up in certain places, and also knowing that it's really important for me as a white woman in this role, even though I am bilingual and I consider myself bicultural, that . . . I can't be the voice of others. I have to stand with my colleagues and parents of color. That's what's really important to me and I also want people to trust that. That I'm not coming at an approach or my approach isn't one of advocacy, it's more of empowerment, right? I think that it's because of my race and because I have positional power in my district. I have to really always be aware of that.

Thus, in referencing "it's because of my race," Linda narrated her awareness of whiteness as a credential in the district organization (Ray, 2019), a form of power that afforded her voice and influence that she felt she needed to be cautious to mobilize in support of colleagues and parents of color (whose voices, in contrast, did not hold the same power or influence in the district).

Differential Psychological, Emotional, and Physical Toll

Finally, the organizational double jeopardy of racial and gendered oppression intersected with the structural vulnerability of the equity director role to exact a significant psychological, emotional, and even physical toll, what scholars have referred to as racial battle fatigue (Arnold et al., 2016; Smith et al., 2007). Equity directors and leaders who centered equity across race and gender mentioned the challenges of the work, and several spoke to the need to address the psychological and emotional toll exacted by equity work in districts. While this toll was felt by all the equity leaders we spoke with, the experience of racial battle fatigue seemed particularly pronounced for equity leaders who identified as Black women. For instance, Tanya, a Black woman equity director, described her role as "fighting a system" composed of people uninvested in change, resulting in impacts that accumulate both daily and over time:

> I think it's a really fragile position and I know this year when—I don't know how much longer I can be in this position because it's not so much a face to face, you are fighting a system. We're trying to push a system to move in a direction. You still have to deal with those barriers that are there because people are not so quick to want to move or change or shift. That takes a toll and . . . that toll is in addition to the toll you're already carrying day to day trying to make it.

Black women equity leaders also implicated the paradox of leading equity work in racialized and gendered organizations as a source of particular strain. For instance, Tracie explained:

> It's one thing to just be a Black woman in a predominantly white space because that's always on your mind. But to be a Black woman in a predominantly white space doing equity work, that just adds another layer. So after five years, I'm tired. I'll be honest with you.

Likewise, April, another Black woman equity leader, was explicit about the need to be "strategic" because she knew her voice would not be heard or respected by particular individuals in positions of power within a white-dominant system that was often actively resistant to change:

> I mean being a Black woman doing race equity work in a White dominant school district—I find that I have to be very strategic. I'm sitting at the table today, what I said about that laundry list of things that all went into equitable learning environments. And I said to the table, and I can't be the one to say that. . . . It's like, no I cannot be the one to say that. Someone else at this table needs to say that. Because I know that my supervisor and the person that reports to him that's overseeing the social emotional learning environment work in our district are very White dominant. Very White fragility, very anti-talking about race. And don't want to have anything to do with the race conversation, but they are leading this equity work. [The district] is all about equity. But they don't even know what it is. And they don't want to know what it is. And they don't want me talking to people about it.

In this quote, April illuminated how the formal rules of the organization—equal voice and consideration in deliberations about fostering equitable learning environments—are often decoupled in racialized ways from actual organizational practice. In this case, the Black woman equity leader's voice holds less weight and is responded to with greater resistance.

Taken together, the dynamics of organizational double jeopardy and racial battle fatigue experienced by Black and other racially minoritized women equity leaders represent a paradox that continues into the present moment of all-out attack on diversity, equity, and inclusion work in education. That is, districts often have inadequate understanding of the investment and organizational conditions required to advance the work of equity. Invariably, equity work necessitates efforts to change policies and practices across a wide range of other departments across a system. Equity leadership requires engaging with and working to change the decision-making, norms, and practices of power-holders, administrators, and educators within white-dominant spaces, many of whom were resistant to even having conversations about race in education. In short, the organizational double jeopardy experienced by Black and other racially minoritized women equity leaders constrains their agency, minimizes their organizational resources, and undermines their legitimacy and influence in pursuing equity-focused change. However, those organizational impacts comprise only half the story. Black women and other racially minoritized women have never been hapless victims in institutions; their experiences navigating oppressive organizations also constitute potent resources for reshaping systems.

LEVERAGING EXPERIENTIAL KNOWLEDGE TO STRATEGICALLY CHANGE THE ORGANIZATION

Despite the double jeopardy in their organizations, Black and other racially minoritized women equity leaders mobilized their race-gendered lived experiences as forms of knowledge and expertise to reshape their organizations. Black women especially talked about building strategic relationships, making strategic comments, and embarking upon strategic endeavors to expand leadership (their own and that of others) to make change. Over time, equity leaders drew on their lived experiences and race-gendered experiential knowledge to (1) build organizational capacity for equity work, (2) restructure the organization, (3) expand organizational resources, and (4) legitimize an organizational priority on equity work. Thus, paradoxically, the race-gendered positionalities associated with organizational double jeopardy are also essential sources of experiential race-gendered knowledge and resources for leading educational equity work and expanding influence.

Building Organizational Capacity for Equity Work

A key aspect of organizational change toward equity relates to the collective capacity of those in the organization to understand, inquire, dialogue, and collaborate with each other in addressing historically rooted structures, policies, and systemic inequities, as well as the current organizational routines, practices, and interactions that perpetuate the status quo (Galloway & Ishimaru, 2019). All the equity leaders of color, but especially the Black women, described their lived experiences of marginalization as an important resource that they drew on professionally to build the organizational capacity of their systems to address inequities. As April explained:

> So, I think being unapologetically . . . Black, proud, mother. I will use my children in any professional context to help people understand how Black boys are marginalized and to give a personal face, because they respect me. I think the fact that I build relationships and I build bridges with people that's a factor that affects my ability to affect change.

For another Black woman equity leader, Tanya, her experiences informed her understanding of the experiences of students and families within the system and the dangers of an assimilative approach to change:

> So I think being aware of either your position in a racialized world or in the system that you're working in [helps]. I mean . . . most people that I've talked to, they have [this] position . . . are also people of color, which may not necessarily be a requirement. I think it helps to have lived an experience where you have been marginalized. I think it's also important to be able to recognize that as much as you are part of a system that you're trying to help and support, you can become a part of that system because of the danger in becoming assimilated into the system that you're also trying to push—which is a fine balance.

Here, Tanya also noted the tension of becoming assimilated into the system by virtue of occupying a district position. That is, equity leaders draw on their own experiences to bring a critical lens to noticing power and avoiding the subtractive dynamics of assimilation to a dominant white patriarchal system.

Loretta, a Black woman, described how her own experiences enable her to connect with families and those who have been "othered" by the system. Such relationships are a crucial starting point for building the organizational capacity of the system, as marginalized families possess what Michelle Fine (2010) calls "specifically revealing wisdom about the history, structure, consequences, and the fracture points in unjust social arrangements" (p. 215). Equity leaders often used their own lived experiences of oppression as a bridge:

> Well, I think I really connect with people who've been "othered" because I have experienced it, you know, throughout my life, in many different ways. And I think that brings sort of a different perspective when working with families. I seem to be able to identify with people who feel disenfranchised or disconnected just because of my experiences.

And Tracie, who also identified as a Black woman, named her racial and cultural practices as shaping her every move and interaction as an equity leader, a dynamic that she was intentional about using:

> I identify as a Black woman, and I walk in that space in everything that I do. I recognize that personally my tone, my posture, my facial expressions and my language can shift the entire atmosphere of a room . . . and I am intentionally unashamed about addressing it in all [situations]. . . . [Laughter] I'm surprised I haven't been fired. So I am not . . . shy about talking about the white dominant approach and expectation that people have in spaces that I operate. . . . So we ended up having this meeting because the principal's like, "I'm uncomfortable talking to you." Well, I'm not here to make you feel good. My job is to build your capacity and some of that . . . some of that might hurt.

In sum, most participants explicitly drew on their racial and cultural identities, lived experiences, and race-gendered knowledge to foster relationships, understandings, and dialogue necessary for building the organizational capacity of their systems to take equity-focused action.

Restructuring the Organization

Black women and other racially minoritized women equity leaders also described efforts to restructure the organizational chart of the district to increase access to executive-level decision-making and expand the human resources dedicated to equity activity. For instance, Loretta, a Black woman equity director, described the necessity of removing reporting layers to have more direct access to the superintendent:

> Initially I was going to report to the . . . Director of Innovation, [who] would then report to the Chief of Innovation, who reports directly to the superintendent. So because nobody really knows what the heck to do . . . initially I was like, okay this ain't gonna work. . . . And so to do the kind of work that I needed to do, I needed to have some of those layers removed and so then I began to report directly to the Chief of Innovation.

Here, Loretta narrated the agency she exercised by changing the lines of reporting in the district hierarchy to enable her to do the work necessitated by her charge. Similarly, Tracie took agential action for about 5 years to change the organizational structures in her district to increase access to the superintendent:

> Okay, so I used to be five people down from the superintendent. Which is a problem, right, if you're really talking about equity. So now, I am two people down from the superintendent . . . and it's taken five years. It's taken five years to do that."

Importantly, these moves were not merely to increase individuals' power, but to enable equity leaders to better influence key decisions about the resources and capacity of the district to realize its equity aims.

Black women leaders, in particular, also narrated their long-term "strategic" moves, sometimes on the order of years, to expand human resources dedicated to equity work. Tracie went on in great detail to explain her efforts not only to reconfigure her access to the superintendent but also to increase her budget and staff resources to carry out different aspects of equity-focused work. Drawing on her experiential knowledge (and awareness of her positioning in organizational double jeopardy), Tracie explained that simply asking for more money would be met with organizational resistance. Rather, she leveraged data and grant funding to strategically restructure positions and resources to build her budget and staff.

Interviewer: So you mentioned earlier how your department went from two to eleven. Can you explain that?

Tracie: The department is a little over five years old. I was the first district equity coordinator. Before I explain, I will say that our district decided to do this work *but didn't know how to do this work*. I don't think that there was any expectation about what this work would actually look like. I'm all about strategic moves.

We have this grant that was funded under someone else. I said, "How about give me those positions under the grant. Let me kind of restructure them and let's see what happens." So they gave me the positions. That was the last year.

So we structured the position for it to have some accountability and some data tracking and we created a system for reporting. And so, we were able to show in that final year that they had made contact with over 220 more unduplicated students compared to what they had years before. And I said, "So if I make these part-time positions and take them off as independent contractors, would you fund them from the general fund for the district?" And they said, "Yeah."

Now I have an Indian education specialist, two equity diversity specialists, and myself that handle professional development. I have two student graduation advocates that work

> in the schools with our Native American, African American, and Pacific Islander students. I have three language instructors that work in the schools cooperating [with] teachers that are funded through another grant.

Tracie made "strategic" moves by leveraging grant funding, using data to advocate for increased budget and staff, and choosing when and how to speak up in various district contexts to increase the organizational resources at her disposal. Likewise, Angela, another Black woman equity leader, described being passed over for promotions as a form of experiential knowledge she subsequently used to make strategic decisions about how to prioritize requests from schools:

> Everything I do is strategic and calculated. Everything. And it's well-thought out, it's—I reflect, I think about—so if I'm invited to a school to do cultural proficiency training, okay, who's inviting me in? Are they somebody who is looking to get a promotion in the next year or two, because I've seen that about five principals who've asked me to come and do cultural proficiency training for them, have gotten promotions within that next year or two, literally. . . . So, I've helped people get promotions and I couldn't get one myself.

In other words, Angela was selective about which schools and principals to support with trainings, as her prior experiences had taught her that her work could be invisibilized and referenced as evidence of leadership for principals who might be promoted over her (another form of organizational double jeopardy within a white normative organization that supposedly prioritizes color- and gender-neutral merit). Instead, she used this knowledge to ensure that she invested her expertise and resources in schools and principals who would continue and expand equity change-making, rather than take advantage of it for their own individual promotion.

Legitimizing Organizational Priority on Equity

Finally, Tanya spoke at length both about the symbolism of the Black woman equity director being the lowest-paid director in the district and the limitations of her access to the executive decision-making table. She implied that others believed she should not have access or higher pay, but she pointed out that the organizational position and compensation for equity leadership should reflect the centrality of equity and "what's really best for the district" in a predominantly white organization that purports to benefit students and families of color:

> I would say the same thing about the whole needing to get closer to the superintendent executive group or whatever. . . . For me it's all about the epitome

> of what equity even is in that statement—who cares how people feel. What's really best for the district? And that's where I think that I can lead a conversation, I want to be at a table [where those] conversations are made. I think the reason why I push [is] because there [are] so many conversations and decisions are being made at that table that I was not aware of yet. . . . So if I could be at the table, it would save all of that extra running around and I can actually be able to put [an] equity lens on conversations [at] a table of white people who are talking about things in our district that are supposed to also benefit our students and families of color.

Tanya subsequently drew on her experiential knowledge as a Black woman about the marginalization of equity work to advocate for her participation in conversations at the executive leadership table and to leverage little-known union policy to build the legitimacy of the position in the organizational hierarchy.

> But there wasn't a guarantee that was happening, and I wanted to see what was happening. I think right now, they have me on as "Sch" Rep which is something where I'm going to get the union around Central Office leadership. . . . And that's my entry so I'm using [it] as an entry. And then my goal is to make that a legitimate position. This is how it should be.

This effort "to make that a legitimate position," in tandem with Tanya's growing budget and increasing (albeit slowly) staff resources, represented evidence of her leadership reshaping district priorities and organizational resources around equity work.

CONCLUSIONS AND IMPLICATIONS

The dynamics of organizational double jeopardy, racial battle fatigue, and the need for long-term, strategic moves will not be surprising or new to most racially minoritized educational leaders at the district level. One telling interaction concerned a conversation with a Black male superintendent with whom we were exploring whether his district might be included in our study. He explained that he had chosen not to have an equity director, quipping that it was a role "where people of color go to have their careers killed." Although we did not include that particular district in our study, this sentiment crystalized the dynamics of marginalization that racially minoritized leaders recognize as a danger of being "pigeon-holed" as an equity leader (yet another example of a kind of racialized knowledge they possess). Yet these dynamics are rarely addressed, acknowledged, or even understood by the majority of white administrators in school districts. And as our study has shown, male-identifying leaders of color and white women leaders largely do not encounter the dynamics of organizational double jeopardy we found for racially minoritized women equity leaders, especially Black women.

Although equity leaders routinely experience organizational conditions designed to preclude their success, district organizations are not totalizing institutions. Black and other racially minoritized women equity leaders narrated long-term, strategic moves to reshape their organization's capacity, structures, resources, and priorities on equity. Paradoxically, the very identities the organization positioned as liabilities were sources of experiential knowledge and practice, vital to these leaders' abilities to lead strategically and make organizational change. Their race-gendered experiential knowledge enabled them to understand and "read" the dynamics of whiteness, patriarchy, and power in the district organization in order to expand the organizational capacity, activity, and people carrying equity work in the district. To be clear, these leaders regarded their strategic moves to change the organization as a means toward realizing more equitable educational systems, not an equity "end" in and of itself. Nonetheless, we argue that their agential moves represented important progress—both symbolically, by elevating the legitimacy and centrality of equity work within their respective districts, and practically and materially, by creating the necessary conditions for equity leaders to transform their systems to become more just.

The dominant research literature frames district central offices as largely neutral organizational bureaucracies in need of greater coherence. When equity leaders fail to single-handedly transform educational systems and produce equitable outcomes (generally narrowly defined in terms of test scores), they are often blamed or assessed as unsuccessful in their leadership. However, our study illuminates district organizations as racialized and gendered spaces infused with historically rooted power inequities and white normative conceptions of leadership. Far from being neutral, district central office organizational structures, resources, and dynamics function to undermine the leadership of Black women in particular, as well as other racially minoritized women educators. As a result of their leadership, however, many districts have been reshaped in important ways—from structures that position equity leaders closer to the centers of power and embed equity across district departments, to building new knowledge and capacity while expanding teams and formal roles dedicated to equity in educational systems. Collectively, these efforts ushered in a new era of midday equity work in education.

REFERENCES

Agosto, V., & Roland, E. (2018). Intersectionality and educational leadership: A critical review. *Review of Research in Education*, *42*(1), 255–285. https://doi.org/10.3102/0091732X18762433

Arnold, N. W., Crawford, E. R., & Khalifa, M. (2016). Psychological heuristics and faculty of color: Racial battle fatigue and tenure/promotion. *The Journal of Higher Education*, *87*(6), 890–919. https://doi.org/10.1080/00221546.2016.11780891

Baldwin, J. (1963, October 16). *A talk to teachers*. [Speech]. https://www.zinnedproject.org/materials/baldwin-talk-to-teachers

Crenshaw, K. (1989). Demarginalizing the intersection of race and sex: A Black feminist critique of antidiscrimination doctrine, feminist theory and antiracist politics. *University of Chicago Legal Forum*, *1989*(1), 139–167.

Crenshaw, K. (1991). Mapping the margins: Intersectionality, identity politics, and violence against women of color. *Stanford Law Review*, *43*(6), 1241–1299. https://doi.org/10.2307/1229039

Diamond, J. B., & Lewis, A. E. (2022). Opportunity hoarding and the maintenance of "white" educational space. *American Behavioral Scientist*, *66*(11), 1470–1489.

Dillard, C. B. (2021). *The spirit of our work: Black women teachers (re)member*. Beacon Press.

Doharty, N. (2020). The "angry Black woman" as intellectual bondage: Being strategically emotional on the academic plantation. *Race Ethnicity and Education*, *23*(4), 548–562. https://doi.org/10.1080/13613324.2019.1679751

Dunbar-Ortiz, R. (2014). *An Indigenous peoples' history of the United States*. Beacon Press.

Fine, M. (2010). An epilogue, of sorts. In J. Cammarota & M. Fine (Eds.). *Revolutionizing education* (pp. 221–242). Routledge.

Galloway, M. K., & Ishimaru, A. M. (2019). Leading equity teams: The role of formal leaders in building organizational capacity for equity. *Journal of Education for Students Placed at Risk*, *25*(2), 107–125.

Lewis, A. E., & Diamond, J. B. (2015). *Despite the best intentions: How racial inequality thrives in good schools*. Oxford University Press.

Poon, O. A. (2011). Ching chongs and tiger moms: The "Asian invasion" in U.S. higher education. *Amerasia Journal*, *37*(2), 144–150. https://doi.org/10.17953/amer.37.2.m58rh1u4321310j4

Ray, V. (2019). A theory of racialized organizations. *American Sociological Review*, *84*(1), 26–53. https://doi.org/10.1177/0003122418822335

Rosette, A. S., & Livingston, R. W. (2012). Failure is not an option for Black women: Effects of organizational performance on leaders with single versus dual-subordinate identities. *Journal of Experimental Social Psychology*, *48*(5), 1162–1167. https://doi.org/10.1016/j.jesp.2012.05.002

Smith, W. A., Allen, W. R., & Danley, L. L. (2007). "Assume the position . . . you fit the description": Psychosocial experiences and racial battle fatigue among African American male college students. *American Behavioral Scientist*, *51*(4), 551–578. https://doi.org/10.1177/0002764207307742

Siddle Walker, V. (1996). *Their highest potential: An African American school community in the segregated South*. University of North Carolina Press.

Woodson, C. G. (1933). *The mis-education of the Negro*. Associated Publishers.

Part II

MIDDAY WORK

CHAPTER 5

Marathons, Not Sprints

Institutionalizing Equity Through Organization-Wide Learning

Teresa Lance

> "When we implement Equity Plan 2.0 with unquestionable intention and focus on the action steps and implementation benchmarks, we will create a school organization that is equitable in both practices and outcomes leading to every student having a sense of belonging and that every student graduates ready for college, career, and civic-life."
>
> —Equity Ambassadors (Equity Plan 2.0)

I started my new role excited for a fresh start. Although the pandemic kept many of us working remotely for several months, my superintendent's cabinet colleagues' welcome was refreshing. I had never heard of the district before the 4 years it became my work home. During my time as superintendent of equity, I designed and led a districtwide effort to institutionalize the district's commitment to educational equity among our 57 district schools that served 35,000 students and employed 2,500 teachers, staff, and administrators.

It was, and remains, a district that struggles to meet the needs of all of its learners. I inherited a district that was required to show how we would decrease overidentification of Black students to special education with an emotional disability indicator. We suspended Black boys at an exponentially higher rate than other racial ethnic groups, even though Black students were only the fourth largest racial ethnic group behind white, Hispanic, and Asian American students. Staff and students of color, people who identified as LGBTQ+, and English language learners, who comprised more than 40% of our district community, felt excluded from decision-making, with no avenue to express their feelings or concerns. In May 2019, the U.S. Department of Education compelled states to identify districts with significant racial disproportionality for 3 consecutive years in special education or, alternatively, be placed on a corrective action plan.

My priority was that our district become an organization where every individual person, regardless of race, religion, sexual orientation, ability level, socioeconomic background, gender identity, and so on belongs. What I did not fully anticipate was my own lack of belonging, or the fact that I would gradually begin to carry the weight of my colleagues' and students' experiences. As a result, I became emotionally, physically, and mentally drained. I experienced racial battle fatigue (Smith et al., 2007), a concept that names the cumulative and unrelenting exhaustion from navigating the emotional, psychological, physiological, and behavioral impacts of racism. Throughout my time, I carried a weight that very few of my colleagues understood, other than the Black women I eventually hired to work with me.

In this chapter I tell the story of how I, a Black woman, selected the work to do, made space and time for people to do the work, and spearheaded learning to advance equity work within the entire school district. This work included every school building, every classroom, and every encounter among and between students and adults, students to students, and staff to families. First, I developed my own understanding. I deepened my learning to sharpen my knowledge of what I needed to accomplish in my role on behalf of the district's students and families. Second, I developed the understanding and knowledge base of my colleagues. I formed a districtwide committee, a learning space where we would shift people's capacities to identify inequities and devise policies and practices that would fix the system rather than "fix" students.

Third, I developed the district's equity accountability. To do this, I expanded and strengthened the district's data collection and reporting activities to account for the experiences of our district's most marginalized students. I leveraged the equity committee to update and revise the district equity plan, which ultimately influenced the district's strategic plan. I used ongoing data collection and analysis to drive all my work—this is where my story begins.

SELECTING A FOCUS: FIGURING OUT THE WORK THAT NEEDED TO BE DONE

As my first order of business, I conducted meetings to determine where to give my attention during my first year or two in the position. I started with my cabinet colleagues: superintendent of human resources, chief of strategic initiatives, two deputy superintendents, three assistant superintendents who oversaw all 57 schools, and one district attorney. I asked three questions:

1. What do you consider the strengths of the district?
2. What do you consider areas of opportunity in the district?
3. What do you consider the greatest inequity in the district?

I found my colleagues to be very forthcoming. I appreciated their transparency and vulnerability. But their responses to my final question were so varied. One person shared that overidentifying Black boys for special education was the greatest inequity. Another named hiring practices and the lack of diverse staff members. At the time of my hire, for example, African American staff made up less than 5% of the total teaching population. Another shared the issue of lack of consistent resources across schools. Collectively, the responses offered no clear or straightforward answers. They also offered no insight about where to start or focus my work. To further complicate matters, my new position entailed a hodgepodge of duties that were not clearly focused on equity, which made it difficult to make the connection between my role and the portfolio of work I needed to lead.

With no clear answers, I returned to the district's existing equity plan for guidance. Several questions advised my focused review. What goals are outlined in Equity Plan 2018? What did the original writers intend to accomplish? By what date? What did they identify as important benchmarks? Who was responsible for implementation or reporting updates on the work? My review surfaced more questions for me. For example, when I saw that more than five positions, including the board of education, were listed under "person responsible" for all identified action steps, I thought to myself, "This will not work." Anyone listed could feign ignorance, blame others, or simply not engage. Who really should be responsible? I couldn't answer my bigger question through my review: Why had the district made so little progress implementing the plan?

From my short time in the role, it appeared that all equity efforts had stalled. I started asking more direct questions. My predecessor, who previously held the role of equity director, developed Equity Plan 2018. Sadly, he died before having the chance to implement it. Understandably, his unexpected death contributed to the stagnation of the action steps. But I still did not fully understand why the work was allowed to pause for more than 2 years. Was it by design? Were people unsure of how to proceed forward? After some time, district staff started to request to meet with me off school district properties. I found these requests odd, so I initially refused to attend. In time, I learned that people wanted to meet off district property because they did not feel protected. Although I wasn't yet clear as to why, I was beginning to understand that people perceived equity work as perilous.

As I listened and learned more about my colleagues' experiences, they described racial battle fatigue that I'd soon come to know firsthand. The very people I assumed would be eager to join me felt a lack of belonging in the organization. I couldn't ask any of them, or any individuals at all, to step up. It was too risky. Within my first 3 months on the job, I determined that two things needed to happen. First, I needed to revamp the district's Equity Plan. Second, our district needed to create the conditions for belonging, especially for those who experienced marginalization. I saw these priorities as mutually reinforcing. And I knew that I was the person who needed to lead these efforts.

MAKING SPACE AND TIME TO COLLABORATE ON THE WORK

I wanted and needed a broad team of stakeholders to participate in updating the Equity Plan in order to create districtwide ownership. Broad participation would ensure stronger accountability and deeper commitment to implementation. I knew it was important to revise the plan in a way that involved input from invested stakeholders. Doing so would ensure the plan would not get shelved as it had after the previous equity director died. As for cultivating belonging and challenging the fear of reprisal for being openly committed to equity, there is safety and power in numbers. I shifted my thinking away from individual leaders as the drivers of change and began to imagine a ground-up approach. I decided I would use my top-down role to create and support affinity groups and form a districtwide equity committee to become leaders of the work.

Affinity Groups

The experiences of some of our African American staff members, coupled with the assistant superintendent of human resources' desire to retain diverse staff members, gave me the leverage I needed to launch several affinity groups during my first year in the role. The affinity groups included African American, Latinx/Hispanic, white allyship, LGBTQ+, and Asian American. I did not need to explain the reason for launching affinity groups to participants or to district colleagues. Affinity spaces provided the reprieve that district staff and community members needed to process, resist, and heal from the harms they experienced in the district. I didn't give them any specific charge. The purpose of creating them was for people to come together.

The affinity groups met monthly; however, I left it to the direction of the affinity group leader to solidify meeting frequency. Some groups, for example, wanted to meet more often than once per month. As the assistant superintendent of equity, I believed it was critical that I met with each affinity group leader in advance of their monthly meeting. During our facilitator meetings, we used that time to codevelop an agenda, answer questions that may have surfaced from previous meetings, and line up resources to ensure the group meetings were a success. For example, the white allyship group wanted to change their name. Prior to engaging in a name change, the affinity group leader and I met to clarify the reason for the name change and, more importantly, to ensure consensus on any new name change. Additionally, because there was no budget for affinity group meetings, I confirmed that if there were needs, such as snacks or outings, that I provided the monetary resources. Although the creation of affinity groups was not directly connected to institutionalizing equity practices, their existence enabled subsequent bodies of work because they became important resources to push our development of policy action steps.

Equity Committee

Members of a defunct districtwide equity committee requested to meet with me. I was not entirely sure of the purpose of the meeting. In hindsight, however, they just wanted to meet with me and hear my vision for how we would re-engage committee members and begin the arduous yet important work of leading equity. The timing was perfect as I had already envisioned forming such a committee. Soon after, I issued a call for district committee members (Figure 5.1).

Figure 5.1. Equity committee call for members

Call for Members

Our school district is seeking teachers, administrators, community members, and students who are interested in joining a committee to review and revise the district's equity plan.

Committee Purpose

The equity committee will review and update benchmarks within the Equity Plan 2018. Additionally, the equity committee will work to (1) expose systemic barriers that block the spread of cultural proficiency; (2) identify institutional patterns that reinforce predictability in opportunity, access, and support; (3) create the shape, format, and content framework of future professional development opportunities; and (4) correct instructional and racist practices that marginalize certain student populations.

Committee Responsibilities

To carry out its purpose, the equity committee will:

- Consistently and actively participate in identified equity professional development sessions.
- Review a common set of research documents and data points, and texts.
- Review and monitor implementation benchmarks of the Equity Plan to include instructional aspects of the school community.
- Propose professional development and other supportive opportunities.

I wanted the equity committee to include staff, families, and community partners who wanted to see transformational equity change. I required a brief application. Besides the typical demographic information such as name, role, and years in the district, I asked applicants to respond to two prompts:

1. Please share any training, academic preparation, or work experience you have that will support the work of the committee.
2. Please share any additional information that you believe would be helpful in securing a position on the committee.

Only 60 people applied. As mentioned earlier, our district serves 35,000 students and employs 2,500 staff members. My hope that more people would be eager to participate was shattered. After reviewing applications, I accepted 50 people to the committee. I was alarmed that the number of applications from Black and Hispanic teachers and leaders was minimal, an unfortunate trend that continued in the years ahead and that I eventually came to accept.

I was excited to start our meeting despite my disappointment with the application pool. For the first year, we met virtually. I started our first meeting with an acknowledgment of my predecessor who passed a couple of years prior to my start. Before jumping into the key activity, a thought exchange about Equity Plan 2018, I led members in an activity to get to know one another. For the bulk of our time, I sought to unearth what the committee members found to be the strengths and areas of improvement with Equity Plan 2018. I used a thought exchange tool to solicit input on what the committee members believed we needed to prioritize. I closed the meeting by sharing a new template we would move to that was more inclusive of leading and lagging indicators, clear action steps, persons responsible, and, most importantly, goals.

SPEARHEADING LEARNING

With the affinity groups and equity committee in place, I started to implement the learning processes that would enable us to collectively develop an informed and transformative equity plan. The process involved an iterative procedure of gathering data and using what was gathered to shift our understandings of what is required to advance equity: focus on fixing the systems, not the students. I wanted members of the equity committee and myself to be system thinkers and leaders. I wanted us to establish an environment where individuals affected by the issues could gather to share truths (e.g., in affinity groups), explore complex situations, consider alternative perspectives, and seek change through continual cycles of action, reflection, and learning.

Understanding the complexity of issues, system leaders foster conditions for the gradual evolution of collective wisdom, leading to innovative thoughts, actions, and identities over time (Senge et al., 2015). In his book, *The Fifth Discipline*, Senge (2006) thoroughly describes the fifth principle: systems thinking. The concept of systems thinking constitutes the fifth discipline within a learning organization. The systems thinking stage entails acknowledging the interrelatedness among various system components while working in tandem to serve a common overarching objective. My objective was to help the equity committee identify the most significant areas of inequity and identify explicit and tangible actions to mitigate, diminish, and, over time, eradicate those inequities. "Select data" was the first rung at the bottom of the ladder of inference.

Learning From Our Equity Audit

I believed a comprehensive equity audit was a necessary first step to assist not just me but also the board of education and superintendent's cabinet to become familiar with the inequities that persisted in our district. Upon receiving authorization to proceed with the equity audit, I convened a committee to assist me in identifying organizations that specialized in large school district audits. Five organizations submitted proposals to conduct our district's equity audit. The equity committee voted on the company we chose to implement the process organized into five overarching areas: vision and expectations, academic achievement, access and equity, culture and climate, and curriculum. The audit confirmed much of what I knew (see Table 5.1). Laid out over 400 pages, the findings were comprehensive and bleak. But they provided a strong basis for acknowledgment and learning what needed to happen over the next 3 years.

The auditors offered several pages of recommendations: overhaul the curriculum and assessment design framework; hire a director for professional development; establish a cycle to review locally created classroom assessments; clarify teaching expectations and recalibrate teacher evaluation tools; develop equity-focused performance tasks and rubrics; and allow the equity plan to serve as the district's strategic plan.

The recommendations were a combination of easy to painstakingly difficult to implement. For example, the auditors recommend that I report directly to the superintendent rather than the deputy superintendent. Redesigning the organizational chart to have my position report to the superintendent could have been a quick adjustment, but that was never accepted. Most of the recommendations would require significant time and thoughtful attention to detail that amounted to second-order change (Senge, 2006). For example, the auditors recommended we review and analyze teachers' use of formative assessment data, which would require classroom observations with a lens on teacher instructional approaches and student tasks.

Table 5.1. Sample Equity Audit Highlights

District Policies and Trends	Audit Findings
Board equity policy states. . . . Invest resources aimed at recruiting and retaining a teacher, support, and administrative workforce that reflects the diversity of the student body.	There was no evidence of a recruitment and retention plan, nor monies explicitly earmarked for this endeavor.
Equity Resolution states . . . the district will be ". . . welcoming, empowering, and recognize students and families of all racial and ethnic backgrounds as essential partners in their student's education, school planning and District decision making."	There was little evidence of this aside from the Bilingual Parent Advisory Committee (BPAC), which is required to be established in school districts that have transitional bilingual education programs with 20 or more emergent English learners (ELs) from the same language background.
Achievement was declining at an accelerated pace. Achievement disparities exist in math, reading, and science. Students who resided in low-income families, students with an identified disability, and African American and Hispanic students comprised the most significant achievement gaps.	Achievement gaps can be attributed to (1) a lack of alignment between content assessments and standard descriptors and (2) teachers' intentional or unintentional lowered expectations of students reflected in their not administering the assessment or developing their own set of assessment questions.

It was all a bit overwhelming. We were flush with data, almost to a detriment. To manage such a large committee and make the analysis of data more manageable, I divided the committee into the four subcommittees presented in Table 5.2.

The Student Success pillar focuses on closing opportunity gaps to ensure equitable access to academic programs for all student subgroups. The Effective and Engaged Staff pillar emphasizes the recruitment, development, and retention of a highly qualified and diverse workforce. The Culture and Climate pillar seeks to create welcoming, inclusive environments for all members of the school community, ensuring that equity is reflected in the district's relationships with families and local stakeholders. Lastly, the Excellence, Efficiency, and Accountability pillar is aimed at promoting transparency and fairness in resource allocation, ensuring that all students benefit from equitable access to the district's structures and services.

Each committee had a leader, but because distributed leadership was not a strong practice in the district, none had ever led a team. I was deeply concerned that we didn't have a process in place to make sense of the data. To systematize our data review and ensure learning, I used the ladder of

Table 5.2. Equity Committee Structure

Subcommittees (Initial)	Subcommittees (2 Years Later)
Culture and Climate	Culture and Climate Community Engagement
Effective and Engaged Staff	Effective and Engaged Staff
Student Success	Student Success (elementary) Student Success (secondary)
Excellence, Efficiency, and Accountability	Excellence, Efficiency, and Accountability

inference process. The ladder of inference process slows down the typical mental model of looking at data to identify a quick fix. It challenges the tendency to think about fixing the student rather than looking internally and wholly at the entire school system for root causes of student experiences or learning problems.

We risked unconsciously selecting faulty data while ignoring other relevant metrics. For example, we requested and received data that detailed our system's exclusionary practices; however, we failed to request data that described students' sense of belonging in our schools. Continuing to figuratively climb the ladder of inference, committee members began paraphrasing and giving meaning to the data through interpreting and exploring assumptions. Next, members drew conclusions from their assumptions and beliefs by writing out statements such as:

> Although 59% of surveyed 4th through 12th grade students feel a sense of belonging as captured by Panorama Survey, 41% of students indicated they do not feel a sense of belonging. This data is more pronounced among our Black and Hispanic/Latinx students.

As conveyed in the example, I guided participants to highlight the strengths and opportunities they saw in the data. Throughout the entire process, I reminded each equity pillar leader to check individual assumptions, especially before we moved to identify action steps. The process was painstakingly slow.

Year 1 Results

As the year progressed, I could see how the demands in front of us wore on people. I wrestled to keep members engaged as the level of initial excitement waned. Each time we met, attendance decreased and participation faded. I asked committee members to meet once a month without financial compensation. I also asked subcommittee leaders to meet monthly in advance of the full equity committee meeting to remain ahead of the work. I had not been clear enough early on about what joining the equity committee would entail. From fluctuating attendance by committee members to no attendance from one of the superintendent's cabinet members, the first year was ripe with bouts of frustration.

On the bright side, by the end of our first year, the committee members reviewed, analyzed, and discussed all the data that was provided to them. And just as importantly, although I had not considered it at the time, I developed leaders who understood how to use data to understand issues of inequity. Moving into year 2, these leaders were crucial partners in the work. I was eager for year 2 for a myriad of reasons, including seeing these four to six leaders show up with increased confidence while working with their respective teams.

YEAR 2: LEARNING FROM OUR OWN STREET DATA

Prior to starting my second year, I was able to sit down with my immediate supervisor to both review my job description and discuss the challenges I faced. I used this opening, afforded me by my supervisor, to express the need and make a request for additional personnel. Equity work is a massive undertaking that, coupled with vast student enrollment of our school district, would hinder significant progress across the district without additional personnel. Fortunately, my supervisor agreed. I was able to write a job description for a director of diversity, equity, and inclusion. This person was integral in allowing me to direct my efforts in a more impactful manner. For example, we divided the 57 campuses between the two of us, which allowed each school to receive ongoing professional learning if they chose.

During the 2021–2022 school year, I relaunched the call to form an equity committee. I asked everyone who participated on the committee in the year prior to reapply. By reapplying, participants would, in my mind, recommit to engaging in the equity work. From my first year coleading the district's equity committee, I knew participation would wane as the school year progressed. So, I intentionally set out to identify more than 40 equity committee members to account for attrition. This time, more than 80 people applied. To account for participation waning, I accepted 60 people with representation from 32 of the 57 school campuses. Most of the school district's departments, from early childhood to curriculum and instruction, had at least one person serving on the equity committee.

I was fortunate to have nearly 60 people, both new and returning equity committee members. I was still disappointed, however, in the lack of diverse representation from across the district. No one from the special education department applied, despite our state mandate to reduce the overrepresentation of Black students in special education. I continued to keep our meetings virtual, as the feedback from committee participants overwhelmingly demonstrated a desire to have the option of participating from home, their work site, or whatever was convenient for them at the time of our equity committee meetings.

We relied on the text *Street Data* by Shane Safir and Jamila Dugan (2021) to ground our work in year 2. The shift into gathering more qualitative data would serve as the linchpin to tie our equity plan together. This was important because, even in year 2, equity committee members consistently made assumptions about the data, which meant we were often making deficit-based assumptions about our students, families, and even some of our staff by relying only on numbers. For example, during one of our meetings, a member of the equity committee shared that Black and Brown students did not fare well because of lack of family involvement.

I could not rely on quantitative datasets alone to guide our work. Safir and Dugan (2021) described three types of data to tell a story that included satellite, map, and street data. Level one, satellite data, relies on measurements such as chronic attendance rates, test scores, and freshmen on-track data. Level two, map data, leans into data a bit more closely and may include measurements such as perception surveys (i.e., Gallup surveys) and algebra readiness–level scores. The third level, street data, Safir states, "is the most important source for understanding the current reality, or at least what people perceive as real" (Safir, 2021, p. 198). It captures the perspectives and experiences of students and staff, helping to inform our decision-making. Our equity audit included all three levels, but an outside firm gathered the information.

The equity committee wanted to capitalize on the equity audit and continue diving into the street data. Although I did not have the language at the time to label my calculated moves, we began employing race-conscious inquiry cycles (Irby, 2021). I formed student and staff focus groups, participated in meetings as both a listener and observer, and questioned entrenched practices that were detrimental to the health of the district. Table 5.3 outlines the additional data I gathered to supplement the equity audit and deepen my understanding of district inequities.

Although the collected data and testimonies within the equity audit had a profound impact on my next steps, there was nothing more powerful than hearing the stories for myself. Some staff members expressed fear of sharing personal experiences because they had witnessed or experienced being the target of discrimination and overt racism. Students recounted stories of being silenced by one or more teachers for speaking in their home language, Spanish, while in class. Students told stories of being called "monkey." A Hispanic teacher told me about a time when another staff member asked a student, "Does your family cut grass?" which to her suggested a

Table 5.3. Street Data Collection Activities

Collected Data	Frequency	Intended Purpose
Focus groups on staff perspectives of belonging	2	Further understand what central office leaders were doing or not that contributed to a lack of belongingness
Gallup survey	2	Understand pain points of staff engagement disaggregated by employee group, race/ethnicity, years in the district, etc.
Student focus groups	7	Dive deeper into the perspectives of students as they relate to their respective school campus
Affinity focus groups	1 per affinity group	Gain deeper insight into the belongingness or lack thereof for each of our staff affinity groups

stereotype that all Spanish-speaking families cut grass and/or engaged in other laborious careers.

Every single story was like a gut punch. After listening to the experiences of students, staff, and families, I needed therapy. I began to carry the horror of my colleagues' and students' experiences, becoming physically and mentally drained. I was carrying a weight that very few, if any, of my colleagues would understand. The urgency to address the experiences that emerged both from the audit and listening sessions was felt by me and my assistant, the director of DEI. Together, we argued for an immediate platform that allowed staff, students, and families to report instances of discrimination and racism. I grew determined that our new plan would be grounded in personal stories.

Increasingly, I realized I had my own street data. In short, I was striving to do the right thing for students, staff, and families based on various times in my life I was pushed to the margins. For example, I recall my high school guidance counselor, who was white, telling my mom that she could not afford to send me to a historically Black college or university (HBCU) and that I would need to attend an in-state school. We lived in New York at that time. At no point in the conversation did that counselor share scholarship or work-study opportunities with me and my mom, and never did he even consider that we may have had access to the funds for me to attend an HBCU. Instead, my counselor made assumptions about me and my mom based on our race.

I was certainly less anxious moving into year 2; my confidence had risen, and I was more self-assured in the work. I often conveyed to my colleagues that I entered the role as assistant superintendent of equity not knowing everything there was to know about engaging in equity-related work; rather, I relied on my lived experiences and my moral compass to guide me. I realized I needed to be more intentional about my own learning.

I felt like we were stuck. I started reading about resistance to equity change. I read Dr. Decoteau J. Irby's book, *Stuck Improving: Racial Equity and School Leadership* to understand the cognitive as well as the "affective feelings of inadequacy, incompetency, anxiety, and frustration" (Milner, 2021, p. viii) that my colleagues were likely experiencing. Many of my colleagues' efforts to improve appeared to be constrained by either self-imposed barriers, external barriers, or systemic barriers that became ingrained into the district's culture. The additional readings, along with *Street Data*, provided us with lessons and tools to confidently ask for and subsequently obtain the voices of the individuals who are too often prodded with new strategies and initiatives while simultaneously being pushed to the margins. What I was learning challenged my current approach. I decided to recalibrate our monthly meetings to focus on learning while doing. We would enter year 3 committed to engaging in book studies, attending professional learning, and meeting outside of our designated monthly meeting.

YEAR 3: FOCUS ON AMBASSADORSHIP

At the start of year 3, I launched another call for equity committee participation. However, I changed the call for committee members to "equity ambassadors" as a way to signal the need to span outside of our monthly meetings and sometimes to meet twice a month. The name change also implies a call to dedicated action, as an ambassador takes ownership in representing, being a proponent, and more. I moved all meetings to in-person. I could feel the energy in the room shift from borderline compliance to excitement. After having selected more than 50 equity ambassadors to continue steering the work, participation remained high for the duration of the third school year. I divided our 2-hour time blocks into two chunks. For the first hour, we discussed books. In the second hour, we examined data. Ambassadors engaged in additional assigned tasks in between sessions. We were deep into the work, and if members returned for the second or third time, I knew without reservation that we could have a solid equity plan by the end of the school year. The previous 2 years of work started to pay off.

Having spent a year studying *Street Data*, for year 3 I selected the book, *Why Race and Culture Matter in Schools* by Tyrone Howard (2010). I opted for this text because I wanted the equity ambassadors to think about the inequities across the school district beyond a Black and white issue and instead as a systemic issue about race and racism. We still kept *Street Data* nearby, especially for new members and to ensure that we stayed grounded in data that told stories from those closest to the work.

The pillar leaders took on more of the work. They maintained the meeting cadence and kept track of assigned tasks. They requested meetings from central office leaders when they had additional questions. They began speaking out against practices and policies that were inequitable. As the equity ambassadors continued to refine their respective sections of the equity plan, they were intentional in thinking about systemic barriers that hindered progress. For example, they grew vocal about removing prerequisites that hindered students of color from accessing advanced placement and other rigorous courses.

The affinity groups I organized during the first year were still going strong. While I didn't anticipate it, they played an important role in supporting our final push to complete the new Equity Plan. We tapped into affinity group leaders to initiate a listening tour with our African American, LGBTQ+, and Latinx/Hispanic affinity groups. Their feedback on our plan development was invaluable. We also held additional student focus groups at our comprehensive high schools. I asked school leaders, many of whom were involved as ambassadors, to identify students who had been suspended at least once during the school year. We asked them, "Do you feel like you belong at your school?" Their responses allowed us to probe further and, as a result, one of our action steps included creating an advising model that ensured each student had at least one trusted adult in their school.

EQUITY LEADERSHIP EXPANDS

By the end of year 3, the equity committee was no longer an equity committee, but a team of equity ambassadors supported by a central office staff that facilitated the implementation of Equity Plan 2.0. Not only did we hire a director of DEI to join the team, but I was approved to hire a districtwide mentor coordinator. The director of DEI and I divided up the 57 school campuses between the two of us so that each school principal and/or other staff members had a direct point person to contact with staff and family concerns.

We designed mentor programs for Black boys and girls in a few select schools, and soon after, almost all our elementary and middle schools wanted a student mentor program. For a time, we didn't have the capacity to bring their wishes to fruition. Hiring a mentor coordinator changed all of that. Within 1 year, our mentor coordinator not only expanded the girls' mentoring program, she also recruited more than one dozen students to participate on our equity ambassador committee. The students' voices and perspectives were the impetus for several additional elements to the final Equity Plan revision.

Our goals were lofty, and our plan demonstrated that system impediments worked against those goals. When we were ready to launch Equity

Plan 2.0, we shared at a board meeting that we wanted to recruit more Black and Asian American teachers and leaders by the start of the 2026 school year. To accomplish this goal, however, we would have to consider a few past and adopted actions that were no longer serving us. Historically, staff from the human resources department traveled to recruit from predominately white institutions (PWIs). They even traveled to Spain to recruit dual-language teachers. They needed to partner with HBCUs. We also emphasized the need for standard interview questions that leaned into cultural competency knowledge and skills from teaching candidates. To me, what was more important than any specific goal or action was that the equity ambassadors were well versed with and believed in our final plan. On their best days, they were enacting it through their advocacy and practice.

CONCLUSION

It took us 4 years to develop Equity Plan 2.0, and that is because we were deliberately slow. Two aspects of the work stand out as the most consequential. First, our comprehensive equity audit of the entire school district was critical. In hindsight, it was important that the committee chose to partner with, and the district invested $150,000 in resources for us to partner with, an organization that visited every district school. The 400-page audit covered every facet of the organization. The time with the auditors was invaluable. The audit lifted inequities that would have taken me, or even a small team, multiple years to uncover. Second, learning and leading learning is an integral part of doing equity leadership that should not be missed. The equity audit mattered because I was intentional about using it to facilitate ongoing learning of my colleagues throughout the district. Throughout our 4 years, after the audit was complete, we continually engaged in our own learning, through book studies, inviting guest speakers, and attending national conferences.

Institutionalizing equity is no small feat. During my tenure as assistant superintendent of equity, I learned quite a bit. I realized through the process that when forming a coalition of people willing to engage in the work, it must be made clear that the work will be long and hard. And that plans don't matter unless a coalition of people work together to develop them. In fact, when done well, developing the plan is itself a kind of equity leadership that is disruptive to the district status quo. As I transitioned to a superintendent position at the end of the 2023–2024 school year, I have continued to reflect on my experience, and I know that many inequities will remain deeply entrenched. At the same time, I remain optimistic that the revised Equity Plan, which was adopted with some modifications, will be implemented as designed. The people and the capacity to do so exist in a way that did not when I started the position. If you are leading equity work or considering it, take heed that racial battle fatigue is real and that there is a real possibility that you will come face to face with it. Take the time you need to rest and recover; equity work is not a sprint, but a marathon.

REFERENCES

Howard, T. (2010). *Why race and culture matter in schools: Closing the achievement gap in America's classrooms*. Teachers College Press.

Irby, D. J. (2021). *Stuck improving: Racial equity and school leadership*. Harvard Education Press.

Milner, R. (2021). Series foreword in Irby, D. *Stuck improving: Racial equity and school leadership* (p. vii). Harvard Education Press.

Safir, S., & Dugan, J. (2021). *Street data: A next-generation model for equity, pedagogy, and school transformation*. Corwin.

Senge, P. M. (2006). *The fifth discipline: The art and practice of the learning organization* (revised and updated edition). Doubleday.

Senge, P., Hamilton, H., & Kania, J. (2015). The dawn of system leadership. *Stanford Social Innovation Review, 13*, 27–33.

Smith, W. A., Allen, W. R., & Danley, L. L. (2007). "Assume the position . . . you fit the description": Psychosocial experiences and racial battle fatigue among African American male college students. *American Behavioral Scientist, 51*(4), 551–578. https://doi.org/10.1177/0002764207307742

CHAPTER 6

Designing Work Routines and Process(ing) Tools

An Infrastructure of Strategic Equity Leadership

Maurice Swinney and Decoteau J. Irby

> People often ask me "How did you accomplish these things? How did you build the equity office to sustain itself?" It's because I strategically designed the office for sustainability with a focus on creating internal and external organizational routines. And I created tools to facilitate the kinds of organizational routines that would drive our work and achieve impact.

In this chapter, we present a condensed narrative, reconstructed from a series of interviews, Zoom calls, and conversations that pushed me (Maurice) to think deeply about organizational routines as a key aspect of how I did the work of equity leadership. Organizational routines are ways of working or processes used to engage teams and others around equity work. They involve mapping time and effort, structures for engaging others, rubrics for assessing our work, and methods for providing support and feedback. When I first took on the role of creating and leading an equity office for my district, I relied on the Cynefin framework (Nachbagauer, 2021; Snowden, 2000; Snowden & Boone, 2007) to diagnose the prevailing operative contexts I was working in and prioritize the problems suited for equity design.

Snowden (2000) argues that the contexts in which we lead are characterized by simple, chaotic, complicated, and complex problems. The effectiveness of leadership depends, in large part, on understanding and responding to these prevailing context problems. Simple context problems can be solved through best practices—effective communication, identifying what's worked in the past, consulting research, and so forth. Chaotic problems leave little time for research and consultations. They demand immediate action to stop whatever acute crisis the organization is facing. I limited the amount of attention I gave to chaotic and simple/clear problems, as I didn't see them as opportunities to create change.

Throughout my tenure as superintendent of equity, I focused on addressing the pursuit of equity and justice as complicated, but mostly complex, work. Complicated problems are those best addressed through diagnosing, analyzing, and responding. Without experiential and academic knowledge, complicated problems may be difficult to pinpoint and thus require expertise to identify. Complex situations have no one answer and are best addressed through continued probing and emergent strategy development. Because I consider school inequity to be complicated and complex, I grounded my leadership practices in seeking out expertise and designing strategies to continually disrupt district business as usual.

I stepped into my role thinking of myself as a systems-level designer of equity and justice innovations. I do not claim to be the first person to take on design as a consequential aspect of equity leadership. In fact, I had the benefit of learning from leaders who came before, both historically from years far gone and more recently from folks who had done the morning work of laying a foundation of resources and materials. I drew from this collective wisdom and experience to think, design, and act in support of our district's over 300,000 students, teachers, leaders, and staff. I kept several resources within arm's reach:

- Boston Public Schools' Equity Impact Analysis Tool
- The City of Portland's Equity Budget Tool and Racial Equity Plans
- The City of Seattle's 2016 Racial Equity Toolkit Assessment Worksheet
- Race Forward's Racial Equity Impact Assessment Toolkit
- Minneapolis Public Schools' Equity and Diversity Impact Assessments
- Oakland Unified School District's Impact Assessment Results-Based Budgeting

All of these resources were created by leaders who were doing and documenting their work between 2012 and 2017. The people and organizations who created these tools were indispensable resources for me as I figured out my own work. The good news was that I wasn't starting from scratch. My superintendent gave me a million dollar budget to start and wide latitude to design the work the way I thought best. And even with all the resources and past knowledge I had with me, I still had to figure out my own local context and problems, create my own localized organizational routines, and establish goals to address the injustices I'd witnessed as a teacher and building principal. In the remainder of this chapter, I share what it means to engage in equity leadership from the mindframe and practice of an equity designer.

Most importantly, I want readers to appreciate that equity work is not about putting out small fires. It is about dismantling and redesigning the system and its processes so that those fires do not keep breaking out in the first place. I describe the importance of using work routines and process(ing) tools as a way to build infrastructures that disrupt system inequities. Throughout, I argue that setting up a system for long-standing equitable improvement requires leaders to establish a leadership infrastructure, which includes three elements: process tools, work routines, and desired outcomes. Working together, process tools support work routines that enable users to achieve desired outcomes. The clearer leaders can be about what each of these elements entails, the better they will be at achieving sustained impact beyond their tenure.

In the remainder of this chapter, I tell four interrelated stories that demonstrate what I mean by using process tools to support work routines that achieve desired outcomes, which are summarized in Table 6.1. I start with the story of how I hired my first leadership team. Next, I explain how I resisted the urge to put out fires and chase rabbits by designing a work routine that allowed my team to minimize noise and distractions and focus our work on high-impact activities. I then explore how our focus allowed us to participate and collaborate with district teams and communities to maximize our impact. I end by explaining why we never created an equity policy and the alternate route we took to impact policy-making at a districtwide scale. In each story, I encourage the reader to pay close attention to the importance of work routines and their relationship to the use of tools. Taken together, the overall story of all four areas of work reveals how *I built out the work*, from myself, to my team, and beyond.

Table 6.1. Work Tools, Routines, and Outcomes

Leaders	Process(ing) Tools	The Work Routine	Desired Outcome
Individual	Equity starter pack	Hire a team	Fully staffed equity office
Internal team: inward	Equity landscape tool	Streamline equity leadership activities to maximize equity office's impact	Highly functioning equity office team that works together to drive district change
Internal team: outward	Plug and play presentations	Provide professional development to district staff and teams	District offices, teams, schools, and community groups understand district equity framework
External team	Policy review rubric and routing form	Help other people and offices to revise policies using an equity lens	Make district policies more equitable for those most burdened by the system

THE WORK OF HIRING A TEAM

To develop the office, I used what I called an Equity Starter Pack. The Equity Starter Pack was a document outlining an initial framework for the advancement of equity efforts within my district. This tool allowed me to clarify and organize my ideas on paper, including how to create and sustain a strong team and defining what I believed I should focus on (workstreams) that would signal where the office of equity is going. Within the Equity Starter Pack I made recommendations for staffing, leadership training, organizational planning, resource allocation, and professional development. The document emphasized the need for systemic change, collaboration, and investment to support marginalized students and promote educational equity.

When creating the Equity Starter Pack, there was no template. I created a document for myself and organized it for how I think and process information. I drew inspiration from several places. For example, I carefully reviewed Seattle's racial equity impact assessment work. I combed through Oakland Public Schools' equity leadership resources. I reached out to select equity directors for advice. I also looked back at my initial interview materials for the superintendent of equity position, which outlined my vision and values of the office: I believed that educators who are in direct contact with students and families will do their best work when they have the right tools and resources to meet the varying needs of students. Designing staff positions for the office, I asked myself three questions:

- How should the positions on the equity team strategically align with the mission to drive high-impact, systemic change and address the most pressing equity challenges?
- What skills, resources, and collaborative routines and tools are essential for these roles to effectively advance equity work and foster sustainable relationships across the district and with community partners?
- How will the impact and effectiveness of these positions be measured and adapted over time to ensure long-term success and responsiveness to evolving equity needs?

The roles needed to be collaborative and interdependent to ensure we were all moving toward the same impact. I wanted to be with other equity-driven people who could bring and share their gifts and talents together with me and mine. Early on, I considered what we would measure outside of student test results to demonstrate our impact and progress. I chose broad impact measures like adult practice shifts, policy changes, and resource flows to the most high-need schools.

My vision included three key team members with distinct strengths. First, I wanted someone with a robust teaching and learning background who understood the diverse needs of young people. Second, I needed a policy expert who could go beyond surface-level fixes and develop a framework to guide policy change. This person would also need to build strategic relationships with external organizations that center racial equity in policy reform. Lastly, I required a team member skilled in data analysis to ensure our work was driven by qualitative and quantitative data toward measurable outcomes. Generally, I wanted team members who could engage across the district schools and departments.

When I started preparing job descriptions, I reviewed other equity office job descriptions in education and the private sector to get a sense of common and current job description language. Next, I collaborated with our district human resources department to write job descriptions. Within a few months, the equity office was staffed with a teaching and learning, policy, and data strategist. Beyond these specific roles, I knew we would need additional hands on deck. I was realistic about our financial constraints, understanding my initial budget of 1 million dollars would only go so far. I hired university interns who needed to complete hours for their coursework. I also partnered with school leaders and teachers who were working on degrees and needed special projects. Once we had a team in place, we had to figure out a way to focus.

THE WORK OF FOCUSING A TEAM

I remember during one of our early team meetings, about 6 months into our work together, I could see something was amiss. So I asked, "What's on everyone's mind?" I looked around and saw facial expressions that I didn't know how to interpret. Then I said to everyone, "Write down what you're feeling." The words that my team wrote down? Overwhelmed. Tired. Foggy. Confused. When we unpacked what we felt about the work we were doing, it was clear—we were doing too much. Despite our early enthusiasm, we struggled to articulate what we were achieving because we were engaged in too many things.

I already knew that the best strategy for doing transformative work wasn't about launching initiatives to respond to years of inequity. It was about firming up the equity office to lead and drive change with others. Early on we fell into the common trap of putting out fires and trying to be everything to everyone. Folks wanted to go down the path of initiatives. I said to myself and to my team, "You know, we're all over this district. We're in everything, at every meeting. But we ain't getting shit done." So we took a step back and paused. We started to seriously question whether the things we were doing were of high value or of high importance or if they were going to have any long-term impact.

Soon after, I hired a consultant to help us recalibrate our *ways of working.* After a 2-day retreat, I drafted emails to colleagues, informing them that we were stepping back from certain projects to prioritize others. I was preparing the office for a strategic shift. Writing those emails was challenging for me, but I felt invigorated by the opportunity to refocus and move forward with purpose. It was around this same time that I designed an Equity Landscape tool. Though the tool itself is not presented in this chapter, Table 6.2 provides a comprehensive view of how the tool helped us organize our work by identifying workstream ownership and assessing workload in real time. It helps evaluate the volume of engagements to determine what to start, stop, or continue, ensuring a focus on the most meaningful and impactful efforts. The goal was to assess whether the equity office's objectives were being met or if efforts were merely sustaining activity without meaningful impact.

Using the tool helped us get into the routine of asking ourselves the question: What are we doing and is it what we need to be doing? People wanted the equity office's support. Some people wanted what we called the "equity sprinkle": just for us to say they are doing the right thing so they could just check off that it was done. But the Equity Landscape Tool provided us with a 360-degree view of where we were spending time and energy. It helped us prioritize where we were going based on clear goals and timelines. The more we dug into the routine of using the tool, the more we could literally see our core work. We began to make clear distinctions about the types of work we were a part of, such as collaborative projects, steering committees, or consultations.

We made it a routine to keep looking at how we were organized. At first, because we needed to create better work priorities, we used the tool at least every 2 weeks. We began to log our work in documents to look at our projects across the year. We could literally see where we were spending our time. We would then ask ourselves: Where do we need to spend more time? Where do we need to spend less time? Where are we? And what are we doing? It was a powerful form of reflective practice for our full team and created clarity and internal accountability. As reflected in Table 6.2, we focused on spending most of our time and energy engaged in high-leverage activities (indicated in bold) that our office owned in terms of responsibility. In other words, there was work that would not be accomplished if we failed to prioritize it, such as designing the equity framework, creating the equity-informed policy review and revision process, and measuring and communicating the impact of our office's work on district operations and performance. Eventually we used it quarterly as a part of our continuous improvement process.

Using the landscape analysis with fidelity led to us making decisions about where we wanted to show up or where we didn't. Of course, there were some places our superintendent and higher-ups wanted us to be

Table 6.2. Sample Activity Distributions Before and After Adopting the Equity Landscape Routine

	Equity Office Responsibilities	Before	After	Standing Committees and Collaborations	Before	After	Steering Committee Participation	Before	After
PD Work	**Equity Framework**	4 hrs	20 hrs	**District Curriculum Committee**	6 hrs	6 hrs	Universal Leadership Work	3 hrs	3 hrs
	Instructional Equity Group	8 hrs	8 hrs	Special Education Equity Group	6 hrs	6 hrs	~~P-12 Curriculum~~	10 hrs	NONE
	Cont. Improvement Plan	3 hrs	3 hrs	~~Curriculum Equity Initiative~~	12 hrs	NONE			
Data Work	**Measuring Equity Office Impact**	3 hrs	10 hrs	5-Year Vision Implementation	10 hrs	5 hrs	School Ratings Redesign	6 hrs	3 hrs
	Equity Reporting to District	8 hrs	5 hrs	~~Status of Women and Girls~~	6 hrs	NONE	Data Governance Council	3 hrs	3 hrs
	Equity Reporting to Schools	20 hrs	10 hrs	Grading Committee	5 hrs	2 hrs			
Policy Work	**Racial Equity Policy Review Process**	6 hrs	12 hrs	**School Board Policy Review**	20 hrs	10 hrs	~~School Ratings Redesign~~	6 hrs	NONE
	Race and Equity Audit Tools	8 hrs	12 hrs	Capital Improvement Project	5 hrs	5 hrs	~~Universal Leadership Work~~	7 hrs	NONE
	Equity/Opportunity Index	10 hrs	10 hrs	Equity Funding Working Group	4 hrs	5 hrs			

present. Board policy stuff. Ongoing law department stuff. Working with our principal quality and human resources office. Working with the budget office. While we initially thought we needed to engage in some relationships year round, we learned that was not the case. Rather, we needed to be present at critical times of the year. So we built the critical moments into the tool for July and August when school budgets are rolling out to ensure an equitable distribution of resources. Other times, we're not even dealing with the budget office, and we let folks know we have enough on our plates.

For other spaces, we just started saying yes or no. Folks would still call on us for everything, and we wanted to be responsive. So, eventually we put ourselves on what we called a "consulting basis," meaning we would say, "Yes, we can help you; however, we cannot take action items from this meeting." That was our way of letting colleagues know we can be in the space with you. We can be a thought partner. But we can't take pieces of work out of the meeting. You have to do your own work. Once we started saying "No," we stabilized our efforts and worked much more productively.

After we were comfortable with the tool and felt more stabilized, we didn't abandon the tool. Instead, we integrated the routine into our cycle of continuous improvement. Pausing and reflecting quarterly became a practice that kept us agile. We now had more space to narrow the focus on completing the equity framework and building capacity of others in a thoughtful way. This practice was key to helping us impact the district more broadly. We began to center our weekly team meetings on building community among ourselves, understanding the complex inner working of the school district, synthesizing our notes from ongoing listening tours, and drafting the districtwide equity framework—the tool that eventually made all of the outward-facing work possible.

THE WORK OF INFLUENCING DISTRICT TEAMS

Our district is huge, so there is no way to champion equity across the system without recognizing that we must build capacity for *anyone* to be able to talk about equity work without us in the room. I knew early on that we needed to set ourselves up to do that over time. The districtwide equity framework we created was the tool that allowed us to go out and deliver a consistent message about the district's commitment to equity and our role in advancing that commitment.

One big question we wanted to respond to was: Who gets to lead? For equity to be transformative, we define leadership by focusing less on positional authority and more on who can be responsible for creating conditions for others. We began by considering the influential people in the district who saw equity as a moral imperative and value and who we deemed to be action oriented. In other words, we identified who was already doing this work before we formed the equity office. We latched onto the idea of *leading for equity*, because many people can lead for equity without a formal position of authority. Next, we thought about how we could organize the learning experiences in a way that did not overtax the team or limit the reach we had. What would professional learning experiences require of us? What partnerships did we need to form? What should the internal team lead, and where do we bring in others with lived experience and expertise?

We started to design a professional learning series focused on understanding the district equity framework—specifically liberatory thinking—which is rooted in understanding your bias, perceptions, and beliefs. We designed the professional development sessions to include thoughtful questions, engaging content, and heart-wrenching calls to action. We piloted the sessions to get feedback. People responded positively. But we were still only a team of five.

Three members of our five-person team, including me since it felt important to be seen leading the work, delivered 90-minute sessions. As excited as we were about the professional development, we found there was not enough time to train everyone who requested a session. When we delivered a productive and positive session, participants suggested more people who would benefit from the experience. We paused and reflected again and used our reflection routines. What were our intentions? What did we want people to do with the learning? We had to create a strategy for moving the work that wasn't just thought provoking but that would equip people with skills and tools to unlock different ways of working. We pivoted to creating professional learning that placed district personnel, teams, and partners into one of four categories, based on the questions laid out in Table 6.3.

When revisiting the goals of our professional development work, we established an inward routine that allowed us to turn outward to support

Table 6.3. Learner Groups and Professional Development Offerings

Learner Groups	Questions	Professional Offerings for Identified Groups
Critical friends, validators, and key leaders	Who needs a one-time professional learning experience to gain a general understanding of the equity framework and/or liberatory thinking?	These are introductory sessions for stakeholders—elected officials, district leaders, community organizers, national networks, union leaders, etc.—to understand the district's equity work including the role of the equity office and the framework.

(*continued*)

Table 6.3. Learner Groups and Professional Development Offerings (*continued*)

Learner Groups	Questions	Professional Offerings for Identified Groups
Sustained communities	Who are the people the equity office needs to develop over a year to increase knowledge and administer application of equity practices rooted in the equity framework and other essential learnings?	The yearlong journey of Future Leaders Mentorship program fits here where we co-construct learning together while supporting them with implementing a practice or change idea.
Working groups/ task forces	Where does the equity office serve in a thought leadership capacity, and what experience should we offer?	The purpose is to develop recommendations or best practices for the work of that team. The work may or may not be directly related to something the equity office is implementing.
District implementers	Where do we need to work collaboratively with offices and departments to make systemic change toward equity for our students?	Collaborating with the budget office to develop a funding formula was a high priority.

the district. This accounted for our limited time and capacity without diluting the learning and development experiences we designed. Every person and team in the district did not need the same support. Some kinds of work required more intensive time and attention. For example, our equity office team spent more time supporting sustained communities and district implementers. We relied on interns, consultants, or members of various district teams to support the equity framework learning of critical friends and working groups or task forces whose work would disband after a period of time. The approach gave the team the ability to go further faster. Mapping and categorizing helped us make our professional development portfolio strategic, enabling the team to determine what levers needed to be pulled in order to accomplish specific equity goals. Policy was one of those levers. And we realized that this was an area that required us to cultivate a routine, not for ourselves to use but for our colleagues throughout the district.

THE WORK OF CHANGING POLICIES

As an equity office, we didn't change policies, per se. Instead of writing an equity policy, we changed the policy design process itself. I am proud of how policy change work happens in the district now as a direct result of our efforts to assess and redesign policies. We figured out what policies needed to remain in place, be improved, or be rescinded. Recently, two former board presidents that came on after my tenure called me to say, "This is a really good process for making changes" because it helped the board and the district know what to look for when addressing policy issues or writing policies.

In 2019, our superintendent created a policy review team to examine all district policies to keep, amend, or rescind each one to make it more equitable for those most burdened by the system. Amending policy was especially rewarding as we aimed to make policies more equitable—ensuring they benefit everyone or, at the very least, do not burden or create barriers for historically underserved communities. But analyzing benefits and burdens of a respective policy was extremely time consuming. Also, those who took on the work of reviewing a policy couldn't help but develop a deep understanding of that particular policy's intended and unintended consequences. Employing a handful of policy experts limits the district's overall equity capacity because only those policy experts participate. They already have a deep understanding of the policy's consequences. Only involving experts robs the people who hold ownership over the policy's implementation from the opportunity to learn and participate in decision-making.

The equity office never wrote or intended to write an equity policy. We didn't consider it necessary since policies, and the resources attached to them, lived in other offices and departments. Because of this, an equity policy would only be a resolution, declaration, or unfunded mandate that wouldn't lead to substantive change. Instead, we partnered with offices and departments to examine their policies based on the belief that ensuring equitable policies has to live in everyone's work. We were all responsible and accountable for the district's policies.

Policy review was a high priority for the superintendent because, at the time, a 5-year vision called for a review of policies to be completed by 2023. In prior years, the superintendent's policy team was examining one policy at a time. Leonard, the equity policy strategist, was assigned from the equity office to be a part of that policy team. His role was to ensure that we looked at policy through an equity lens. It was tedious work. He read each policy, analyzed its intent, and supported the policy team and policy owners to gather insights from students, school leaders, families, and communities who may have been impacted by the policy. Gathering insights meant that district employees who are working on the revisions had to participate with internal and external stakeholder groups to understand the policy impacts.

For every policy, teams brought data that showed the positive and negative impacts. The equity lens helped policy owners gather data to unpack what the policy was intended to do and what the policy actually does. As you can imagine, this was a laborious process, and it began to consume too much of Leonard's time. In addition, too many policies were handled by different people. For instance, the office of academics could handle one policy, but the data review was handled by another group. And while these groups were not coordinating, a change in one policy could impact the work in another office or department. So then I thought, "We need to redesign the policy design process." This step was important because it was a transparent way of using quantitative and qualitative data to make decisions.

We took a step back to think about what a policy revision process could look like: a process with clear professional learning experiences, instructions, expectations, and tools to help offices and departments examine and revise their own policies. As I already explained, the equity office team had a common practice of pausing and reflecting when the work began piling up. This time was interesting, though, as we realized the need to develop a process and tool to decrease the burden on the district teams working on policy revisions. We turned to local and national policy and advocacy groups for advice and resources.

Leonard, the policy strategist at the time, knew a lot of people who did policy work, both locally and in other districts. I requested that he get a list of folks to find out how they approach racial equity impact assessments and policy review frameworks. We talked to groups like Race Forward, Policy Link, and City United for Equity to make sure we didn't make up something way out in left field or off base. Then, in collaboration with members of the district law department, we created an equity-focused policy redesign process and rubric to support teams. Table 6.4 provides an overview of the policy review flow we created.

Here's how the policy review process and rubric worked. As the first step, we required any department or team involved in policy change work to participate in a professional learning session with the equity office and interdepartmental policy team. The session provided an overview of the policy review process and, most importantly, helped them understand the intent of the process to ensure every policy was shaped by a commitment to equity. The next step, understanding and analysis, required the team to identify and engage stakeholders to assess the policy for equity and impact.

Steps 3 and 4 involved the work of actually writing up the policy, in which a team of collaborators put the ideas on paper and forwarded this to the policy team for comments, revisions, and final drafting. As a fifth step, we required every team to prepare a policy brief that broke the policy down for the superintendent's cabinet. The final step before presenting to the board was public comment. And to be clear, this wasn't just an exercise. The public comments were used to make final revisions before briefing the board and asking for a vote. A policy that had not been ushered through the entire process with fidelity would not be brought to a vote. In some cases, the superintendent's cabinet required departments to go back to satisfy a step in the process that they deemed inadequate.

Table 6.4. Who and what of the equity-informed policy review process

Who . . .	Equity Office and Interdepartmental Review Team . . .	District Department or School . . .	Equity Office and Interdepartmental Review Team . . .	Superintendent and Board . . .
What . . .	1. Delivers **professional learning** to explain policy modification requirements and process	2. Involves impacted community to **understand and analyze** policy change benefit and burdens	5. Collaborates with department or school to prepare and **deliver policy briefing** to superintendent's cabinet	7. Submits policy change for **board vote**
		3. **Drafts policy changes**	6. Collaborates with department or school to **revise policy** in preparation for board review	
		4. Hosts forum to present proposed changes for **public comment** by impacted communities		

Now, to clarify, we tested the review process itself before requesting that the board adopt it. We did not put it in front of the school board until we tested it out with community groups. Interestingly, this turned into an effective way for everyday people to have a little insight into what was developing policy-wise. This allowed them to know what was happening with policies that affected them before the board of directors discussed these topics in public meetings. The community members would say things at board meetings like, "Thank the equity office for engaging us. I know y'all are thinking about how to redesign policies." So, then I get calls from board members saying, "Hey, can you tell us a little bit more about this policy?" I responded like, "Yeah, you know, it's an experimental phase." But that was my process of testing out an idea. We put together a process. The people who own a particular policy are accountable for following the established process.

Once the process was strong and solid and had been tested a few times, our superintendent told me to present the process to board members. She also indicated that when a policy comes to her, she trusts it has gone through an equity audit or review *before* it goes to the board. So I made sure to let board members know that when people are bringing policies to the board, they need to tell you how they engaged the community and what data they used. They should find out the risks and mitigation strategies, all in order to make an informed decision. And because we did the policy review as a process strategy, the policy change work can now continue without us. Because if you take away the process, people are going to say, well, where did the policy redesign process go? When I was the superintendent of equity, there were about 20 policies that went through based on our policy rubric. At that point, our equity policy strategist's role shifted from working with every team who was working on a policy revision to providing professional learning experiences and tools that empowered teams to take up the work on their own.

DISCUSSION AND CONCLUSION

I recently went to speak at a meeting of principals, and the equity office staff were meeting in the same building. They now have a staff of 14 people plus interns. I had five team members. It was especially cool that it was the first time people saw me and the current superintendent of equity in the same room—a full circle moment. I thought, "Wow! This team has really grown." There are many more tentacles and initiatives in the district that are focused on academics, social and emotional well-being, and much more that weren't happening when I left.

Sustainability in equity work has the potential to outlast a leader's tenure if the leaders embed these elements into the day-to-day operations of a district, ensuring that equity is not just an agenda item, but a guiding framework for systemic change. At the heart of this work is the understanding that equity cannot be achieved in isolation, which can lead to frustration and disorientation. It requires deep, sustained relationships, partnerships, and coalition building, both within the district and beyond. Transformative change happens when leaders invest in people, create structured yet adaptive processes and tools, and build the capacity of others to carry the work forward.

We want to emphasize the critical importance of avoiding the constant cycle of "chasing rabbits"—the tendency to react to every emergent issue, crisis, or request that arises. It's easy to get trapped in immediate responsive/crisis management, which at times is required. The COVID-19 pandemic was one clear example. But reactionary leadership is not likely to shift how the system functions overall. Rather than taking on every issue or responding to every immediate crisis, we found that focusing on long-term systems change through collaboration was the most effective strategy for creating lasting impacts on the system—a solid office, policy changes, stronger coalitions, embedded and far-reaching professional learning opportunities, and processes to ensure equitable resource distribution.

While urgency is often a reality in equity work, a purely reactionary approach does not lead to systemic change. Instead, we learned to prioritize structured reflection, strategic alignment, and clear boundaries to ensure that our efforts were always contributing to a larger, more sustainable vision for equity in the district. True equity work is not about putting out fires—it is about redesigning the system so that those fires do not keep breaking out in the first place. Although I've focused heavily on organizational routines and tools, it's absolutely critical to understand that ensuring the work continues beyond any one leader or moment in time is about centering relationships, building coalitions, and leveraging collective power. Without a doubt, relationships are essential for weathering the challenges that evenings bring about.

REFERENCES

City of Boston. (2013). *Boston Public Schools Equity Impact Analysis Tool.* bpsracialequityimpacttoolinword.pdf

City of Portland. (2017). *Equity budget tool and racial equity plans.* https://www.portlandoregon.gov/citycode/ article/634752

City of Seattle Government. (2016). *Racial equity toolkit assessment worksheet.* https://www.seattle.gov/Documents/Departments/RSJI/RacialEquityToolkit_FINAL_ August2012.pdf

Great Cities Institute. (2016). *Chicago community area economic hardship index.* https://greatcities.uic.edu/wp-content/uploads/2016/07/GCI-Hardship-Index-Fact-SheetV2.pdf

Nachbagauer, A. (2021). Managing complexity in projects: Extending the Cynefin framework. *Project Leadership and Society*, *2*, 100017.

Oakland Unified School District. (2015). *Oakland Unified School District impact assessment results based budgeting.* http://proxient.com/wp-content/uploads/2016/03/dell_Impact_Assessment_Results-Based_Budgeting.pdf

Minneapolis Public Schools. (2017). *Equity and diversity impact assessments.* https://www.mpschools.org/departments/equity-school-climate

Race Forward. (2015). *Racial equity impact assessment toolkit.* www.raceforward.org/practice/tools

Snowden, D. (2000). Cynefin: A sense of time and space, the social ecology of knowledge management. In C. Despres & D. Chauvel (Eds.). *Knowledge horizons: The present and the promise of knowledge management* (p. 34). Butterworth-Heinemann.

Snowden, D. J., & Boone, M. E. (2007). A leader's framework for decision making. *Harvard Business Review, 85*, 68–76.

CHAPTER 7

A National View of Equity Leadership Activities

Andrew Matschiner and Ishmael Miller

> That's the thing that I would need to do a better job . . . because my role has multiple hats, right? I am the director of equity, but if I were to look at . . . a time scale, I probably spend about 30% of my time doing that role. And then I'm also the director of [state accountability plan], which I spend probably 60 to 65% of [my] time focused on the [state accountability work], because the [state accountability work] . . . seems like every single part of this district, all departments, all sites, because those are the funds coming in. . . . Now, I also manage school sites. . . . I oversee certain school sites, and I work with principals. So I'm also a director of schools. And so my time is stretched. So for me to say [I'm at] a hundred percent fidelity on one of these areas, I'd be lying. It's because of the multiple hats I wear. . . . So it's a job that's done okay, [but] I would love to do a great job of it.
>
> –Latino male equity director reflecting on his role[1]

As referenced in the epigraph, the job responsibilities of equity director roles vary based on many factors, including role resources (e.g., budget, staff) and forms of equity leadership activity. While researchers have examined who holds equity director roles, we know much less about job responsibilities, daily activities and tasks, and support received for this emergent position. In this chapter, we explore and analyze trends in leader demographics, resources afforded to leaders, and equity directors' diverse forms of equity leadership activity. We draw data from 34 responses collected from the 2022 "Lead for Equity Survey of Equity Leaders," during the midday of equity leadership, a time where formal equity leaders were plentiful and when leadership activities were at a high point.

Survey trends point to discrepancies in the work equity directors report to be important and the types of work accomplished over the last year, with limited areas of alignment; the pivotal role of organizational conditions and resources in equity director work; and the central importance of family and community engagement as a core equity leadership activity. Ultimately, we argue that supporting equity directors as leaders (and individuals) requires an ongoing understanding of the role, so it can be redesigned, reimagined, and aligned with district priorities to achieve intended outcomes (Irby et al., 2022). Understanding roles and, when necessary, shifting them is vital to transforming unsupportive organizational contexts, addressing unclear and misaligned role configurations, and challenging oppressive racial-gender experiences (Ishimaru et al., 2023). As we will address, these factors undermine the transformative potential of equity director roles, contribute to leader burnout, and ultimately leave the inequitable school systems that harm far too many children unchanged.

SURVEY DESIGN AND RESPONSES

The 2022 Lead for Equity Survey of Equity Leaders was developed by Dr. Decoteau Irby, Dr. Ann Ishimaru, and Dr. Terrance Green and administered using Qualtrics in summer 2022. While the survey was intended to capture the experiences of central office leaders working in formal equity leadership roles (i.e., roles explicitly invoking diversity, equity, and inclusion [DEI]), respondents fell into three roles: school-level leaders (e.g., assistant principals), district-level central office leaders in roles that did not explicitly invoke DEI (e.g., director of social and emotional learning), and district-level "equity directors" (e.g., director of educational equity).

Among the survey respondents, 13 served in building-level leadership roles; 8 served in other district-level roles that did not explicitly invoke "equity," "diversity," or "inclusion"; and 34 served in "equity director" roles (i.e., district-level roles invoking "equity," "diversity," and/or "inclusion"). In this chapter, we focus on equity directors. By "equity director," we mean leaders working in formal district-level leadership roles with "equity," "diversity," and "inclusion" as part of their role title and charge (e.g., director of educational equity, coordinator of diversity and equity).

The survey contained approximately 30 open-ended and Likert-scale questions addressing the following: leader demographics (open-ended), role characteristics (open-ended), equity leadership activity (e.g., developing equity programs and initiatives; Likert scale), forms of support (e.g., my district had my back when equity work was questioned or attacked; Likert scale), and district characteristics (open-ended). Among the 34 equity directors, approximately 70% reported working in "suburban" districts, whereas the remaining 30% reported working in "urban" districts. The 34 equity director respondents worked in districts across 13 states and all four U.S. Census regions.

FINDINGS

We share data related to the racial and gender identities of equity directors before exploring key findings related to equity leadership activity and role resources. Regarding equity leadership activity specifically, we echo Ishimaru et al. (2023) who described, "Equity directors' primary leadership activities involve working to transform organizational structures, policies, and practices to improve the social, emotional, and academic experiences and outcomes of minoritized children" (p. 365). Findings then provide a preliminary picture of the leaders who hold equity director roles and the work these leaders carry out most frequently.

First, equity director survey data reveals discrepancies between equity leadership activity *importance* and *engagement* over the last year. Next, amid importance-engagement discrepancies across many forms of equity leadership activity, *community engagement* stood out as one form of equity leadership activity that equity directors rated both important and engaged in frequently. Finally, limited role resources and challenging organizational contexts appear to limit equity director efficacy and likely contribute to importance-engagement discrepancies.

EQUITY DIRECTOR RACE AND GENDER DEMOGRAPHICS

Examining equity director roles begins with understanding the identities and experiences of the leaders who hold such roles. Table 7.1 details the self-identified racial and gender characteristics of surveyed equity directors. Thirty of thirty-four equity directors (88%) identified as people of color. Nineteen respondents (56%) self-identified as Black: 12 identified as Black women and 7 as Black men. Multiracial, Latino/Hispanic, and white equity directors accounted for 12% of those surveyed. Twenty-two of thirty-four equity directors (65%) identified as women. The diversity of equity directors presents an opportunity to understand better how these leaders' racially and culturally diverse backgrounds inform their ability to address systemic inequities in addition to analyzing how these leaders understand the toll of navigating and addressing systemic racism as a person of color.

Table 7.1. Equity Director Demographics (n=34)

Demographic	Sample (%)
Black	55
Multiracial	12
Latinx	12
White	12
Asian American	9
Female equity directors	65
Male equity directors	35

Table 7.2. Equity Leadership Activity Importance and Engagement Responses, Five Highest Averages

Engaged in Most Often During the Last Year	Identified as Most Important for Advancing District Equity Work
Develop equity programs and initiatives (M=4.03, SD=1.06)	Learning from and working with students (M=4.73, SD=0.51)
Engage families and community partners (M=3.97, SD=0.67)	Strategic planning, goal setting, budgeting, and progress monitoring (M=4.68, SD=0.59)
Represent and communicate district equity efforts (M=3.94, SD=1.15)	Engaging families and community partners (M=4.59, SD=0.61)
Visit schools (M=3.79, SD=0.91)	Visiting schools (M=4.59, SD=0.61)
Coach district staff and employees (M=3.71, SD=.80)	Developing and revising district policies (M=4.47, SD=0.66)

Note: Appendix 7.A and B provide averages for all 16 equity leadership activities.

Survey questions asked equity directors how important they believed a range of 16 equity leadership activities were for "advancing equity in your district." Equity directors were also asked how frequently they engaged in each of the same 16 equity leadership activities over the last year. Table 7.2 provides equity director averages and standard deviations based on 5-point Likert scale responses for the five highest-rated activities for each question.

EQUITY LEADERSHIP ACTIVITY DISCREPANCIES

An initial discrepancy emerged across all 16 forms of equity leadership activity: Average importance scores were higher than average engagement scores. Importance scores were 0.86 higher on average than engagement scores across all 16 forms of equity leadership activity. Social desirability bias—the reality that equity directors may have felt pressure to report all equity leadership activity as "very important" or "extremely important"—may have contributed to higher importance averages. Still, as analyzed throughout this chapter, other factors such as limited staff and financial resources likely influenced this discrepancy.

Comparing the highest-rated forms of equity leadership activity in terms of importance versus engagement reveals other discrepancies. The equity leadership activity most engaged in was developing equity programs and initiatives ($M = 4.03$, $SD = 1.06$). Notably, this form of equity leadership activity did not appear among the five most important forms. Based on survey data, it is unclear what programs and initiatives equity directors had in mind when answering this question or which ones equity directors engaged in most often (e.g., programming supporting minoritized students, school-based equity teams). We return to consider equity programming in the "Discussion" section.

Three forms of equity leadership activity were rated among the most important and did not appear among the most commonly engaged forms of activity. These activities were "learning from and working with students"; "strategic planning, goal setting, budgeting, and progress monitoring"; and "developing and revising district policies." These three forms of equity leadership activity were subject to the largest differences in average importance and average engagement scores: "developing and revising district policies" (1.38 difference in averages); "strategic planning, goal setting, budgeting, and progress monitoring" (1.32 difference in averages); and "learning from and working with students" (1.12 difference in averages). These discrepancies point to important questions about how misaligned role configurations limit equity directors' ability to carry out prioritized work, how superintendents may expect equity directors to carry out conflicting or additional forms of equity leadership activity, and how equity director role placement and design influence equity leadership activity.

EQUITY LEADERSHIP ACTIVITY ALIGNMENT

Survey results show alignment between two of the five forms of equity leadership activity equity directors reported engaging in most often and rated most important for advancing district equity work. "Engaging families and community partners" was the second most engaged in activity (M = 3.97, SD = 0.67) and rated third in importance for advancing district equity work (M = 4.59, SD = 0.61). "Visiting schools" had the fourth highest engagement average (M = 3.79, SD = 0.91) and was fourth in importance for advancing district equity work (M = 4.59, SD = 0.61). Based on survey data, it is unclear what "Engaging families and community partners" and "Visiting schools" entail. For example, an equity director could visit a school for multiple reasons, including providing professional learning, meeting with students, or supporting the site administrator in addressing a biased incident. This alignment suggests the importance of equity directors actively connecting with their community to build relationships, collect data, and address issues rather than working in isolation. In addition, there is a need to understand equity directors' interactions better when they engage with their communities.

ROLE RESOURCES

Survey responses point to a second important trend: equity director role resources. Data indicates that equity directors often have limited staff and financial support for district equity work but often have access to the superintendent based on the position of their role. Nearly 60% of equity directors reported having one or fewer full-time equivalent roles to support district equity work, leaving many equity directors as the only person formally charged with leading equity work in their district. Limited staff capacity almost certainly undermines equity directors' ability to pursue the forms of equity leadership activity they deem most important, particularly time-intensive activities such as developing and revising district policies—among the least-engaged-in equity leadership activities.

Furthermore, 65% of equity directors reported a budget of less than $150,000 annually (excluding equity director salaries) to support district equity work. Alarmingly, 38% of equity directors reported no dedicated budget to support district equity work. Limited and precarious budgets likely force equity directors to engage in a limited set of equity leadership activities while focusing on less resource-intensive forms of equity leadership activity. Only 4 of the 34 equity directors reported budgets of $500,000 to support district equity work.

Regarding the organizational position of equity director roles, over 60% indicated they reported directly to the superintendent or were one level removed from the superintendent. Still, 18% of equity directors reported their role was positioned three or more levels from the superintendent. Findings signal support for equity directors' work from many superintendents and suggest equity directors are often "at the table" for critical district conversations. Yet positional authority without staff and financial resources likely reduces the scope of equity leadership activity and the likelihood of equity directors engaging in more resource-intensive activities. This "rank without resources" dynamic (Matschiner, 2024) likely reduces some equity director roles to primarily symbolic roles without adequate resources and support (Lewis et al., 2023; see also Tichavakunda, 2021).

DISCUSSION

Centering Race and Gender in Educational Leadership Literature

Leaders of color comprised 88% of equity directors analyzed in this chapter. This percentage is particularly notable at the central office level. Rogers and Tieken (2020) conducted a national survey of PK–12 superintendents, obtaining a sample of 1,218 participants, of whom only 8.2% identified as people of color. The demographics of this sample provide an opportunity to analyze how race and gender influence equity director leadership practice and impact experience.

Historically, educational leadership literature has often forwarded a color-evasive conception of leadership standards and practices (Davis et al., 2015; Khalifa et al., 2013; Lopez, 2003). Research on Black superintendents has documented their racialized experiences and the unique gifts these leaders bring to address persistent disparities (Alston, 2005; Joseph, 2023). For example, Peters and Nash (2021) investigated how Black women superintendents' racialized and gendered experiences support their praxis to be "(a) explicitly anti-racist; (b) explicitly anti-sexist; (c) explicitly acknowledges the multiplicative influences of marginalization centering race and gender, and across planes of identity; and (d) explicitly leverages authority to serve and protect historically underserved communities" (p. 7).

Similarly, burgeoning scholarship within the equity director literature has begun to document the leadership practices of Black equity directors. Miller (2024) described the equity director–type leadership practice of Black community advocacy utilized by W. A. Robinson. Robinson was a Black male central office leader who supported integrating Black students and staff in response to the 1953 *Phillips v. Phoenix Union High Schools and Junior College District* case, which led to school desegregation in Arizona. Robinson addressed forms of anti-Blackness and systemic inequity by hosting community conversations on school integration issues, partnering with a community organization to obtain resources for students in need, supporting a Black candidate's run for school board, and partnering with district and community librarians to obtain books and other learning material representative of recently integrated students. While these studies focus on the experience of Black equity leaders specifically, leaders of color across racial and gender backgrounds bring unique and important understandings to address inequity in P–12 systems. Such findings and further research would contribute to disrupting color-evasive educational leadership discourse.

Second, since equity directors are overwhelmingly people of color, they are navigating racialized and gendered organizations that often push these leaders out of systems. For example, scholars have documented that teachers and leaders of color navigate racially hostile work environments (Dixon et al., 2019; Joseph, 2023; Weiner et al., 2022). Similarly, Black women equity directors experience "organizational double jeopardy," which is a form of racialized and gendered injustice that limits their ability to create transformative change in P–12 systems effectively (Ishimaru et al., 2023). Equity directors are positioned as chief respondents and have to navigate systems that reproduce forms of racism. Future research might further investigate the impact of racialized and gendered experiences on equity directors and the strategies that support these leaders to process and heal from these persistent forms of oppression.

Resourcing Equity Director Roles

Results addressing equity director role resources highlight how insufficient resources make a challenging role more difficult. Given the normative and political dimensions of equity work (e.g., Oakes, 1992) and the systemic nature of racial inequity, resources are an indispensable aspect of realizing the potential of equity director roles.

Considering the nature, scope, and scale of the change equity directors are charged with supporting, it appears roles are often inadequately resourced. Our findings here complement other research using equity director survey data (Matschiner, 2024), which similarly found that equity director roles were often designed with limited resources and authority despite elevated rank and access to district leadership spaces. Although not directly examined here, many equity directors are likely provided fewer resources than leaders in similar central office roles (e.g., equity directors receive far less financial support than other director-level roles—a topic worthy of future investigation).

Limited equity director role resources likely constrain the vision equity directors develop for their district equity work and their ability to carry out such work. Insufficient resources may force many equity directors to reduce their work to what is possible with limited staff and financial resources. This likely contributes to equity directors being unable to engage in equity leadership activity to the degree they might, being forced to deprioritize more time- and resource-intensive forms of equity leadership activity. Thus, with many equity directors working to create what the role will become, limited role resources likely circumscribe equity directors' visions for equity leadership work before such work even begins. Inevitably, this contributes to importance-engagement discrepancies for many equity directors.

Limited resources render equity director roles further structurally and psychologically vulnerable (Irby et al., 2022; see Mitchell et al., 2017). Irby et al. (2022) explained, "structural vulnerability reflects a work role that actually minimizes a person's ability to carry out what they believe is the right work" while "psychological vulnerability is the feeling of decreased self-efficacy, frustration, and self-doubt that emerges when a person experiences a gap between the work that they believe is the right work to undertake and the work tasks they are assigned to carry out (Gronn and Lacey, 2004)" (p. 422). Limited role resources minimize equity directors' ability to carry out envisioned work (i.e., contributing to structural vulnerability). The inability to carry out envisioned work likely reduces equity director self-efficacy and increases frustration, given equity directors' inability to support prioritized work across district systems.

Limited role resources also take a personal toll on equity directors. For example, equity directors with no additional staff supporting district equity work (41% of leaders surveyed) are responsible for designing, delivering, supporting, and evaluating this work—a massive task that almost certainly limits the impact of district equity work and contributes to burnout and role turnover (e.g., Ishimaru et al., 2023).

Limited role resources induce structural and psychological vulnerabilities that restrict equity directors' ability to carry out prioritized equity leadership activity, likely increasing leader burnout. Compounded by nationally coordinated attacks on district DEI work and leaders since late 2020, equity director roles remain particularly vulnerable.

Equity Leadership Activity as Executing Programmatic Responsibilities

Importance-engagement discrepancies provide a provisional picture of equity leadership activity trends. Survey analysis suggests equity director role responsibilities tend to be execution focused, largely programmatic, and often reactive. Equity directors spend much of their time executing programmatic responsibilities in response, at least partly, to racist incidents and other crises.

Notably, importance averages were higher than engagement averages for all 16 equity leadership activities. Three factors likely shaped this trend. First, as described in the epigraph at the beginning of the chapter, equity directors' time and attention are spread across many activities, potentially leaving limited capacity to address activities that equity directors also believe to be important. Next, equity director roles may be established without specific priorities and outcomes to focus time and attention, with equity director efforts spread thin across many areas. Last, equity directors may believe that all forms of equity leadership activity are important, given the vast range of district norms and practices reproducing racial and other inequities.

Equity directors rated "developing equity programs and initiatives" as the form of equity leadership activity they engaged in most often. Similar to "visiting schools," the breadth of the "developing equity programs and initiatives" activity category invites questions about what specifically equity directors were engaged in. Equity programs and initiatives could be anything from identity- and advocacy-focused clubs for students to working with school board members on an equity-focused rezoning initiative. Future research might pair a survey and interviews to assess the range of "programs" and "initiatives" to discover which ones equity directors engage in most often.

Equity directors rated "learning from and working with students" as the most important equity leadership practice, yet the practice did not appear among the five most commonly engaged in practices. Equity directors, many of whom have worked in schools previously (see Matschiner, 2024), may believe learning from and working with students is important but find their district central office role does not often expect or allow for such work. Furthermore, even when equity directors visit schools, they may do so, for example, to coach principals on equity issues as opposed to working directly with students.

Equity directors rated "strategic planning, goal setting, budgeting, and progress monitoring" as the second most important equity leadership activity. Yet this activity also did not appear among the five most commonly engaged activities, ranking 11th in engagement. This suggests that equity directors have limited time and attention for strategic planning and progress monitoring amid myriad responsibilities such as leading meetings, facilitating professional development, coaching principals, and more. A heavy focus on execution with limited time and attention for larger strategic planning is consistent with equity director roles established with limited DEI staff capacity (e.g., no additional staff).

Equity directors may find that, despite valuing strategic planning and goal setting, they are forced to deprioritize this more intensive form of equity leadership activity that requires significant time, collaboration across stakeholder groups, and institutional support. Contrasted with potentially less intensive forms of equity leadership activity such as "representing and communicating district equity efforts" (e.g., leading a monthly stakeholder meeting or attending a weekly meeting), limited role resources may force equity directors to deprioritize strategic planning.

Reactive crisis-driven attention may divert focus from strategic planning, progress monitoring, working with students, and other forms of equity leadership activity. "Putting out fires" captures the reactive nature of equity work in many districts as superintendents and other leaders ask equity directors to respond to the latest racist incident—forcing equity directors to reprioritize or drop work underway. Equity directors rated "putting out fires" as the least important form of equity leadership activity. Still, putting out fires had the ninth-highest engagement average among the 16 equity leadership activities. This reactivity likely contributes to engagement-importance discrepancies and undermines equity directors' visions for the role.

Comparing *programmatic* equity leadership activity with *policy-focused* equity leadership activity (i.e., "developing and revising district policies") invites important questions for future scholarship. While "developing equity programs and initiatives" was the form of activity equity directors reported engaging in most often, "developing and revising district policies" had the second-lowest engagement average. This discrepancy is particularly surprising because developing and revising district policy was one of the five highest-rated activities in terms of importance. Thus, survey findings suggest equity directors engaged in policy-related work far less frequently than programmatic work and far less likely than expected based on the corresponding importance average. The discrepancy in policy averages could be due to the nature of equity-oriented policy development: It often takes longer to identify, develop, and approve district policy compared to, for example, executing programmatic work such as leading professional development for a group of principals. Furthermore, revising or establishing a new district policy can be more difficult as it often requires formalizing districtwide changes through time-intensive processes such as developing a board-approved equity policy.

Equity Director Interactions With Community

The survey results indicate alignment between engaging families and community partners visiting schools, and the vagueness of those terms suggests a need to better understand the type of interactions equity directors have with their community. Engaging families and community partners was a focus of attention in many districts before the rise of equity director roles (see Ishimaru, 2019b). It was common for central offices to conduct family engagement activities by providing programs and expecting youth, parents, and community to be passive supporters of the district's agenda (Ishimaru, 2019a). The orientation of school districts to conduct family engagement through discrete and passive programming is important because the survey reveals the most enacted activity of equity directors is developing equity programs and initiatives.

The literature suggests school leaders working with youth, parents, and community can lead to impactful and longer-lasting change on issues of inequity (Rodela & Bertrand, 2018; Welton & Freelon, 2018). For example, Ishimaru (2019b) describes equitable collaborations as a movement from family engagement toward school leaders partnering with parents and communities to drive systemic transformation. Thus, investigating equity directors' interactions with their community is crucial. A future study might examine equity director interactions when they engage families and community partners or visit schools. Understanding how much equity director leadership activity focuses on visiting schools to engage in discrete programs, such as a cultural fair instead of working with youth, parents, and community on committees that reform policies and practices, could identify the organizational structures that prevent equity directors from positioning their community to address systemic inequities.

CONCLUSION

Survey results from the 2022 Lead for Equity Survey of Equity Leaders provide the first national effort to contextualize central office "equity director" roles. Drawing on 34 equity director responses nationally, this chapter examined trends of equity leadership activity and the resources afforded to equity directors.

Equity director roles are most often held by Black leaders (55%), women of color (61%), and Black women specifically (35%). Across 16 forms of equity leadership activity surveyed, equity directors reported engaging in "developing equity programs and initiatives" and "engaging families and community partners" most often over the last year. Equity director roles were often senior central office roles (e.g., director, assistant superintendent), with 63% of equity directors either reporting directly to the superintendent or positioned one level from the superintendent. Despite such rank, equity directors often reported inadequate staff and financial support, with 60% of equity directors reporting only one or no additional staff to support purportedly districtwide equity work.

Findings in this chapter underscore the importance of resourcing roles in ways that support equity director impact and attend to how organizational dynamics constrain such impact. Supporting equity directors as leaders and individuals requires designing and evolving roles in ways that clarify the intended outcomes and central responsibilities of roles, align role configurations with intended outcomes (Irby et al., 2022), and provide the staff and financial resources necessary to carry out system-wide equity work. Without such alignment and resources, unsupportive organizational contexts, unclear and misaligned role configurations, and experiences of racial-gender oppression (Ishimaru et al., 2023) will continue to undermine the transformative potential of equity director roles and lead to burnout and turnover among the leaders of color that most often hold these roles. In a moment when equity work is under attack nationally and misrepresented for political gain, district support and resources for equity director roles are urgently needed.

REFERENCES

Alston, J. A. (2005). Tempered radicals and servant leaders: Black females persevering in the superintendency. *Educational Administration Quarterly*, *41*(4), 675–688. https://doi.org/10.1177/0013161X04274275

Davis, B. W., Gooden, M. A., & Micheaux, D. J. (2015). Color-blind leadership: A critical race theory analysis of the ISLLC and ELCC standards. *Educational Administration Quarterly, 51*(3), 335–371.

Dixon, D., Griffin, A., & Teoh, M. (2019). *If you listen, we will stay: Why teachers of color leave and how to disrupt teacher turnover*. Education Trust. https://edtrust.org/rti/if-you-listen-we-will-stay/

Ishimaru, A. M. (2019a). From family engagement to equitable collaboration. *Educational Policy*, *33*(2), 350–385.

Ishimaru, A. M. (2019b). *Just schools: Building equitable collaborations with families and communities*. Teachers College Press.

Ishimaru, A. M., Barajas-López, F., Sun, M., Scarlett, K., & Anderson, E. (2022). Transforming the role of RPPs in remaking educational systems. *Educational Researcher*, *51*(7), 465–473.

Ishimaru, A. M., Irby, D. J., & Green, T. (2023). The paradox of organizational double jeopardy: PK-12 equity directors in racialized and gendered educational systems. *The Urban Review, 55*(3), 364–392.

Irby, D., Green, T., Ishimaru, A. M., Clark, S. P., & Han, A. (2021). *K-12 equity directors: Configuring the role for impact.* Center for Urban Education Leadership. https://files.eric.ed.gov/fulltext/ED624002.pdf

Joseph, S. (2023). A call for Black superintendents to document their experiences through autoethnography. *Urban Education*, *58*(6), 1415–1434.

Khalifa, M., Dunbar, C., & Douglas, T. R. (2013). Derrick Bell, CRT, and educational leadership 1995–present. *Race Ethnicity and Education*, *16*(4), 489–513.

Lewis, M. M., Modeste, M. E., & Johnson, R. M. (2023). The rise of the school district chief equity officer: Moving beyond mimetic isomorphism and promoting anti-racist systemic change. *Educational Administration Quarterly*, *59*(1), 143–178.

López, G. R. (2003). The (racially neutral) politics of education: A critical race theory perspective. *Educational Administration Quarterly*, *39*(1), 68–94.

Matschiner, A. (2024). *A national portrait of P–12 equity director roles and role design*. [Manuscript submitted for publication].

Miller, I. A. (2024). Historicizing the equity director position: Black community advocacy at the start of school integration. [Manuscript submitted for publication]. Submitted to *Journal of School Leadership*.

Mitchell, C., Armstrong, D., & Hands, C. (2017). "Oh, is that my job?": Role vulnerability in the vice-principalship. *International Studies in Educational Administration*, *45*(1), 3–18.

Oakes, J. (1992). Can tracking research inform practice? Technical, normative, and political considerations. *Educational Researcher*, *21*(4), 12–21.

Peters, A. L., & Miles Nash, A. (2021). I'm every woman: Advancing the intersectional leadership of Black women school leaders as anti-racist praxis. *Journal of School Leadership*, *31*(1–2), 7–28.

Rodela, K. C., & Bertrand, M. (2018). Rethinking educational leadership in the margins: Youth, parent, and community leadership for equity and social justice. *Journal of Research on Leadership Education*, *13*(1), 3–9.

Rogers, C., & Tienken, C. H. (2020). *The American superintendent 2020 decennial study*. AASA: The School Superintendents Association.

Tichavakunda, A. A. (2021). A critical race analysis of university acts of racial "redress": The limited potential of racial symbols. *Educational Policy*, *35*(2), 304–322.

Weiner, J., Garrett-Walker, W., Strickland, T., & Burton, L. (2022). Reifying discrimination on the path to school leadership: Black female principals' experiences of district hiring/promotion practices. In *Frontiers in Education* (vol. 7, p. 925510). Frontiers Media SA.

Welton, A., & Freelon, R. (2018). Community organizing as educational leadership: Lessons from Chicago on the politics of racial justice. *Journal of Research on Leadership Education*, *13*(1), 79–104.

CHAPTER APPENDIX

Appendix 7.A. Equity Leadership Activity Importance Descriptives (n = 34)

How important do you think the following activities are for advancing equity in your district?	Mean	SD
Learning from and working with students	4.73	0.51
Strategic planning, goal setting, budgeting, and progress monitoring	4.68	0.59
Engaging families and community partners	4.59	0.61
Visiting schools	4.59	0.61
Developing and revising district policies	4.47	0.662
Supporting behavioral and climate improvement	4.46	0.67
Developing equity programs and initiatives	4.44	0.66
Leading administrator professional development and learning	4.44	0.82
Supporting instruction and curriculum improvement	4.44	0.75
Coaching district staff and employees	4.38	0.65
Managing up to district leaders and board members	4.32	0.77
Representing and communicating district equity efforts	4.32	0.64
Leading teacher and staff professional development and learning	4.29	0.91
Implementing district policies	4.23	0.85
Interfacing with external power brokers (e.g., elected officials, philanthropists, universities, etc.)	3.85	0.92
Putting out fires (addressing incidents of racism and injustice)	3.79	0.95

Note. n = count, M = mean, SD = standard deviation

Appendix 7.B. Equity Leadership Activity Engagement Descriptives (n = 34)

In the past year, how frequently did you engage in the following activities to advance equity in your district?	Mean	SD
Develop equity programs and initiatives	4.03	1.06
Engage families and community partners	3.97	0.67
Represent and communicate district equity efforts	3.94	1.15
Visit schools	3.79	0.91
Coach district staff and employees	3.71	0.8
Learn from and working with students	3.62	.95
Lead administrator professional development and learning	3.47	1.05
Support behavioral and climate improvement	3.47	1.02

Appendix 7.B. (*continued*)

In the past year, how frequently did you engage in the following activities to advance equity in your district?	Mean	SD
Put out fires (addressing incidents of racism or other injustice)	3.47	1.13
Support instruction and curriculum improvement	3.41	0.99
Strategic planning, goal setting, budgeting, and progress monitoring	3.35	1.18
Implement district policies	3.32	1.27
Lead teacher and staff professional development and learning	3.29	1
Manage up to district leaders and board members	3.2	1.22
Develop and revise district policies	3.09	1.19
Interface with external power brokers (e.g., elected officials, philanthropists, universities, etc.)	3	1.07

Note. n = count, M = mean, SD = standard deviation

Appendix 7.C. Sixteen Equity Leadership Activities in Alphabetical Order for Reference

1. Coach district staff and employees
2. Develop equity programs and initiatives
3. Develop and revise district policies
4. Engage families and community partners
5. Implement district policies
6. Interface with external power brokers (e.g., elected officials, philanthropists, universities, etc.)
7. Lead administrator professional development and learning
8. Lead teacher and staff professional development and learning
9. Learn from and work with students
10. Manage up to district leaders and board members
11. Put out fires (addressing incidents of racism or other injustice)
12. Represent and communicate district equity efforts
13. Strategic planning, goal setting, budgeting, and progress monitoring
14. Support behavioral and climate improvement
15. Support instruction and curriculum improvement
16. Visit schools

ENDNOTE

1. Data collection methods for this chapter did not include interviews. This epigraph comes from a 2022 equity director interview conducted by the authors for a different project.

Part III

EVENING WORK

CHAPTER 8

Sisterhood as Leadership Beyond the Central Office

Constance Daw, Fannie Martinez, and Ann M. Ishimaru

Who knew that pink T-shirts on a Wednesday could cause such a ruckus? In the spring of 2020 as the world plunged into a pandemic, the four Black women principals in Sky Mountain Public Schools (SMPS) (all district, school, and individual names are pseudonyms) started to meet online weekly as a professional learning community. Three years into their collaborative partnership, the group had become a sisterhood: the Black Lady Principals (BLPs). They encouraged each other professionally and personally, expanded their networks of support and influence, and kept each other sane in the work of SMPS school leadership in a time of major upheaval. The decision to find partners in the work of educational leadership for equity was a conscious one, and they were clear it was time to lead by example.

In 2023, the BLPs made their sisterhood visible when they wore their new pink shirts to attend sessions together at the summer leadership institute of SMPS, a mid-size urban district in the West of about 30,000 students, a majority from communities of color taught predominantly by white educators. Some of the other administrators stared. Some smiled. Others cut their eyes. Many approached and said, "Where's my T-shirt?" In a quieter voice, a school director said to them, "I love what you all are doing today. We all need to see you and see what you do."

Although the 2020 global pandemic and ensuing racial reckoning enabled new visibility during a midday of systems equity work, the current offensive against such efforts illuminates the need to consider the long arc of leadership in schools and communities, particularly as the dark of repression falls. Even in the absence of formalized district structures, roles, and resources, though, systemic equity leadership can exist and grow. This chapter moves us beyond the focus on the central office to offer an expansive vision of systems leadership emerging across schools and communities. The BLPs in Sky Mountain suggest that the collective leadership of Black women has never been about waiting for institutions to grant them permission or formal authority to foster educational justice. As we approach a new era of education reform, we argue that understanding and enacting equity leadership requires not only systemic, strategic moves from multiple leaders in a system but also humanizing practices; fugitive spaces (Kelley, 2022); and visions of wholeness to hold, push, and support those doing the work. This chapter offers insights about how a group of Black women leaders worked to sustain each other as they collectively disrupted inequity in their system.

Both historically and into the present, Black women educators are often at the forefront of leading equity in educational spaces (Dillard, 2021; Ishimaru et al., 2023; Murtadha & Watts, 2005; Peters & Miles Nash, 2021). Despite many intersectional marginalizations (Crenshaw, 1991) and differential (negative) assessments of their leadership (see Chapter 4), Black women are often driven to transform their communities on behalf of their children and generations yet to come, recognizing their work as essential to the progress and well-being of future generations. Their ongoing leadership of social justice movements persists across time despite racialized and gendered organizational conditions that systematically minimize their influence and contribute to a sense of racial battle fatigue (Pizarro & Kohli, 2020; Smith et al., 2007).

The story of the BLPs in Sky Mountain demonstrates how Black women leaders organized in both formally recognized and subversive ways to advance equitable learning opportunities for children. While many districts focus on creating formal equity positions, unrecognized forms of leadership can *also* disrupt inequity and creatively advance more just education. However, sustaining the change-making led by Black women requires holistic care and relational accountability (Wilson, 2008) in moving toward equitable educational experiences for students and their community.

In SMPS, a group of Black women leaders found in each other what Indigenous scholars call survivance (Vizenor, 2008). That is, rather than merely surviving the status quo in an oppressive educational system, the BLPs worked to collectively disrupt systemic inequities and realize more just schooling while also tending to their well-being beyond the narrow role of the principalship. Though each had chosen a path toward equity in their individual leadership, they found synergy and support along the way through their sisterhood. By creating a fugitive space and leaning into their spirituality as Black women, they leveraged their collective relationships to receive the encouragement, vision, push, and affirmations necessary to sustain their work. As Dillard (2021) affirms, "When Black women are able and willing to marshal their spirits in pursuit of teaching and learning, everything we touch can be transformed, including our students" (p. 3).

In this chapter, we first contextualize the leadership of these Black women in a district without a formal equity director. Then, we offer vignettes of the BLPs' equity-focused practices to "seed" equity-based change, help the town reckon with a racist past, mobilize the community toward holistic well-being, and partner with families and communities to enact collective systemic equity leadership across a time of enormous challenge.

BEYOND THE CENTRAL OFFICE: EQUITY AS EVERYONE'S WORK, NOBODY'S WORK?

In the decade prior to the pandemic, the superintendent of SMPS wanted to ensure that educators across the system—regardless of their role—would feel a sense of responsibility for the success of all children because "equity is everyone's work . . . people need to own the equity work." The decision *not* to designate an equity director or department was, thus, an intentional move to preclude a common "checkbox" approach in which districts *claim* they are doing equity work but relegate responsibility for it to a designated few. As other research has shown (Trujillo, 2013), this performance of equity—through equity plans and equity roles—can mask the reality of a status quo that remains largely intact (Lewis-Durham, 2020). The small group of Black women district and school leaders in SMPS was also aware of the danger of this approach. That is, without a formal equity role or office, equity work could still be easily dismissed at the building level, especially without accountability measures. In an interview, Jamila James, SMPS's AVID and advanced programs equity director, explained:

> I'm passionate about this work. I love this work. But don't keep saying things like we're doing so well with equity implementation, and we have this districtwide plan and equity is everyone's work and then not have any accountability measures that go along with it.

A number of district and school leaders in SMPS, including the superintendent herself, perceived substantial variability across schools with regard to addressing racial disparities; as the BLPs saw it, many schools continued to maintain the status quo as a result of the lack of accountability.

Any accounting of Black women's leadership in the SMPS must begin with Caroline Smith, the Black woman superintendent who led the district until her retirement in 2021. When Caroline was named superintendent in 2012, the district had an infamous reputation as a "dropout factory," with dropout rates of 55% (Sky Mountain Tribune, 2015; all identifying information in this chapter is masked for confidentiality). At the time, she was one of the only Black women superintendents in the region. However, the city of Sky Mountain itself continues to be racially diverse, and over 60% of SMPS students identify as Black, Indigenous, Asian, Pacific Islander, Latinx, or multiracial. Sky Mountain is a tight-knit community, and many of SMPS's educators grew up in the town—this is especially true for the BLPs. The district size is such that you can "put your arms around" it, as former Superintendent Smith shared; enrolling about 30,000 students means "you can know everybody." Across Smith's superintendency, Black women have increasingly taken formal leadership roles, from district central office roles (including those related to supporting community partnerships and equitable instruction) to a Black woman board chair starting in 2020, as well as principal and assistant principal roles.

Beyond the increase of Black women in leadership roles, the conversation about equity has evolved in the district over time as well. Only a few years after Smith's arrival, the district came to national attention for its "whole child" approach to turning around the dropout crisis. Using data beyond test scores and partnering with community organizations, the superintendent and her assistant superintendent, Dr. Jerry Gutierrez (who became her successor), focused on after-school extracurricular programming, social–emotional learning, early learning, re-engagement programs for those who dropped out, and rigorous coursework expectations.

Meanwhile, Superintendent Smith had been laying the groundwork for change in the broader community. In 2016, after the first election of Trump, Smith presented a policy to assure the public that the students and families of Sky Mountain would be granted "sanctuary" in public schools. Through a feature in the *Sky Mountain News Tribune*, she appealed to the collective responsibilities of community members and leveraged the peer pressure of virtue signaling as "good neighbors." In these efforts, Smith frequently used the local newspaper to direct the public toward equity-focused policies impacting Sky Mountain residents. She hired the former editor of the *Sky Mountain News Tribune* to be the communications director at SMPS, activating his network of newsrooms around the nation, even to the extent that the district and its superintendent were applauded for major gains in graduation rates in a national magazine in 2016.

By 2020, a more explicit focus on "equity" in SMPS could also be seen in professional development opportunities, like Critical Conversations, and book studies, such as Zaretta Hammond's *Culturally Responsive Teaching and the Brain*. Every school had an equity action team, with representatives who met monthly for professional development and support. However, district and school leaders noticed that the group of educators who participated remained limited to those already motivated to do equity work. As Jamila, the district leader for equity in advanced programs, explained, "equity" came to mean "a lens that you could put on if you wanted." Pushback came from within school buildings as well as from some families such that when equity champions returned to their buildings, they were stymied in their efforts to lead change. Near the end of her tenure, Superintendent Smith signaled a change in her thinking about the need for an equity director, expressing concern about what would happen after her departure. By the time Smith retired in 2022, the graduation rate had risen to 90.2%, and she decided to stay on an additional year on special assignment to see through the equity initiatives developed by the equity design team (described later), particularly around training district employees in cultural awareness and bias.

As the few Black women school leaders in SMPS compared notes about the lack of central accountability and sustainability around these efforts, they began to make moves that exercised their individual leadership for advancing equity at the ground level. And through their network, they began to enact collective leadership across the system at multiple levels. The following four vignettes illuminate different aspects of equity leadership within an emergent systemic network—*a sisterhood*—for advancing equity and fostering care to sustain each other in risky change work. We turn next to understanding how the sisterhood seeded equity, helped the city to reckon with a racist past, mobilized the community in the face of adversity, and partnered with families and communities to dream an "otherwise" system in SMPS. The focus and strides of their collective work made good on the notion that *equity work is everyone's work.*

"SEEDING" EQUITY IN SKY MOUNTAIN PUBLIC SCHOOLS: JAMILA JAMES

A self-described "Sky Mountain Girl," Jamila recalls being bussed from the Eastside of Sky Mountain to one of the first magnet schools in the United States on the other side of town. She talks of her determination to be a teacher and her energy to transform the academic opportunities afforded to low-income children and children of color. That calling pushed her into leadership. Kids across the Eastside knew that "Ms. James don't play." Her no-nonsense approach with students extended to her work with teachers. As a teacher supervisor, she demanded high-leverage instructional strategies consistently implemented as a lever for meaningful and rigorous learning for every Sky Mountain student. As an administrator, she talked about students going to college, achieving excellence, being bright lights for their families and communities, and educators' responsibilities to provide a way. Always specific and precise in her tools, Ms. James championed AVID at the schools she led. She encouraged colleagues to adopt the strategy through her secondary professional learning communities (PLCs). She mentored students, teachers, mothers, and other community members even as she led her school with determination and pride. This walk/talk for Sky Mountain has made her a true matriarch in the city. A few Sky Mountaineers are also honored to call her "Auntie Jamila."

SMPS doesn't have an equity office or a formal equity director role, but SMPS has Jamila James. Jamila James initially refused to become the equity director for SMPS. After decades of equity-focused school leadership as a humanities teacher, assistant principal, and principal, Jamila resisted the calls from Superintendent Caroline Smith to succeed the prior equity director in 2016. She refused to leave her school, fearing disconnection from the work of justice-centered instructional leadership, from students, and from her call to ensure generational well-being. She felt that the role of equity director might be vulnerable to budget cuts in the event that an incoming superintendent was politically disconnected from equity work. Instead, Jamila became the director of AVID and academic advancement and was determined to press on the "what" of district functioning with the "why" that guided her for 20 years—*justice for every child, justice for the little Black girl in Sky Mountain that she once was and will forever be.*

However, SMPS and the community have an unspoken understanding that Jamila James is the unofficial equity director. Neither Caroline nor Jamila wanted equity to be seen as another add-on, but rather as something integrated and embedded into each day and throughout buildings. It became clear, though, that educators and building administrators who were part of the equity action teams were "already about the work"—and those who were not committed were creating barriers for educators who sought to facilitate conversations about equity in their buildings. For instance, a number of principals refused to give their equity action team representatives time with school staff so they could share resources and learning. To address this, Jamila (with support from Caroline) created the equity design team (EDT), comprising mostly building and district leaders, to increase accountability for the work at the ground level. Jamila explained:

> For this to work, we have to have some really clear guidelines around equity leadership in this district, it has to be equity leadership, it can't just be somebody who's really passionate about the topic, trying to move a whole building. Not gonna work, right? So the Equity Design Team was created to include principals on it, to give voice to the process, so that we could create something that might be able to help building administrators and level directors to effectively implement district equity leadership consistently, that then we could say—yes, we truly have a district-wide equity implementation plan that includes every school.

The purpose of the EDT was to enable the proliferation of equitable practices from the district to the buildings. To make that happen, Jamila worked to provide stipends, extend resources districtwide, and partner with a local university on various equity-focused training initiatives. Some of those initiatives included creating state department–required diversity and equity trainings that teachers would need so they could maintain their certifications. The EDT created modules and tools, such as an extensive resource bank including a video library of "best practices" in culturally responsive teaching, efforts intended to make these resources and information accessible to all educators in the district. Their work continued even during the COVID-19 pandemic shutdown; Caroline Smith continued to lead the charge through the end of her final year with the district, though the EDT did not continue under the new superintendent.

At its core, the EDT was about increasing the accountability of principals' implementation of equity practices. This was one of the many ways that Jamila used her organizational influence to make equity work proliferate into buildings to foster change on the ground level. Jamila leveraged her position at the district level to build the capacity and networks of educators and principals so that they could collectively lead the equity work. This "seeding" of equity work in the district—like that of some equity directors (see Chapter 3)—set the stage for the BLPs.

HOPE AND HEALING FOR FUTURE GENERATIONS: FORMATION OF THE BLPS

With COVID-19 restrictions limiting their access to colleagues, students, friends, and family, Black women leaders first sought community through an affinity support group. The principalship is an isolated position, and even more so when in lockdown while the nation grappled with racial inequality, police brutality, and health disparities. They were four lifelong Sky Mountaineers, each identified as Black women, who were dedicated to the well-being of the city. But the BLPs became more than an affinity group for socializing and venting frustrations.

Across time, the BLPs evolved into a PLC that provided resources and information about district functions. They coplanned professional developments and revised each other's leadership plans. They reviewed problems of practice and advised each other through administrative decisions. Each leader was consciously pursuing racial equity goals for their schools and community. The BLPs pushed each other to be more ambitious and more intentional. They showed each other ways they might not have discovered on their own. Incorporating antiracist curriculum and equitable practices within schooling systems is challenging for any leader. However, when the leaders who are attempting to move toward equitable practices also hold intersectional marginalized identities, they face additional layers of tension and pushback. The BLP space was born from an understanding that to keep "the work" moving forward, Black women leaders needed to be sustained in ways that went beyond the typical professional supports tailored for white male colleagues in the principalship.

Sustaining equity leadership for the BLPs also meant attending to the crucial role of community, healing, and holistic well-being. While formal policies help with making equity moves visible, informal practices make the work sustainable so the passion that ignites the flame for the work doesn't burn out. Instead, the bonds and support system can help fan the flames to keep the light and warmth alive. The BLPs affirmed and supported each other through family challenges and health scares. They made each other laugh and cry and dream and demand. Once distancing regulations were lifted, they visited each other at their schools and in their homes, always affirming, always imploring each other, in love, to be well so they can help others pursue well-being. The BLPs encouraged each other to live wholly.

This work came to life for them because, as Black women from Sky Mountain, they understood the stakes. Equity work for them was always about more than data and outcomes, more than checkboxes and standards. Equity for the BLPs meant Black liberation and Indigenous sovereignty; equity meant indisputable excellence for all students and world-class public schools in low-income neighborhoods; equity meant deeply supported staff and administrators of color in culturally sustaining spaces; equity meant love exemplified through the education system. The BLPs felt a shared responsibility to ensure "the work" of equity changed their practices and the experience of schooling for the students, families, and communities of Sky Mountain. The BLPs understood their schools, neighborhoods, and people as home and as family. They pursued the hope, healing, and well-being of that family for the present *and* for generations to come.

RECKONING WITH A RACIST PAST: BERNICE REDMOND

Bernice Redmond is one of those people who has never met a stranger. She has rich auntie vibes while exuding a perennial down-to-earthiness that embodies the warm demand of urbane high expectations rooted in the community's best interest. Bernice was a kindergartener in the Eastside neighborhood, played water polo for her high school, taught English in a neighboring high school, and became the proud principal of her alma mater, Wilson High School, in 2018. But there was a hitch. By then, Superintendent Caroline Smith had already been working with a local racial equity consulting group to determine ways to advance equity in the district. The team determined that renaming schools in alignment with the antiracist movement nationally would be an opportunity for impact and lasting change. Woodrow Wilson High School was the first school selected for change.

When the superintendent told her about the name change, Bernice was terrified. She knew that being a biracial Black woman leading change was an exceptionally difficult undertaking. The Wilson community was passionately tradition-oriented with active booster clubs that kept the Sky Mountain community connected to the school's programs. Principal Redmond anticipated resistance to the school's name change and resistance to her as a woman of color leading the school name change. She feared threats to her person, long nights of board meetings, and the unknown. But Bernice also understood that she was in a place to transition this school onto a path of equity for all—and most importantly, because of the BLPs, she would not have to do it alone.

When Bernice took the helm at Wilson High School, institutions and monuments named to honor the country's racist and colonizing past were under attack everywhere. During the eulogy for the congregants murdered at Bethel AME in Columbia, South Carolina, during the summer of 2015, President Obama called for the removal of the Confederate flag from every statehouse. Bree Newsome climbed a flagpole and brought down the Confederate flag at the South Carolina State House later that week. Monuments to Confederate generals were pulled down by protestors in New Orleans, Memphis, and across the United States. Activists were calling for the dissolution of police departments in the wake of public outcry against the extrajudicial police killings of Tamir Rice, Freddy Gray, Michael Brown, Philando Castile, Sandra Bland, and other Black Americans. Public spaces were being renamed as communities realized that many essential elements of American life have depended on the maintenance of racist structures and white supremacy. Past presidents also came under scrutiny, including the 28th president of the United States, Woodrow Wilson, who was an open advocate of the anti-Black racist terrorist organization, the Ku Klux Klan.

Bernice knew she had to move strategically. She partnered with the superintendent's cabinet to engage community listening groups. They surveyed stakeholders to determine the will to change and brought together focus groups to investigate alternative names for Wilson High School. It became clear that youth were more likely to support and—in many cases *require*—a school name change. Bernice used the district's communications channels to talk about the past president's racist connections and to communicate about the need for change. "When we know better, we do better," she told the community.

Bernice fielded hate mail, crude emails, livestream spamming, and rude interactions, as she had feared. The school got called out for its so-called "woke agenda." Bernice leaned on her personal network—her parents, friends, colleagues, and especially the BLPs for support.

On July 1, 2021, Woodrow Wilson High School was renamed after the first Black woman administrator in SMPS, the first Black woman to serve on the Sky Mountain City Council, and a former president of the Sky Mountain Chapter of the National Association for the Advancement of Colored People (NAACP). In the Black church community, it is often said, "Give me my flowers while I yet live." Dr. Height was still living when she received the flowers of community recognition, celebration, and appreciation for a life of service in Sky Mountain. There is a beautiful photograph of her standing in front of the newly renamed high school with Principal Bernice Redmond, Superintendent Caroline Smith, the school board president and the Sky Mountain mayor—all Black women at the time. Dr. Height passed away later that same month in 2021 at the age of 95.

After the Height High School renaming, two more Sky Mountain schools undertook similar renaming processes to address community dissatisfaction with associated histories. A middle school—originally named after a white missionary who participated in the genocidal Indian reeducation movement—was renamed for the Eastside neighborhood around it. An elementary school had been named for a settler and city founder who helped establish the racist apartheid that continues to disadvantage people of color in Sky Mountain. The school was renamed for a local female pastor and activist whose leadership has combated the systemic inequalities experienced by the neighborhood most impacted by poverty and racism. While these efforts were not easy, the leaders and district were able to follow the path forged by Principal Redmond to help the community reckon with its racist and colonizing past, honor those who fought for justice, and chart visions for more equitable educational spaces and futures for all the children of Sky Mountain.

CULTIVATING LEADERSHIP IN OTHERS: DR. NATALIE WATSON

"I'm a Black woman. I'm a principal. And I'm a lot," says Dr. Natalie Watson by way of introduction, with a laugh. A statuesque Black woman, a basketball mom, and a cancer survivor, Dr. Watson is the principal at Fawn Elementary, and she is one of the most popular women in Sky Mountain. She builds deep bonds of love and support with almost everyone she meets and keeps a close eye on each of those relationships. She tells everyone, "Call me Watson" because while she is the homie, she's also in charge. She has a clear vision of what is right, bringing integrity to schools as a PE teacher, a counselor, and a middle school assistant principal prior to becoming an elementary principal. Watson's dedication to equity work stems from witnessing her mother engage in equity work throughout her childhood in Sky Mountain. Rooted in a commitment to educational equity, Watson turns to the strengths within her community as a resource to move through times of adversity and struggle.

Watson is no stranger to adversity. Like other Black women educators across time (Dillard, 2021), her commitments to showing up with and for her school and community persisted through profound personal health challenges, a global pandemic, and a largely unresourced systemic call to foster culturally responsive teaching and learning in her school and across the district. Watson claims no heroics in her role as leader; rather, she leans on family, spiritual strengths, the BLPs, her school, and the broader Sky Mountain community. She pulls them all together toward a vision of holistic well-being.

From the beginning of the equity action teams at the district, Watson leveraged district book studies and learning sessions to educate and lead other educators in fostering more culturally relevant schools. Yet she also recognized that periodic district-led sessions alone would not lead to the profound changes necessary in the system. Drawing from her own doctoral studies, she stepped forward to lead a few districtwide trainings on race, equity, and culturally relevant teaching. In 2020, Watson created and has continued to facilitate an African American educator affinity group on a volunteer basis. When staff transitions arose, she brought more racially diverse staff to her building to better reflect her students. And she has been intentional and effective in bringing her school community into conversation with each other.

As an integral part of her equity efforts at Fawn Elementary, Watson launched community circles in the mornings for teachers, parents, and students to come together and hold discussions. Watson saw these as crucial moments for engaging the school community and embedding restorative practices into the school's daily routines. For instance, one question in a community circle was, "How can you lift each other up?" Watson also created a group called Leaders of Change, where students met to voice their needs. The question at their last meeting was, "What are you needing?" When students voiced complaints about the bathrooms, Watson accompanied them to the restrooms and encouraged them to take leadership for making change. While traditional school structures and power dynamics often reinforce an organizational hierarchy with educator voice at the center and student voice at the margins (Rodela & Bertrand, 2018), Watson worked to change that incrementally through the Leaders of Change student group. She encouraged teachers to be inclusive of student voices through prompts like, "Have you asked students?" Restorative practices and community circles became embedded in the culture of the school, and Watson envisioned students developing guiding questions for the circles.

Watson's focus on well-being and giving back to her community came into even sharper focus as she navigated a breast cancer diagnosis in December 2021. Through her diagnosis and treatment, Watson found ways to narrate and share her journey. She launched an inaugural breast cancer awareness walk to bring together families and community members with a common goal to help others. The walk is now an annual event. Like the rest of the BLPs, Watson perceived a need for the system to enact evaluative authority for equity practices across the district. At the same time, she recognized the power of building level action and brought her spirituality and focus on holistic well-being to her equity leadership across the system.

PARTNERING TO DREAM AN OTHERWISE SYSTEM: DR. CAROL MOORE

Carol is a young warrior for joy and justice, a Black woman whose smile lights up her eyes and whose warm firmness with her students calls to mind generations of Black educators and mothers. Originally a school orchestra teacher, she came to leadership early in her career as an educator. Carol claimed for herself a vision of leadership as a grassroots organizer: inspirational, aspirational, leading from beside and toward a vision of justice.

In a time of immense upheaval, Carol became principal of her first school and grew her equity-focused systemic leadership with an eye toward multigenerational dreams for children and community. The school had no assistant principal, no family liaison, no social worker, and was a Title I school with a 78% free and reduced lunch student population, with low performance and high-growth goals as its academic data norm. Carol promptly wrote a leadership framework rooted in the hopes and "otherwise" futures collectively held for the children and community she and her staff would serve. When she presented it to district supervisors, she was met with eye rolls and questions about the prudence of "hope" and "belief." From that response, she understood that she would need to be devoted to the "why" of the work and would need to build coalitions with the stakeholders for whom the "why" was most important: parents. Carol's efforts to creatively disrupt the status quo—with the BLPs at her back—illuminate partnering as a strategy for dreaming futures of thriving in everyday systems.

From the outset, Carol saw families as key to imagining and realizing a more liberatory educational experience for the young people in her community. She started by shifting the typical open house classroom presentations to a whole-school community circle that would foster relationships between parents and teachers and enable them to share their hopes and aspirations for children. Carol partnered with a community leader to craft a listening session in which staff members would sit down with parents to record their thoughts on questions like, "What is a 'more-perfect' school?" and "What are your hopes for the children in this community?" When she presented the format to the Site-Centered Decision Making committee, made exclusively of staff members at the time, Carol got her first indicators of how challenging such a seemingly simple shift would be.

After sharing the questions in a staff meeting followed by an email emphasizing the opportunity for community building, staff said they did not know what to do. She said, "Just sit with families, ask the questions, take notes." Staff bemoaned the lost opportunity to set their own expectations for their classrooms. The night of the event, staff clumped beside the food tables and had to be prompted to go sit with families in groups of six to ten. Staff members were stressed, but parent feedback was joyous, grateful, excited, hopeful. Without prompting, the parents stacked the chairs and reset the cafeteria—a feat that had not been witnessed by the school staff prior. In the postevent feedback session, staff shared everything from resentment over the lost opportunity to establish their own leadership in their classrooms to the importance of connecting personally with families of students and even some excitement about families requesting field trips, homework, and high-quality teaching and learning. Nonetheless, the resistance was clear.

When COVID-19 hit and schooling went remote, Carol witnessed the exhausted struggles of her staff teaching online (a third of whom retired at the end of 2020) and conducted virtual meeting after meeting with no idea how to lead remote instruction. Yet pandemic-era leadership also meant no behavior intervention, no state improvement reporting, and no state testing. The holds of the time afforded Carol and other leaders the rare space to think, dream, ideate, and connect. She had time to build a professional learning community alongside the other Black women leading schools in her district. The BLPs provided professional support systems and a network that Carol did not have access to prior to the pandemic. She began to perceive her leadership as part of a broader set of partnerships and work to change the district.

Along with most of the other BLPs and a number of other principals, Carol joined the district EDT to realize the equity work Superintendent Smith was emphasizing as she transitioned out of the district. The EDT built on the post-2020 momentum to design and teach online modules to develop principals' racial literacy, develop tools to guide teachers in developing their culturally responsive instruction, and position equity work at the school level as an opportunity to lead the broader system.

When Carol re-engaged with staff and families at her school, she leaned on the BLPs and her network to creatively strategize about resources and situate partnerships in the broader community. Amidst dwindling resources and staffing at the school, Carol initiated critical partnerships with families, teachers, and students to reimagine schooling as a vehicle toward "otherwise futures" of generational well-being through pro-Black, pro-Indigenous, healing-centered learning and community. While building staff awareness of their own biases and self-regulation through cultural conflicts, Carol leveraged Title I school improvement funds to provide professional learning with literacy and racial equity specialists, launched a pedagogical leadership team with teachers and families called the Racial Justice League, and organized staff learning cycles of Universal Design for Learning. Partnering with a community organization, they together codesigned a schoolwide literacy program that enabled each student to contribute to a classroom-based film concerning Black liberation, food justice, Indigenous sovereignty, and water protection, culminating in a film festival for the community. By the end of the second year, students had made considerable academic progress and were removed from "at-risk" designations with the state school improvement office, downgraded from level four to level one consideration with the state. The school made remarkable progress toward the goals of high achievement without race-based performance discrepancy.

As Carol moved on to lead a new school, she reflected on the relational conditions that made such tremendous growth possible; the people and partnerships with that community taught her "that love is a verb, a noun, an adjective, and an adverb." She also realized that it was time to make the collective equity leadership of the BLP sisterhood visible to the system.

CONCLUSION: VISIBILIZING BLP LEADERSHIP

Carol's text was to the point: "Send me your T-shirt sizes—I'm gonna do something!" Three years into their collaborative partnership, Carol was considering the power of the visibility of leadership moves. The group had become a sisterhood. It was time to lead by example. The BLPs wore matching shirts to the August 2023 SMPS Admin Institute. The shirts said "PRINCIPAL" boldly across the chest, with the preferred name of the principal in script beneath: Dr. Moore, Ms. Redmond, Mrs. Tyler, Dr. Watson.

The public declaration of the BLPs' collective leadership prompted discomfort, surprise, and curiosity from administrators at all levels of the system. No longer hidden, the BLPs' equity leadership in SMPS emerged as a center for "the work" outside the district central office, despite the lack of systemic accountability each had observed and felt lacking. The BLPs are quick to say that they and the district do not have it all figured out. District and school data continue to reveal inequities for Black and Brown youth in academic and school experiences, particularly at the intersections of gender and special education status. The work of principals continues to be bounded by the limits of time and resources, and often the requirements lead to unattainable goal setting. The BLPs frequently discuss the struggle of attempting balance in their lives and the perception of impossibility in their work. In holding the responsibility of equity work, leaders who make visible equity moves face outsized criticism for disturbing the status quo and judgment of their methods. Being visible is risky. Nevertheless, these leaders continue to show up for the children of Sky Mountain, their communities, each other, and themselves—and to realize change in their system.

The BLPs did not wait to be invited or bestowed with formal equity titles or resources. At a time of unprecedented challenge, they instead took up the responsibility to do what they could collectively to move the system toward equity for their community by holding each other accountable and sustaining each other in the work. As we finalized this chapter, Carol texted a photo with the note: "Look who's grown?? 9 in the Sisterhood!" A large group of Black women smile proudly, all wearing Black t-shirts with the word "Sisterhood" emblazoned in gold script across the front: *"There is strength in Sisterhood. Encourage. Support. Uplift One Another."*

REFERENCES

Crenshaw, K. (1991). Mapping the margins: Intersectionality, identity politics, and violence against women of color. *Stanford Law Review*, *43*(6), 1241–1299. https://doi.org/10.2307/1229039

Dillard, C. B. (2021). *The spirit of our work: Black women teachers (re)member*. Beacon Press.

Ishimaru, A. M., Irby, D. J., & Green, T. (2023). The paradox of organizational double jeopardy: PK-12 equity directors in racialized and gendered educational systems. *The Urban Review*, *55*(3), 364–392. https://doi.org/10.1007/s11256-022-00653-2

Kelley, R. D. (2022). *Freedom dreams: The Black radical imagination*. Beacon Press.

Lewis-Durham, T. (2020). "All lives matter": How districts co-opt equity language and maintain the status quo. *Education Policy Analysis Archives*, *28*(141), 1–25.

Murtadha, K., & Watts, D. M. (2005). Linking the struggle for education and social justice: Historical perspectives of African American leadership in schools. *Educational Administration Quarterly*, *41*(4), 591–608. https://doi.org/10.1177/0013161X04274271

Peters, A. L., & Miles Nash, A. (2021). I'm every woman: Advancing the intersectional leadership of Black women school leaders as anti-racist praxis. *Journal of School Leadership*, *31*(1–2), 7–28. https://doi.org/10.1177/1052684621992759

Pizarro, M., & Kohli, R. (2020). "I stopped sleeping": Teachers of color and the impact of racial battle fatigue. *Urban Education*, *55*(7), 967–991. https://doi.org/10.1177/0042085918805788

Rodela, K. C., & Bertrand, M. (2018). Rethinking educational leadership in the margins: Youth, parent, and community leadership for equity and social justice. *Journal of Research on Leadership Education*, *13*(1), 3–9. https://doi.org/10.1177/1942775117751306

Smith, W. A., Allen, W. R., & Danley, L. L. (2007). "Assume the position . . . you fit the description": Psychosocial experiences and racial battle fatigue among African American male college students. *American Behavioral Scientist*, *51*(4), 551–578. https://doi.org/10.1177/0002764207307742

Trujillo, T. M. (2013). The politics of district instructional policy formation: Compromising equity and rigor. *Educational Policy*, *27*(3), 531–559. https://doi.org/10.1177/0895904812454000

Vizenor, G. (Ed.). (2008). *Survivance: Narratives of native presence*. University of Nebraska Press.

Wilson, S. (2008). *Research is ceremony: Indigenous research methods*. Fernwood Publishing.

CHAPTER 9

Breathe and Rest

Designing Networks of Critical Care for Equity Leaders

Dayna Muñiz

> When we talk about that which will sustain and nurture our spiritual growth as a people, we must once again talk about the importance of community. For one of the most vital ways we sustain ourselves is by building communities of resistance, places where we know we are not alone.
>
> —bell hooks (*Yearning: Race, Gender, and Cultural Politics*, 1999 p. 213)

It was a late afternoon, and like many in the late fall of 2020, I was in my makeshift home office, finishing up with the umpteenth virtual call of the day, when my phone rang. It was a dear colleague of mine, sharing that, like her, there were educators in nearby districts who had been leading equity efforts in their districts without a formal equity title who were now being named as equity directors. She wanted to request that our organization, the Education Partnership, provide support to the group, and I was happy to say yes.

After discussing with the organization's director, Dr. Frank Samuel, we decided that convening the group to determine their needs was a necessary first step. Our first meeting was held virtually in late November and included a handful of equity directors. Most were newly appointed, with only one or two having been in the role for a year or more. After brief introductions, we asked people to describe their roles and to share what supports they thought they might need going forward. The conversation was lively and open; folks shared their experiences originating the role, pressures they were facing given the demands for change after the murder of George Floyd, uncertainties of COVID schooling, and pushback some were beginning to see with electoral politics. They discussed the structural supports necessary in order to lead change efforts (e.g., budget support for increased professional development, need assessment studies) and their desire to meet monthly to share resources with one another.

I recall thinking it would be important to provide resources that addressed their concerns directly, so I sent out a bibliography and information about upcoming professional development opportunities with our organization. The meeting helped me realize that although many of these educators had been leading equity efforts for a long time, their new roles provided a different platform with attendant benefits and risks. Given the nascent nature and broad mandates of the equity director positions, I reflected on how to provide the most effective support. As follow-up to the meeting, I had received multiple messages expressing a sense of gratitude for the connection with colleagues who were facing similar challenges *and* had similar commitments to equity. This insight has guided my efforts since.

In this chapter, I argue that peer networks provide essential support to equity leaders. The development and depth of our group illustrate how being in community can benefit equity directors (educators pursuing educational equity), while simultaneously supporting their well-being and sustaining and affirming their humanity. Using the concepts of healing-centered care (Wilson & Richardson, 2020) and germinal networks (Baker-Doyle & Mawhinney, 2024), I elaborate on the benefits of networks for equity directors. Throughout the chapter, I draw from my own experience convening a network of equity directors and from *testimonios* (Delgado Bernal et al., 2012; Reyes, Curry Rodriguez, 2012) of equity directors (all organization and individual names used in this chapter are pseudonyms) collected during my dissertation research (Muñiz, 2024) to weave a "reflexive narrative of liberation" that seeks to "bring light to a wrong, a point of view, or an urgent call for action" (Reyes & Curry Rodríguez, 2012, p. 525).

My goal in this chapter is to bring light to the experiences of equity directors, experiences that are still not widely understood in roles that are ever evolving. I highlight qualitative data that demonstrates the importance of networks to the sustainability of equity leadership. Having demonstrated the importance of networks in equity leadership roles, I call for direct support from philanthropic organizations, school districts, higher education institutions, and governmental agencies to create, maintain, and grow equity director networks.

MEETING A NEED: BUILDING INTENTIONAL, GERMINAL NETWORKS FOR EQUITY LEADERS

As research indicates, the role of equity director can be isolating, due—at least in part—to the racialized and gendered dynamics that often come from being the "first and only" district leader tasked with driving a district's equity efforts (Ishimaru et al., 2022; Martinez-Maldonado, 2023; Matschiner, in press; Muñiz, 2024). Keaton (2023) finds that Black women working as athletic diversity and inclusion officers (ADIOs) in Division 1 programs frequently find themselves putting their feelings in "the back seat" and embodying the strong Black woman stereotype to navigate their racialized and gendered workplaces. Across studies, scholars argue that DEI leaders carry a heavy load *and* use their identities to resist and persist as equity leaders. Studies also find that intraorganizational and interorganizational networks can help educators navigate these dynamics and provide spaces for cultivating respite, growth, and collective power (Baker-Doyle & Mawhinney, 2024; Bristol & Shirrell, 2019; Keenan, 2020; Muñiz, 2024; Pour-Khorshid, 2018).

In their analysis of teachers engaged in teacher activism networks, Baker-Doyle and Mawhinney (2024) use a critical social network perspective to understand how formal and informal relationships, and structures within networks, help to shape social power. Their study finds that network participants in affinity-based subgroups foster what they call germinal networks. Germinal networks are typically grounded in affinity (both racial and ideological) and supply participants with affirmation, personal renewal, professional development, and resilience. Baker-Doyle and Mawhinney identify three features of germinal networks that can help us better understand what it takes to build these networks intentionally. These three features are network activities that humanize participants and their work, pursuing expertise and valuing lived experiences, and germinal influence through collaboration.

In the following section, I share the emergence of the Education Partnership's network to set the stage for the reader. I then share how the three features highlighted in Baker-Doyle and Mawhinney's work are reflected in the evolution of the Education Partnership's network and how these features have enabled the group to continue growing and to now serve over 50 educators across six states.

COMING TOGETHER

After our first meeting, I sent out a Doodle poll and organized a monthly Zoom meeting for the group. Meetings were held during the school day, and participants were welcome to attend as schedules allowed. Equity directors were encouraged to invite other colleagues. I also announced the group to our superintendent listserv and encouraged them to share the names of newly hired directors. These recruitment strategies helped the group grow to over 15 members by the end of the 2020–2021 school year.

The first few meetings we held were informal forums focused around an organizing question. For example, one of our earliest meetings in 2021 asked attendees to share professional development efforts in their district and how they were structured. There was also a focus on community building.

During these early months, I listened closely to the challenges shared and the resources requested. Some themes that emerged centered on community engagement, curriculum and equity assessments, and board relations. Starting in the spring of 2021, and with those themes in hand, Dr. Samuel and I called upon our personal and professional network to recruit speakers for our meetings. I also searched academic databases to identify and contact researchers that could share relevant expertise with the group. As a result of these efforts, presenters have ranged from a school district solicitor sharing strategies for policy development to former equity directors sharing experiences in the role, as well as academics sharing research on school leadership, ethnic studies, curriculum development, policy, and a host of other areas. Most people we reached out to have eagerly supported the group and generously donated their time.

Starting with the 2021–2022 school year, we developed a cadence for our meetings, with presenters taking 30–40 minutes of time to share some of their expertise and then engaging in a question-and-answer period with attendees. The informal environment has encouraged folks to attend as they are able to, and attendance has ranged from 8 to 30 attendees for any given session. I continue to stay in close contact with most group members and solicit the group's input on programming at least twice a year. As the group has continued to grow, equity directors have highlighted the value of engaging in a professional learning community, one that is both responsive to their needs and based on a feeling of safety. The work of supporting the group has been a privilege. In the section that follows, I discuss how the development of the group has mirrored the three germinal network features highlighted by Baker-Doyle and Mawhinney.

HUMANIZING WORK

Germinal networks take a "whole person" approach to creating spaces of community. They are not just places to learn, they are places to *be*. Baker-Doyle and Mawhinney describe this aspect of this work as "reflective and humanizing" (p. 127). Equity directors who participated in my research echoed Baker-Doyle and Mawhinney's findings and highlighted the support garnered when participating in networks that served equity directors specifically. Elyse, a veteran equity director in the Mid-Atlantic, described being part of an equity director network thusly:

> We support each other . . . we are sensitive to each other's needs . . . [because] *you get tired of explaining what a DEI director does, because no one knows what we do* [emphasis added] . . . being around people who know . . . that's the healing part . . . [it allows us to] go on and continue to fight the fight.

For Elyse, a significant respite comes with being with people who "get it," and she finds restoration and rejuvenation from the equity director network with which she engages. Nicole, another equity leader in the Mid-Atlantic, frames the group she engages with as a "rescue" and elaborates:

> Those networks become like home for equity officers. Like rescue, a rest, and you don't have to explain it, because everybody has experienced it, and we get it. And we get each other, and we see the strength in each other. . . . We are able to help each other keep going on. And that's what people need in these roles. Because yes, you're navigating it as your profession, but you're also navigating it as a person, you're navigating it as your family and you're navigating the loyalty to your culture. And when all of those roads meet, you're going to need support to come and go forward.

As noted by Nicole and Elyse, networks can play a pivotal role in the experiences of equity directors. The ability to connect, to vent, to be in community can be thought of as a restorative strategy that can heal and sustain. Wilson and Richardson see this kind of "caring for the caregivers as a political, communal, and fugitive act of resistance" (Wilson & Richardson, 2020, p. 80).

In the Education Partnership's network, humanizing work has manifested itself in a variety of ways. For example, from our first meetings in early 2021, equity directors requested that we consider meeting in-person for a social event, but it took some time to make that a reality given COVID-era restrictions. Finally, after a year of virtual meetings, we hosted our first get-together in December 2021, and in a somewhat risky move, we decided to host our holiday gathering outdoors to comply with university guidelines. I anxiously monitored the weather and was relieved and delighted to see the forecast in the mid-70s for the week of our gathering. We met at our university office, and the excitement was palpable as we walked to a nearby restaurant. People were chatting with natural camaraderie, and we were all thrilled to get seated by the patio's firepits. The meal was lively with lots of laughter and easy conversation. At my table, we celebrated the news of an attendee who had recently led her district's efforts to adopt a new policy to support marginalized students. Old colleagues and friends warmly welcomed newcomers, and a photograph from the gathering depicts a smiling group of equity directors basking in sunshine together. While this moment may seem insignificant, many in our network have expressed that the lunch served as a buoy when facing resistance in their districts and communities.

In addition to prioritizing opportunities for socialization, I have learned that networks can also recognize and honor the humanity of participants by being inclusive, regardless of a participant's fiscal resources. In the network I support, this means that although many of the equity directors in the Education Partnership's network worked in districts affiliated with the organization (and thus paid membership fees), I made the choice not to limit participation to those who were members. Thankfully, both Dr. Frank Samuel and the Education Partnership's current director, Faith Willis, have been supportive of this decision despite potential financial implications. This inclusivity has proven to be crucial to the growth and sustainability of the group for two reasons. First, in these last few years, equity directors have reported the need to reduce budgets due to declining district budgets and, more recently, due to the expiration of the Elementary and Secondary Emergency Relief Fund that provided additional financial support to schools in response to the COVID-19 pandemic. Participants who have not been able to continue or renew membership with our organization have expressed appreciation for our open-door policy. Second, the choice to separate fiscal support from participation in the group has signaled that our goal is to support equity directors as *people*, beyond their roles and organizational affiliations. As a result of this approach, we have had continued engagement by some former equity directors who have changed roles or organizations.

Our commitment to the personal and professional development of equity directors has also been evident in the growth of programming for the group. For example, in addition to our monthly meetings, we have hosted a virtual retreat in conjunction with another organization, as well as two in-person retreats focusing on systems change and on nurturing connections across the group. Our continued evolution and responsiveness have defined and distinguished us from other networks that have disbanded due to a lack of funding, transitions, or lack of support among leadership at their host organizations.

In short, given the subtext of isolation faced by many equity directors as they navigate racialized and gendered dynamics, networks of support must be created to provide an anchor or a buoy in challenging times. These networks, serving as steadfast spaces, can attend to the breadth of professional and personal experiences faced by equity leaders in their organizations while providing opportunities for connections to develop over time.

LIFTING AS YOU CLIMB

Baker-Doyle and Mawhinney (2024) highlight the emphasis placed *on pursuing expertise* from "mentors, elders, and leaders" (p. 129) as another feature of germinal networks. Teacher activists in their study saw mentorship as a way of sustaining themselves and sustaining the work of advancing racial equity. Veteran equity directors like Shawn found themselves serving as the first link in the chain of mentorship. He describes it as follows:

> What ended up happening was starting in the 2021 school year . . . I became the support network for a lot of folks who were new to the position . . . I laugh

> about it now, [but] I would see the headline of "district hires" person. . . . Next thing you know . . . I am gonna get an email.

Given his status as a "regional first," Shawn served as a first point of contact for newly hired equity directors in his region and underscored the connections he worked to foster and facilitate for folks who reached out. In other cases, equity directors and their networks leaned on experienced leaders of color who had been championing equity work in school districts for years without formal titles or structural support. Jada, an equity director in the West, described the significance of support from veteran colleagues "who had been in the trenches" and had navigated similar challenges. Elyse described the critical support offered by an administrator in a neighboring district:

> Dr. Donna Sinclair, from one of our neighboring districts, from the first moment, when I became a principal . . . [she has] provided support and mentorship. . . . There has been this pouring in, because, as I'm sure you've heard people say, it's exhausting to do this work like it never ends. You feel like you've finished one fight and then there's something else, so it's taxing on you, your family, your mental health.

It makes sense that equity directors draw strength from the wisdom and support of the lived experience of veteran colleagues. Group members have often highlighted intergenerational support as a "life raft" that can help equity directors navigate complex systems.

The Education Partners' network was well situated to foster intergenerational mentorship. The organization, in existence for over 20 years in the region, has deep roots as an organization focused on supporting equity leaders *and* connecting them across districts. This proved particularly helpful given the emergent nature of equity director roles and, in some cases, equity work at the district level. By connecting with an established organization, equity directors could plug in to an ecosystem of support that helped them to better understand their roles and the broader landscape of equity work in the region. For example, at a recent meeting, someone brought up their struggle to frame an initiative for a senior colleague whose buy-in was necessary for the initiative to advance. Promptly, several other equity directors chimed in, relating to the situation and asking questions that inspired reflection and consideration of different approaches to the issue. The person who initially raised the challenge expressed gratitude for the respectful support and earnest engagement, deeming the whole experience illuminating and empowering.

In another meeting, someone shared a handout they had created to engage with families, and the group provided feedback on the language and structure. These are just some examples of a myriad of interactions that occurred during our meetings and that illustrate how participants benefit from the extensive experience of group members. The collective has thus served as a brain trust, with participants acknowledging a felt sense of empowerment in response to being in community with "people who get it."

COLLABORATING ACROSS ORGANIZATIONS

In addition to benefitting personally and professionally from networks, equity directors leveraged their networks to nudge their districts into trying new initiatives. Gina, an equity director in the Midwest, shared:

> I find it helpful when I can [tell our] district . . . [the] district next door . . . they're doing this . . . and it's working really well . . . [which allows us] to put some pressure on the districts as we share what's happening.

Gina's connection with other equity directors has allowed her to advocate for programs and policies that she was told were unattainable. This points to the fact that equity efforts exist within a larger context, and districts are often cognizant and sensitive to how they are seen vis-à-vis neighboring districts. Gina's experiences are representative of the third feature of Baker-Doyle and Mawhinney's germinal networks: *germinal influence*. Germinal influence is borne out of the space created by a network where "new, alternative ideas could germinate and take root" (Baker-Doyle & Mawhinney, 2024, p. 130). My study participants explained that networks provided a space in which to learn from colleagues whom they considered brilliant and in the vanguard. Like Gina, several participants were emboldened to revisit previously dismissed ideas when colleagues shared the positive impact similar ideas had on their district. In one instance, a participant shared being able to forge a connection with a nearby superintendent through his equity director colleague. He later called on that superintendent to share the outcomes of an equity initiative with his supervisor, which led to renewed conversation about a previously dismissed idea. Relationships forged in networks can facilitate change and influence the trajectory of equity work; being in community with other highly skilled, savvy professionals allowed equity directors to plant seeds within their systems that could later germinate into new policies and practices, as evidenced by Gina's comments earlier.

In addition to the impact of peer influence, having a space for exchanging expertise was important for participants who did not always experience access to the same level of expertise or engagement within their district. They reported that their peer networks were spaces in which they could engage in conversation about "real" system-level work. Toni explains:

> They [equity directors] are some of the brightest people you're going to meet in your life. However, we are all put in these situations . . . they [districts] don't want you to do real systemic work.

The exchange of ideas in the networks around policies and practices sparked opportunities for collaboration. In the Education Partners' network, participants have shared language from recently adopted district equity policies as a way to support colleagues in the process of developing their own. Others have offered insights and strategies after they led specific initiatives to address disproportionality in access to coursework or in discipline. As intended, network participants share artifacts, consult with one another, connect colleagues with service providers for support, and develop tools to help plant seeds and shift mindsets. I found that equity directors, despite a range of role configurations, worked to influence district-level equity work from whichever seat they occupied (Irby et al., 2022). Directors sometimes faced resistance given their system-level impact, and some had to decide whether they could stay in their roles or leave their districts. When making those decisions, they often reached out to colleagues in our network to discuss their options, solicit advice, and determine their exit plan. Importantly, directors who had to leave their positions often considered acts of seeding and nurturing as a salve.

In addition to the impact these relationships had on their own practice and systems, equity directors also recognized their influence on each other. Jeremy, an equity director in the Mid-Atlantic, speaks of the direct influence a nearby colleague had as they both served in their new roles:

> In the district where I live, they hired a DEI director at the exact same time [I started] . . . I knew him already . . . so he and I just started meeting that summer and just started kind of sharing ideas. And their district had already been doing the work as a district where they already had committees set up, they had that infrastructure in place . . . because their district had already moved forward with a lot of the work . . . I was able to kind of lean on him get some ideas, and he was able to help me focus my attention.

Jeremy was able to accelerate some of his work by learning from the experience and advice of a colleague with more equity infrastructure in his district. Similarly, Shane reached across districts to build capacity regionally, with a focus on supporting student voice efforts and equity efforts at large. Expanding outreach for creative collaboration allowed Shane to dream bigger, to bring regional recognition to his district, and to build momentum for the district's equity efforts.

This type of collaboration has also flourished in the Education Partnership's network. Working closely with district leaders who have more experience doing the work, we have provided substantial professional learning about systemic change and strategy development that equity directors can leverage to address systemic inequities. Tackling systemic change as a group has been particularly productive, as equity directors often face similar challenges in dissimilar contexts. For example, many of our equity directors would agree that racialized disproportionality in access to honors courses is a common issue across districts. Discussing common root causes, as well as the individual policy and practice "flavors" in each of their districts, has helped equity directors to consider and apply various approaches for the best outcome. The network has functioned as a laboratory, providing participants with a safe space to explore issues from a different lens, an aspect of the community often touted as a significant benefit.

NETWORKS AS SPOTLIGHTS

In addition to the features of germinal networks highlighted by Baker-Doyle and Mawhinney, equity directors in the Education Partners' network have also noted the importance of having a strong and visible presence beyond their district boundaries. Participating in networks has brought visibility to their work, thus helping to sustain momentum for their work in a highly politicized environment. In the excerpt that follows, Jeremy highlights the benefits of being part of networks and the impact additional visibility and resources has on his efforts:

> I'm a part of a network that meets monthly at the university . . . it allows me to connect with different people on campus and different community organizations throughout the area . . . it just allows me to continue to build networks, and now to be on boards and on committees. And so that looks good for our district. *But it also helps me do the work, and to bring in additional resources to our school community* [emphasis added].

Similarly, equity directors in the network often mention the positive impact of connecting at a regional level, where they get to amplify each other's successes in a public way through events and connections offered by the network. Unfortunately, people who fill equity leadership positions do not often have access to formalized support that caters to their roles. Shawn, a former principal from the Mid-Atlantic, framed the necessity of these leadership networks this way:

> As a superintendent, there's a Superintendents Association. Principals, like there's a Principal's Association . . . as an equity officer, there is no affiliation or organization . . . And earlier on [before 2020] . . . there weren't even colleagues.

As discussed earlier in this chapter, Shawn saw this lack of support as a significant challenge and served as a "connector" for newly hired equity directors in the region. Ben, an equity director in the Southeast, shared that he sought out advice and connection by cold-calling colleagues across the country. He described his efforts as "a listening tour" where he could tap into the experiences of others to help guide his own efforts. Ben later became a part of several regional and national networks of equity leaders, appreciating the networks as valuable spaces to hone his craft. Like Shawn and Ben, many of my equity director colleagues around the country sought each other out and worked to create spaces of connection. Sometimes, those networks were hosted by educational organizations, higher education institutions, and others.

STRATEGIES FOR CREATING NETWORKS OF SUPPORT

Across this chapter, I have sought to highlight the importance of networks to equity leaders. Germinal networks, which focus on humanizing leaders, elevating lived experience, and fostering collaboration for action can serve to buoy equity leaders (Baker-Doyle & Mawhinney, 2024; Keenan, 2020). Not only do networks counter isolation, they also provide rich spaces for community and healing that help to sustain leaders and their work (Wilson & Richardson, 2020). However, creating and sustaining these networks is delicate work that requires attentiveness to the needs of the group and to the contexts they inhabit. In the section that follows, I reflect on my experience convening the Education Partners network and share strategies and practices that have helped to sustain the work and the equity directors we support.

Tailored Support

Equity directors are in full agreement about the importance and benefits of staying connected with networks that provide relevant support, center humanity, and foster connection. As mentioned earlier, building responsive programming has been fundamental to the sustainability of the Education Partners group. Thus, in order to best understand the needs of the equity directors, I had to stay closely connected and attuned to them. It was also crucial to adapt and vary programming and meeting format as we emerged from the COVID-19 pandemic. For example, to serve directors from across the country, we meet virtually once a month. We also meet later in the day so those from other time zones could join. To meet the socialization needs of the group, we meet for a holiday lunch that is mostly attended by those in the Philadelphia region. However, our annual retreat draws attendance from a larger geographic area, as it occurs in the summer and extends over 2 days. Providing a range of opportunities in which to engage has fostered an inclusive environment that acknowledges equity directors' variable schedules and fluctuating capacity to engage in out-of-district meetings.

Equity directors have also reported a need for challenging and dynamic professional growth opportunities within their respective networks. Many equity directors, new to central office roles, spoke of the need to better understand governance, finance, and other aspects of central office leadership. Superintendents can support equity directors by encouraging and supporting access to high-quality, job-specific training and development opportunities. This might involve setting aside professional development funds or approving additional professional development hours. Superintendents can also connect equity directors with organizations and leaders that can help them navigate their roles. For example, a participant in my dissertation study noted the impact on her career trajectory when a colleague invited her to a network meeting with superintendents and other central office administrators present. Her experience as a guest in that space fostered connections that led to significant professional advancement. This is noteworthy, as ambiguity in role configuration impacts not just the day-to-day of equity directors but can also impact their trajectory. One equity director framed it this way:

> We will see what it [the role] brings . . . this role is not really understood . . . I do feel I am well prepared for larger roles [assistant superintendent, superintendent] but I am not sure . . . boards are still pretty traditional [in their hiring].

Given the emergent nature of equity director roles, it is important for networks to establish new and viable connections with superintendents and other central office colleagues across districts. Expanding professional opportunities will undoubtedly reap benefits for equity directors as they forge ahead in their careers.

Formalizing Support

Equity directors in our network and those in my study have expressed a desire for the work of existing networks to be formalized. Some envision a national organization with regional chapters. However, while most equity directors would appreciate having access to folks nationwide, many have highlighted the crucial role played by *regional* networks given the local nature of school politics. Our organization has tried to balance these requests for expanding and centralizing support. Annual meetings open to all, such as the Education Partners' equity director retreat, serve as important touchstones, providing protected time for professional development and community building. Concurrently, we provide spaces to focus specifically on regional connections through our holiday gathering and other events. While providing support through these organizations and gatherings can be both labor and resource intensive, it is clearly an invaluable way to sustain the ongoing work of equity directors.

Sustaining the Network

Networks can play a pivotal role in the experiences of equity directors. They provide targeted and responsive professional development, foster a sense of community and support, invoke creative collaboration, and help equity directors advance equity efforts in their respective systems. Having witnessed and experienced the importance of these networks, I encourage philanthropic organizations, higher education institutions, government agencies, and K–12 school districts to support the work by providing fiscal and logistical support. By nurturing these networks, educational leaders at all levels can amplify the unique contributions of equity leaders who bring a wealth of experience to the work of systemic change. The investment to build and maintain spaces that affirm and sustain equity leaders doing the work will undoubtedly make an impact within and across systems.

REFERENCES

Baker-Doyle, K. J., & Mawhinney, L. (2024). From a spark, a mighty flame: How germinal networks support teachers of color to promote change in activist organizations and beyond. *Teachers College Record*, *126*(3), 110–138. https://doi.org/10.1177/01614681241262622

Bristol, T. J., & Shirrell, M. (2019). Who is here to help me? The work-related social networks of staff of color in two mid-sized districts. *American Educational Research Journal*, *56*(3), 868–898.

Delgado Bernal, D., Burciaga, R., & Flores Carmona, J. (2012). Chicana/Latina testimonios: Mapping the methodological, pedagogical, and political. *Equity & Excellence in Education*, *45*(3), 363–372.

hooks, b. (1992). Yearning: Race, gender, and cultural politics. *Hypatia*, *7*(2), 177–187.

Irby, D. J., Green, T. L., & Ishimaru, A. M. (2022). PK–12 district leadership for equity: An exploration of director role configurations and vulnerabilities. *American Journal of Education*, *128*(3). https://doi.org/DOI: 10.1086/719120

Ishimaru, A. M., Irby, D. J., & Green, T. L. (2022). The paradox of organizational double jeopardy: PK-12 equity directors in racialized and gendered educational systems. *The Urban Review*. https://doi.org/10.1007/s11256-022-00653-2

Keaton, A. C. (2023). An interpretative phenomenological analysis of Black women Diversity and Inclusion Leaders in sport organizations. *Journal of Sport Management*, *38*(1), 12–25.

Keenan, H. B. (2020). The Trans Educators Network: A reflection on community organizing and knowledge production. *Teaching Education*, *31*(1), 84–97. https://doi.org/10.1080/10476210.2020.1714580

Martinez-Maldonado, G. J. (2023). *Leading equity change: A phenomenological study of Massachusetts public school directors of diversity, equity and inclusion (DE&I)* [EdD, Boston University]. ProQuest Dissertations Publishing. https://www.proquest.com/docview/2812329044/abstract/86C332E435C3449CPQ/1

Matschiner, A. (in press). A national analysis of P–12 "equity director" role establishment. *American Educational Research Journal.*

Muñiz, D. (2024). *Superintendent and equity director perspectives on the equity director position in suburban school districts* [EdD, Temple University]. ProQuest Dissertations Publishing. https://www.proquest.com/docview/3099620629/1526649379C94A18PQ/4?sourcetype=Dissertations%20&%20Theses

Pour-Khorshid, F. (2018). Cultivating sacred spaces: A racial affinity group approach to support critical educators of color. *Teaching Education*, *29*(4), 318–329. https://doi.org/10.1080/10476210.2018.1512092

Reyes, K. B., & Curry Rodríguez, J. E. (2012). Testimonio: Origins, terms, and resources. *Equity & Excellence in Education*, *45*(3), 525–538. https://doi.org/10.1080/10665684.2012.698571

Wilson, A., & Richardson, W. (2020). All I want to say is that they don't really care about us: Creating and maintaining healing-centered collective care in hostile times. *Occasional Paper Series*, *2020*(43). https://doi.org/10.58295/2375-3668.1342

CHAPTER 10

Holding Space, Holding On

Precarity and Turnover as a Feature of Equity Leadership Work

Ahreum Han and Decoteau J. Irby

> I am holding space as Acting Superintendent of Equity. And now, this week alone, it was announced that our founding Superintendent of Equity will transition out of the district. So, the position and this office now is left . . . we're meeting this week to find out exactly what that vision is for our Office with our new district superintendent. More information is forthcoming.
>
> —Sophia, Acting Superintendent of Equity, Pine Oaks School District

We hope that by now, the preceding chapters have conveyed the importance of strong and sustainable equity leadership as essential to improving minoritized students' educational experience and outcomes in K–12 education. At the same time, people in formal equity roles (and the many others who informally do the work) experience numerous challenges in their fight to create and expand opportunities from within hostile and oppressive education systems. Many equity leaders leave their jobs to retreat from the adverse experiences and hostile conditions they experience at work. In fact, almost all of the equity leaders who participated in our research over the past several years reported holding their positions from 2 to 6 years maximum. While we have not yet systematically explored why formal equity leaders leave their positions, we do understand that leaders at our study sites tend to leave their roles due to job-related stress and burnout from facing resistance to their work. In the best situations, they left for promotions offering more expansive resources and influence under new titles. But, consistently, a relatively short job tenure and precarity are characterizations of formal equity leadership roles.

As trailblazers, equity leaders enter their jobs fully awake, aware that it will take some time before the sun sets on their efforts. Indeed, many step into their designated role and swiftly establish goals and priorities that will inch the district closer to system-wide changes to benefit marginalized students. They lay foundations and stack bricks for others to build on where they leave off. To be fair, leader turnover in districts and schools is a problem across the board, regardless of leadership position. School leaders take on complex, difficult, tenuous—and often thankless—work.

Principals are one example. Levin and Bradley, in their report *Understanding and Addressing Principal Turnover* (2019) reviewed 35 published principal studies and found that as of 2016–2017, the average tenure of school principals was 4 years. An alarming 35% of principals remained at their school for less than 2 years. Only 11% of principals remained at their school for 10 years or more. In high-poverty schools, the turnover rate was twice that of low-poverty schools. Levin and Bradley (2019) found five main reasons that principals left their positions: inadequate preparation, poor working conditions, low salaries, lack of decision-making authority, and high-stakes accountability policies. Principals who lead for justice and equity often face additional, unnamed, and unappreciated challenges (Capper & Young, 2014; Dantley & Tillman, 2006; Irby, 2022; Santamaria, 2014; Theoharis, 2007). Two examples are racial battle fatigue and inadequate access to resources.

As Irby et al. (2022) note, superintendents also play an important, albeit typically indirect, role in leading equity change by leveraging their institutional authority to allocate resources and create policies at a systems level. Their tenures, usually 3 to 6 years in duration, are consistently grueling. As public-facing leaders, superintendents work long days, nights, and weekends. They must respond to external policy demands and school boards and act as liaisons between their school district and local communities (Holme et al., 2014). Superintendents are always in the center of the culture wars at play in the United States. They navigate book bans, union demands, and mascot renaming. In the time frame covered in this book, they have worked alongside the rising sociopolitical and cultural tide of Black Lives Matter, #MeToo, MAGA, xenophobia, anti-immigrant, anti-CRT, anti-DEI, and anti-LBGTQAI+ that emerged when Barack Obama was elected as president in 2008. The backlash reached a crescendo on January 21, 2025, when Donald Trump signed the executive order 14151 "Ending Radical and Wasteful Government DEI Programs and Preferencing."

But superintendents' relationship to diversity, equity, and inclusion was at best tenuous for years before Donald Trump launched a federal campaign to eradicate all efforts to make schools more just, equitable, and supportive for students and staff. In many districts across the United States, a superintendent's slight hint of supporting equity and, in particular, speaking about race and racism, could set off a firestorm of criticism and resistance from the broader community (Villenas & Angeles, 2013). Given the potential for public scrutiny and resistance, many superintendents have been unwilling to directly engage in racial equity leadership.

But even superintendents willing to be outspoken in their support of equity in theory are often unprepared to move their district toward realizing their promises (Tienken, 2021).

Equity leaders are nestled in between principals, who face a myriad of challenges leading for equity, and superintendents, who, even if supportive, may act as if their hands are bound or may lack capacity to be effective in their equity leadership. Understanding their precarious position helps us understand why equity leadership activities start, stop, grow, and become difficult to see and appreciate. For people who take on the work of equity leadership, "inadequate preparation" is a misnomer. Formal equity leaders persist in their roles despite the outright absence of formal preparation, guidance, associations, or standards that principals and superintendents have within reach. As demonstrated throughout this book, oppressive working conditions make it so equity leaders have to fight for decision-making authority. Their ability to influence their superintendents and direct reports has proven to be paramount. It is no surprise that they remain in their roles just long enough to accomplish "something."

In this final chapter, we explore how leadership turnover impacted equity leadership activities in the three districts presented. Specifically, it became clear that superintendent support matters. When a superintendent who supports equity leadership leaves a district, the leaders themselves—as well as their activities, initiatives, and priorities—become vulnerable. For each case, we focus on the three elements illustrated in Figure 10.1. We describe the superintendent, equity leaders, and leadership activities that existed before the hiring superintendent departed and what happened after they left.

In our analysis, we identified three key individuals or groups that engage in equity leadership work in most districts. These include formal equity leaders, district-supported teams, and informal leadership teams. Formal equity leaders are district employees whose job is to advance equity within the district and who hold a specific title or designation indicating the focus of their employment, such as equity specialist, director, assistant superintendent of equity, and so forth. For the purposes of our analysis, we categorize

Figure 10.1. Case Elements

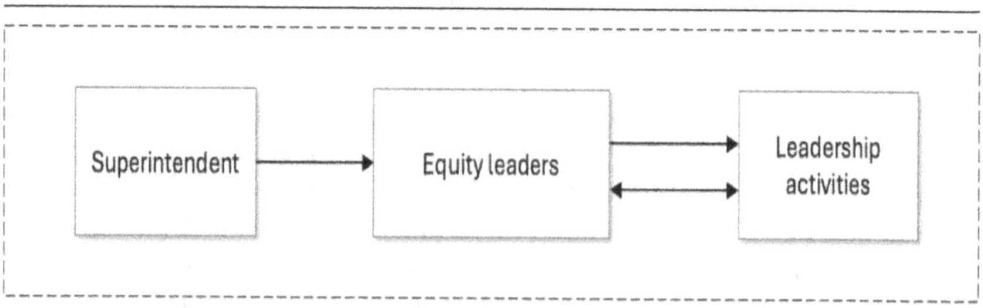

equity leaders who sit in the superintendent cabinet as formal equity leaders because their job requires a focus on advancing equity.

District-supported teams consist of district employees whose primary roles are not explicitly tied to equity work but who contribute to these efforts as part of their additional responsibilities. This group typically includes principals, teachers, and other district staff. Although equity work is not central to their job descriptions, they frequently participate in initiatives under the guidance of formal equity leaders. For example, a principal might lead school-based equity projects in collaboration with district equity specialists. In our cases, district-supported leadership teams include equity committees and similar groups that support the enactment of equity policies, activities, or initiatives.

Finally, we categorized informal leadership teams as ones that consist of a combination of family, community, or business volunteers and/or district employees who engage in leadership activities off the clock or with limited district-supported guidance and resources. For example, informal leadership teams or groups might meet in district facilities, which, by definition, are a district resource. But they could just as easily meet offsite, independently setting their own agendas and self-directed leadership activities. In our cases, informal leadership teams include affinity groups and principal-directed networks.

Equity leadership activities refer to the broad areas of work that the leaders and teams carried out, including but not limited to developing and implementing equity plans and policies; designing learning materials; and organizing and delivering teacher, staff, and principal professional development sessions. As we illustrate, both formal and district-supported leadership are essential forms of equity leadership because they ease the disruption to activities that occur when superintendents turn over.

CASE PRESENTATIONS

For each case, we present a high-level narrative of the equity leaders and teams and activities that existed before the superintendent departed and after the superintendent position was filled. We supplement each narrative with a timeline summary figure. Each summary figure illustrates the superintendent, equity leaders, and activities, as well as the movement related to superintendent departures in our three case districts. In each figure, we shaded the areas that reflect periods of superintendent turnover. Our goal is not to offer a granular-level analysis of change within each district, but to look across cases for broad patterns. Therefore, we do not present an exhaustive list of personnel or activities.

Overall, we determined that organized structures and relationships are the two elements that drive and grow equity leadership momentum and activities. We begin by presenting the case of Evergreen School District (all district names and individual names are masked with pseudonyms), where the equity leadership efforts persisted largely based on relationships. In the second case, we present Cherry Blossom School District, where relationships and structure sustained the efforts. In Pine Oaks School District, the third case, we explore the role that structure, in the form of an equity office with clearly defined positions, played in sustaining their work during a period of superintendent transition.

Case 1: Relationally Sustained Equity Leadership

Evergreen School District's equity work was driven by a philosophy: Equity work is everyone's work. People throughout the district took this proclamation and its constant refrain to mean that no one single person can be, or should be, responsible for leading for equity. People in Evergreen held various opinions as to whether this approach was best. Regardless of different opinions, with long-standing buy-in and relationships as a foundation, the district, with its de facto equity leaders and district-supported teams, was able to accomplish equity commitments through loosely structured, relatively informal equity leadership teams. Unlike other cases in our study, Evergreen School District's leadership comprised insiders who worked together to negotiate roles and timelines for activities. When hiring and program planning to bring the work forward, the district appointed staff with insider knowledge and histories. Overall, the lack of formal leadership structure and reliance on long-standing relationships as the primary accountability mechanism for doing the work led to numerous equity activity starts and stops, characterized by varied intensities and durations. An overview of Evergreen School District's case is presented in Figure 10.2.

Case Context

Evergreen School District is a medium-sized urban district approximately 35 miles from a major West Coast city. Evergreen School District educates approximately 30,000 students. In 2020, the first year of our multiyear case study research, the district's racial-ethnic demographics included about 40% white, more than 20% Latinx, almost 15% Black/African American, 15% multiracial, 9% Asian, 3% Pacific Islander, and 1% Native. The district operated 60 schools and a range of early childhood education programs and alternative programs. Evergreen School District utilizes a combined neighborhood school and *choice enrollment* model that automatically assigns students to a neighborhood school and also allows students' caretakers to apply to magnet schools.

As we began our research, Monique Carter had served as superintendent for almost 10 years. In 2021, she announced her intention to retire

Figure 10.2. Summary of Evergreen School District Leadership and Activities

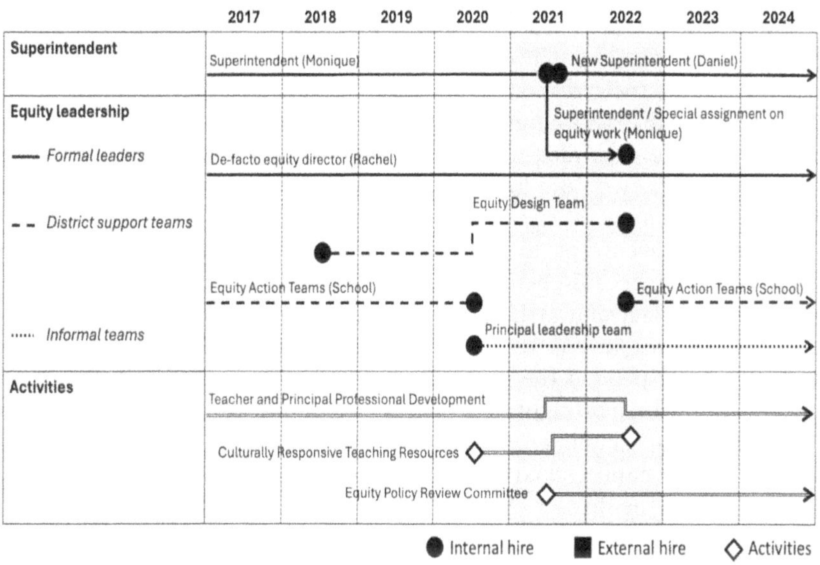

at the end of the academic year (June 2022). When the board selected her successor, Assistant Superintendent Daniel Harper, as the next superintendent, Monique assumed a 1-year appointment as "superintendent on special assignment" that overlapped with Daniel's first year. Monique used the 1-year special appointment to organize and streamline the district's equity activities in a way she had not been able to do throughout her superintendency. Evergreen School District never hired a formal equity director, nor did they establish an equity office because Monique and other equity-focused leaders held a strong conviction that "equity work is everyone's work."

The Work: Leadership and Activities

Prior to her special assignment year, Monique tasked several different district employees to implement the district's nondiscrimination and equity policy; she believed that giving a single person or office this charge would undercut her "equity is everyone's work" philosophy, so rather than hire an equity director, she distributed the work required. Rachel Adams, the district's AVID (Advancement Via Individual Determination) and advanced programs equity director, worked in the Curriculum and Instruction department under the assistant superintendent of teaching and learning. Many people in the district regarded Rachel as the unnamed de facto equity director. Despite having no equity office and few resources, Rachel ran equity-focused professional development and workshops for teachers and principals interested in engaging. She created equity action teams with representatives from each school to participate in equity-focused professional development, with the expectation that they would share the trainings and resources with their respective schools. In short, Rachel initiated or led almost all the district's equity-focused professional development, meetings, and events; she depended on a ripple effect where school-level educators, mostly teachers, would educate others in their buildings about culturally responsive teaching.

However, according to Rachel and Monique, the equity action teams were ineffective because many building principals refused to give them time to share their learning at faculty meetings or resisted the suggested focus on culturally responsive teaching. In 2020, at Rachel's urging, Monique temporarily suspended the equity action teams and prioritized the equity design team, which brought together district administrators, such as Rachel, the assistant superintendent of teaching and learning, the partnership director, and seven hand-picked principals from elementary, middle, and high schools across the district. Monique also employed a seasoned community consultant, Malik, to facilitate the equity design team in its first year. A parent in the district (and a founding member of the Black Parent Alliance), Malik brought consulting experiences with select Evergreen School District schools as well as the district office itself.

The equity design team focused on developing a series of online learning modules to introduce basic equity concepts and support educators in developing more culturally responsive teaching practices. These modules became central in the online culturally responsive teaching library of resources that the team continued to build. In particular, the equity design team intended every principal in the district to complete the series of modules and then use them to facilitate the professional learning of their staff. Members of the equity design team also sought out and created short videos of remote, culturally responsive teaching practices and initiated tools to support principal evaluation of teachers based on culturally responsive, teaching-informed refinements to their district teacher evaluation framework. In her transition year, Monique recruited a project manager to steward several additional projects, including a focus on teaching and equity standards, equity and cultural competency training for operational and classified staff (like bus drivers and nutrition workers), an "elevator speech" about the importance of equity in Evergreen School District, and modules for all newly hired certificated staff.

The Turnover and Aftereffect

The new superintendent, Daniel Harper, was not actively engaged in the equity design team or other district equity activities. While he was aware of the activities, he regarded his predecessor's efforts as exceedingly narrow and not particularly impactful. For Daniel, the most crucial equity work happened at what he referred to as "the margins," outside of classrooms and even schools. He believed that since schools were so ingrained in a traditional approach to teaching and learning, that attempting to change teacher practice was an ongoing challenge. Instead, he focused on increasing access and opportunity in spaces outside of the realm of teachers, such as ensuring student access to after-school activities ("Beyond the Bell") and access to early learning, monitored through an extensive data dashboard using multiple measures to ensure accountability.

When Monique retired, she sunset the equity design team but handed off the projects she worked hard to put into motion to three leaders in different district departments. Although Daniel brought Malik to launch the following school year with a rousing equity summit attended by all the administrators in the district, the work at the district level appeared to resume where it had left off. The informal principal leadership network continued to grow through new hires into school leadership roles, intentional women of color leadership mentoring spaces, ongoing African American and other affinity groups for educators, and collective support for school-level equity leadership; these activities proceeded without formal district supports or resources.

CASE 2: RELATIONAL-STRUCTURALLY SUSTAINED EQUITY LEADERSHIP

Evergreen School District reflects a district where structured leadership and relational connections coalesced to sustain equity leadership activities during a superintendent transition. Cherry Blossom School District's commitment to equity started in the first wave of equity leader hires. As in many suburban districts between 2014 and 2016, the Cherry Blossom superintendent and board created formal positions to address the state's scrutiny of its persistent racial disparities. By the time Linda Chapman assumed the role of assistant superintendent of equity and innovation, equity seeding was already underway, offering Linda a foundation from which to build. As an external hire completely unfamiliar with the district's prior efforts, Linda prioritized structure while also strategically working to build strong relationships with her colleagues. An overview of Cherry Blossom School District's case is presented in Figure 10.3.

Case Context

Cherry Blossom School District is a large, diverse school district that serves nearly 40,000 students. Located about a 60-minute drive from

Figure 10.3. Summary of Cherry Blossom School District Leadership and Activities

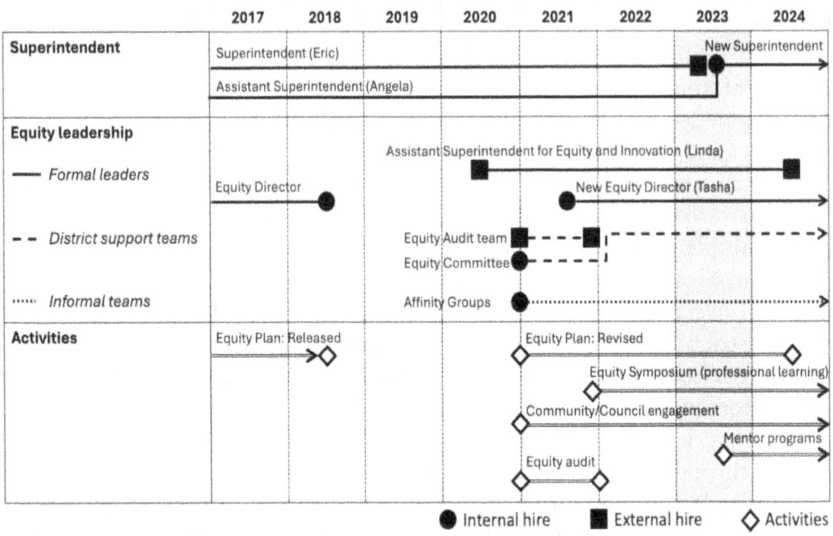

a major U.S. city, the district encompasses a 90-square-mile enrollment catchment that spans 11 distinct municipalities. Because of its sprawling geography, the district's schools serve a wide range of neighborhoods, communities, and students, a majority of whom identify as Latinx. The district's suburban shopping options, single-family-home communities, and curving streets and turning lanes that befuddle visitors mask pronounced racial, cultural, and economic differences within and across school buildings.

Assistant Superintendent of Equity and Innovation Dr. Linda Chapman (all names are pseudonyms) was hired in 2020 under Dr. Eric Bennett, who served as superintendent since 2014. Linda did not report to Eric, but to Dr. Angela Crawford, the assistant superintendent for the district. Linda was the district's second equity leader; however, her position in the superintendent's cabinet distinguished her role from her predecessor who worked as a director, a step lower than an assistant superintendent. Notably Eric and Angela had long histories in the district, working in various roles for 15 and 20 years, respectively. The district and, by extension, Linda benefitted from stability, colleagues' historical memory and experiences, and a deeply ingrained way of doing things, as reflected in the district retention of employees and common practice of promoting from within. In 2015, the district's Board of Education approved its strategic plan that sought to address the persistent achievement gaps faced by historically marginalized students by reorganizing district structures and systems.

The Work: Leadership and Activities

Dr. Linda Chapman was hired in 2020 to implement the district equity plan. With an initial hybridized role configuration that encompassed seeding, innovation, management, and community collaboration activities, her responsibilities extended across a portfolio of programs aimed at ensuring educational fairness. In about 2 years, she expanded her influence to include a team of seven direct reports, including Mrs. Tasha Robinson, a district insider whom she hired as the director of diversity, equity, and inclusion. This expansion followed an equity audit conducted in collaboration with the equity audit team and supported by the district. Beyond this critical achievement in formalizing leadership, Linda streamlined her role to focus on oversight and innovation, enabling her to drive systemic change through high-impact initiatives.

Linda's efforts to advance equity within the district were evident in her leadership of monthly equity committee meetings, where she brought together administrators, teachers, counselors, and community representatives to review the district's four equity pillars, identify gaps in quality service, and develop actionable solutions to address the identified disparities. Her collaborative approach also extended to working with key community groups—such as the Faith Leaders Council, African American Council, Bilingual Parent Advisory Committee (BPAC), and Community Advisory Council (CAC)—to align equity strategies with community needs and address the concerns of historically underrepresented populations.

After Linda hired Tasha as the director of diversity, equity, and inclusion, they worked together to expand the district's equity initiatives. Together, they launched the equity symposium, a multiday professional learning event focused on critical topics such as achievement gaps, staff diversity, and culturally responsive teaching, providing actionable insights for district staff and community members. Recognizing the importance of mentorship, they also collaborated to develop and implement a mentoring program within the district. Through these joint efforts, Linda and Tasha exemplified a shared commitment to fostering sustainable and inclusive systemic change.

Turnover and Aftereffects

Eric, Cherry Blossom School District's superintendent, ended his tenure in January 2023. Angela Crawford stepped in as the interim superintendent for the 2022–2023 academic year. In June 2023, Angela was officially appointed as superintendent. Having worked in Cherry Blossom School District for more than 25 years, Dr. Crawford brought extensive experience within the district. This leadership turnover occurred at a pivotal time for Cherry Blossom School District's equity work. Despite the change in the superintendent position, Cherry Blossom School District's equity work experienced minimal disruption. We believe that this continuity was largely due to Linda's prior direct reporting relationship with Angela, which will be discussed more in the cross case analysis.

CASE 3: STRUCTURALLY SUSTAINED EQUITY LEADERSHIP

The equity office in Pine Oaks School District has established itself as a cornerstone of the district's efforts to address and eliminate opportunity gaps through its clear roles, well-defined responsibilities, and strategic initiatives. Despite challenges posed by leadership transitions, the office demonstrated remarkable resilience and adaptability guided by a strong equity framework, collaborative team culture, and commitment to actionable policy work. By balancing institutional memory with fresh perspectives, the team has not only sustained its impact but also expanded its reach and capacity. The Pine Oaks School District Equity Office demonstrates how a clear vision with an aligned framework, structured leadership, and a commitment to equity can drive meaningful, sustainable change in a large, diverse school district.

Case Context

Pine Oaks School District is a large urban school district that serves a culturally, linguistically, and socioeconomically diverse student body of about 350,000 students in over 600 district-operated or charter public schools. The district's founding assistant superintendent of equity, Dr. Malcolm Hayes, was hired in 2018 under the leadership of Dr. Julia Morgan, a Black woman who assumed her superintendency a year earlier in 2017. The current Pine Oaks School District equity efforts trace back to Dr. Julia's appointment as the assistant superintendent in 2015. Under her leadership, a race and equity working group was formed in 2016. The working group spent a year developing a set of recommendations for the superintendent to implement, including the proposal to hire a superintendent of equity and to create an equity office.

When Dr. Julia assumed the role of superintendent in 2017, she expanded the equity agenda and hired Malcolm to create a brand-new district equity office. Reporting directly to her, Malcolm's initial leadership activity proved consequential for the sustainability and growth of subsequent leadership activities. Notably, the call for a new stand-alone office differed from the more typical approach of districts to place equity leaders within existing offices or units (see Chapter 3).

The Work: Leadership and Activities

Figure 10.4 illustrates the 2018 leadership activities that yielded a new stand-alone office as a formal equity leadership entity, with its own staff

Figure 10.4. Summary of Pine Oaks School District Leadership and Activities

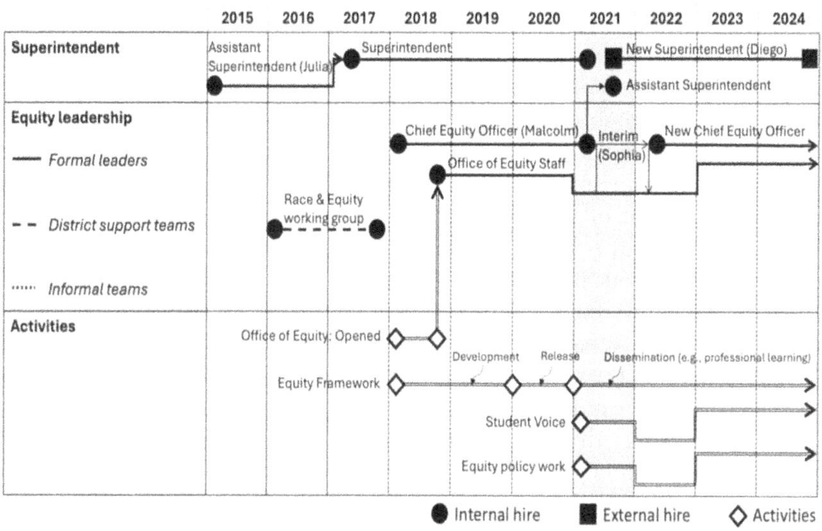

and budget. By the end of the first year, Malcolm established the Pine Oaks School District equity office to develop, support, implement, and monitor district efforts to eliminate opportunity gaps in educational quality, policies, and supports for students and adult teachers, administrators, and staff. With the launch of this office, he dissolved the race and equity working group and integrated its initiatives into the new office's functions. The equity office reflected a centralized and hierarchical structure with eight members, including roles such as director of professional learning, equity data strategist, and director of racial equity initiatives. Superintendent of Equity Malcolm oversaw the entire office, while Sophia, the newly appointed director of professional learning, served as second in command. A dedicated administrative assistant and various equity interns supported the office's activities.

The equity office engaged in diverse initiatives at the district, school, and community levels, beginning with a listening tour, as well as a policy and data review. The office's efforts, anchored in the Pine Oaks School District equity framework, developed over 2 years following Malcolm's appointment. Described as a "living document," the framework outlines four dimensions of an equity lens: liberatory thinking, inclusive partnerships, resource equity, and fair policies and systems. This framework provided a philosophical foundation and priorities that enabled the office to thrive and contribute significantly to districtwide equity activities. Some examples of equity policy projects include the school renaming initiative, collaboration with external organizations to amplify student voices, and professional learning opportunities for educators and other professionals, such as medical staff.

The Turnover and Aftereffects

In early 2021, Julia Morgan announced her intention to step down from her role as superintendent. Although the district publicly conveyed a smooth transition, the equity office team was surprised to learn of her planned departure. As is common, Julia's announcement precipitated more departures in the superintendent's cabinet, including within the equity office. For example, soon after Julia announced her intent to leave, her second in command, the superintendent of academic affairs, followed suit. Malcolm was called to act as interim superintendent of academic affairs, which suddenly left the equity office without its founding superintendent. To fill this void, Sophia, formerly the equity director for professional learning, assumed the role of acting equity superintendent. Such crucial transitions happening throughout the district created tension and uncertainty for the equity office, impacting its ability to carry out its portfolio of equity leadership activities.

In just a 2-month period, the equity office staff shrank to nearly half its original size. Staff expressed concerns with comments like "people are leaving" and "hands are not active" (check-in interview with Dr. Hayes and Sophia, June 29, 2021). As acting superintendent of equity, Sophia described the unprecedented nature of the transition, noting widespread changes across all levels of the district—from teachers and principals to central office and senior leadership positions. By the end of 2021, approximately 9 months after Julia Morgan announced her intent to leave the superintendency, the board unanimously approved Diego Alvarez to fill the district's superintendent vacancy. At that point, rather than remain in the superintendent's cabinet or return to lead the equity office he established, Malcolm Hayes decided to leave the district.

Despite a tumultuous 9-month period of rapid turnover and challenges, the office quickly rebounded. In 2022, Diego Alvarez hired a new superintendent of equity, this time a Black woman. Under her leadership, the office expanded once more, growing to a seven-member team, including new hires such as learning specialists, data strategists, and more equity interns. Buoyed by ongoing involvement and renewed commitment, Sophia returned to her previous role of equity director of professional learning, and the equity office team resumed its previous leadership activities. Soon after, the equity office also played an important role in developing the district's new 5-year strategic plan as it began to interface with and influence other district offices.

Several factors contributed to the resilience and sustainability of the Pine Oaks School District equity office during the leadership transition. As Sophia expressed during one interview, the seeding work of the initial team ensured that "team member roles are clearly defined. People know what they are supposed to do" even when there is not one person giving direction over the work. Another key factor was the presence of clear and active policy agendas, which ensured that the team maintained focus and continued progress on critical equity initiatives, such as their equity framework and districtwide projects. A strong team culture also played a crucial role, as the team prioritized equity of voice, collaboration, and shared commitment to their values and goals, fostering a sense of unity and purpose.

STRUCTURE, RELATIONSHIPS, AND LEADERSHIP CONTINUITY (OR NOT)

Superintendent turnover destabilizes the top of the organization, the very location where equity leadership researchers and practitioners advocate the most transformative equity work is possible. Progress can be easily affected by or compromised when district leadership transitions occur. As noted in other leadership studies in education, turnover in district leadership positions—particularly the superintendency—has become a fact of contemporary school life. In our analysis, it appears this may also be the case with the people who do the work of equity leadership. However, the degree of vulnerability depends largely on the presence of formal structures and strong relational connections. We find that more formalized leadership roles are better able to withstand the shocks of top-level leadership transitions.

The cases of Evergreen School District, Cherry Blossom School District, and Pine Oaks School District offer valuable insights into how structure and relationships influence the sustainability or disruption of equity leadership during periods of transition. While structure is crucial for maintaining consistency, relational ties within the system can serve as both strengths and vulnerabilities.

The importance of structure becomes evident when comparing how these three districts managed leadership transitions. In Pine Oaks School District, a formal equity office with clearly defined roles, a dedicated budget, and a guiding framework allowed the district to withstand disruptions with minimal impact. The office's structure ensured that the new superintendent leadership could seamlessly continue advancing equity initiatives. Cherry Blossom School District similarly benefitted from a formal structure. Dr. Linda Chapman, as the superintendent of equity, played a pivotal role in expanding and solidifying the district's equity efforts. Under her leadership, equity initiatives grew across multiple areas, and the establishment of the formal equity director position ensured that the work continued even after her departure.

In contrast, Evergreen School District lacked formal structures, which left its equity work fragmented and vulnerable to leadership changes. When key figures like Monique Carter stepped down, taking on a yearlong appointment as superintendent on special assignment to streamline and organize the district's equity activities, the absence of a centralized system made it difficult to sustain visibility and coherence in districtwide initiatives. While equity work continued at the individual school level, it became disconnected from the larger district framework, limiting its long-term effectiveness and impact. These contrasting cases highlight the critical role that formal structures play in sustaining equity leadership through periods of instability.

Relationships, on the other hand, played a complex and varied role in sustaining equity leadership across the cases. In Evergreen School District, where no centralized equity office or formal leadership structure existed, equity work was largely carried out by individuals with other responsibilities, such as Rachel Adams, whose official role was not directly focused on advancing equity system-wide. Informal teams led by school-level leaders helped sustain some momentum, but the work remained highly dependent on supportive relationships. After Superintendent Monique Carter stepped down, district-wide equity efforts became fragmented, with no consistent oversight to coordinate or align initiatives across schools. This lack of structure left the work vulnerable to leadership changes and shifts in priorities.

In Cherry Blossom School District, relationships played a stabilizing role due to the presence of a formal equity leader, Dr. Linda Chapman. Equity initiatives expanded under her leadership, and her direct reporting relationship to district leaders—including the future superintendent—helped sustain the work after she stepped down. This relational connection between the equity leader and the district's leadership created continuity during the transition, allowing equity efforts to continue without major disruptions.

In contrast, Pine Oaks School District relied less on relationships and more on a hierarchical structure. The equity office had a well-defined framework, clearly delineated roles, and strategic initiatives that institutionalized collaboration. During the superintendent transition, the office staff expressed uncertainty about the new superintendent's direction, but the established structure enabled them to maintain and advance equity initiatives without relying on relational support.

These cases demonstrate that while relationships can provide essential support for equity leadership, they are fragile, fluctuating, and highly individualized. Without formal structures, relational networks are vulnerable to disruption during leadership changes. However, when combined with structured roles and frameworks, as seen in Cherry Blossom School District and Pine Oaks School District, relationships can complement and reinforce equity leadership by providing both stability and adaptability.

SUNSETS

Turnover in superintendent positions impacts the sustainability of reform initiatives. This is true for district equity initiatives; however, turnover could create even more challenges for people engaging in equity leadership because, as a relatively new position in school districts, their work is often highly vulnerable. While role ambiguity allows equity leaders a great amount of freedom, flexibility, and creativity, their work can also be affected by or compromised when district leadership transitions occur.

As demonstrated in the firsthand accounts offered in this book, the ambiguity of the equity leadership role often affords equity leaders a great deal of autonomy to approach their work as they see fit. The backing of supportive superintendents is paramount to equity leaders' success (Muñiz, 2024), making the ambiguity and autonomy an asset rather than a liability. For example, in the first chapter of this volume, Dr. Latish Reed described how support from her Black woman superintendent turned the tide in her LGBTQIA+ nondiscrimination policy development and implementation work. The extent and duration of the vulnerabilities depends in large part on the leadership—formal, district supported, and informal—and what kinds of activities and initiatives occur, especially in the earlier years and as part of the ongoing seeding leadership that grows after a specific leader's tenure expires.

Turnover can often feel like a sunset in the life cycle of equity leadership. The departure of a key district leader (or leaders) can cast uncertainty over activities and initiatives, especially when the organization lacks formal structures to sustain its work. In some cases, transitions without a robust structure leave districts in a prolonged state of darkness, where equity efforts lose visibility and coherence. While the work may not come to a complete halt, it is less visible and potentially less impactful at a systems level. However, when a district has strong structures and supportive relationships, the work is more likely to be sustained over time. Structure and relationships provide continuity and stability, enabling the district to move forward despite leadership transitions. But even if and when work sunsets, it doesn't mean that people aren't continuing to do the work. They may approach it from a different direction or on a revised timeline. For example, as illustrated in Chapter 8, school-level leaders may take it upon themselves to carry forward the activities a district abandons. Others, like leaders in the Cherry Blossom School District highlighted in this chapter, continue the existing work but do not expand their efforts. More importantly, shifts in leadership may give people who are committed to equity and justice the opportunity to do work that sets the stage for a new morning. This is the kind of work that is best done out of view and is made possible precisely because leaders refuse to be repeatedly attacked, to acquiesce, or to remain committed to broken systems.

REFERENCES

Capper, C., & Young, M. (2014). Ironies and limitations of educational leadership for social justice: A call to social justice educators. *Theory into Practice 53*(2), 158–164.

Dantley, M., & Tillman, L. (2006). Social justice and moral transformative leadership. In C. Marshall & M. Oliva (Eds.). *Leadership for social justice: Making revolutions in education* (pp. 16–30). Pearson/Allyn and Bacon.

Executive Order No. 14,451 (2025)—Ending Radical and Wasteful Government DEI Programs and Preferencing. https://www.govinfo.gov/content/pkg/DCPD-202500118/pdf/DCPD-202500118.pdf

Holme, J., Jellison, J., Diem, S., & Welton, A. J. (2014). Suburban school districts and demographic change: The technical, normative, and political dimensions of response. *Educational Administration Quarterly, 50*(1), 34–66.

Irby, D. (2022). *Stuck improving: Racial equity and school leadership.* Harvard Education Press.

Irby, D. J., Green, T., & Ishimaru, A. M. (2022). PK–12 district leadership for equity: An exploration of director role configurations and vulnerabilities. *American Journal of Education, 128*(3), 417–453.

Levin, S., & Bradley, K. (2019). *Understanding and addressing principal turnover: A review of the research.* Learning Policy Institute and National Association of Secondary School Principals. https://learningpolicyinstitute.org/product/nassp-understanding-addressing-principal-turnover-review-research-report

Muñiz, D. (2024). *Superintendent and equity director perspectives on the equity director position in suburban school districts* [EdD, Temple University]. ProQuest Dissertation Publishing. https://www.proquest.com/docview/3099620629/1526649379C94A18PQ/4?sourcetype=Dissertations%20&%20Theses

Santamaría, L. (2014). Critical change for the greater good: Multicultural perceptions in educational leadership toward social justice and equity. *Educational Administration Quarterly, 50(3),* 347–391.

Theoharis, G. (2007). Social justice educational leaders and resistance: Toward a theory of social justice leadership. *Educational Administration Quarterly, 43*(2), 221–258.

Tienken, C. (2021). *The American superintendent 2020 decennial study.* Rowman & Littlefield.

Villenas, S., & Angeles, S. (2013). Race talk and school equity in local print media: The discursive flexibility of whiteness and the promise of race-conscious talk. *Discourse: Studies in the Cultural Politics of Education, 34*(4), 510–530.

Conclusion

Dream

Ann M. Ishimaru and Decoteau J. Irby

If you stay awake long enough—through the morning, midday, and evening—the sun will disappear from the horizon. As we write this conclusion, night has fallen. The "sun"—supportive policy, resources, and public commitments to an education that serves every child—has set. Night brings with it existential threats, not only to equity leadership but to public education and its centrality to the premise of democratic governance in the United States.

Our hope is that this book reminds us of the persistent determination, creativity, and sustained strategy of those "doing the work" of bending educational systems toward justice in the era ushered in by the election of the first Black person to the presidency of the United States. This decade of equity-focused systems work advanced meaningful change in schools, districts, and the lives of young people, even if it rarely realized the full-scale transformation leaders sought.

Even in the dark, educational and community leaders will continue the work of reshaping educational systems and schools to foster the learning and well-being of all children. Perhaps underground, moving under cover of darkness. Perhaps as distant beacons of light for others. Evening is also a time to take stock of the day's work. We point readers to the lessons that weave across the chapters and work of morning, midday, and evening—and argue that they can continue to light the way as we find ways to rest, reflect, and continue the work into night and the long season ahead.

LESSONS FOR A NEW DAY

First, sociopolitical and racial-historical contexts are dynamic, unfold across time, and profoundly shape both the possibilities and constraints on the work. There is no such thing as a one-size-fits-all playbook for equity leadership across every place and time. But equity leaders can ensure that they understand the histories of their communities, their organizations, and prior equity efforts. As Latish Reed (Chapter 1) and Teresa Lance (Chapter 5) both suggest, they can assess not only the disparities and barriers to access experienced by students but also take a frank look at how power plays out in their system and local community. The work of equity leadership is complex, multifaceted, and potentially overwhelming, as Maurice Swinney (Chapter 6) points out, so leaders must move beyond putting out daily fires and develop structures and processes that account for local histories and contexts to *prioritize* their focus and effort where it will most deeply root in the system.

Second, superintendents and other formal leaders play a crucial role in narrating commitments to ensuring high-quality education for every student and navigating the inevitable politics, but leadership for systems equity work requires multiple people in a variety of roles with a broad range of expertise. As Andrew Matschiner and Ishmael Miller (Chapter 7) illuminate, equity leaders' expertise spans policy work and governance, educator professional learning, instruction and pedagogy, racial and data literacies, human resources, and collaboration with youth, family, and communities. In short, no individual can single-handedly realize change across the often-siloed areas of district activity. In addition to these challenges, Ahreum Han and Decoteau Irby (Chapter 10) describe how constant leadership turnover at multiple levels impacts the sustainability of equity work and compounds the precarity of change-making efforts.

To foster change in such complex systems, equity-focused leaders must not go it alone. Dayna Muniz (Chapter 9) argues for the importance of finding each other and building networks both internally and externally to the district. Leaders can move collectively and strategically to influence the organization and embed organizational structures, routines, tools, and *learning* into the fabric of district work. They can cultivate politicized trust with minoritized families, community-based organizations, justice-focused advocacy groups, intermediary organizations, and tribal or racially minoritized communities. For instance, Latish Reed sought the support of LGBTQIA+ advocacy groups (Chapter 1), and Carol Moore partnered with parents and a local community-based organization (Chapter 8).

Third, systems are gonna system, and leaders who bring crucial lived experiences of oppression in tandem with their formal education and professional skills are often the least well supported and sustained. As in many other aspects of society, Black and other racially minoritized women often take the lead in education—and bear the brunt of the negative reactions and backlash as systems default to racialized and gendered organizational dynamics, a dynamic of "nice white districts" described by Shannon Paige Clark (Chapter 2). Ann Ishimaru, Decoteau Irby, and Terrance Green (Chapter 4) illuminate how the constant undermining of Black women's leadership erodes their efforts and their well-being. Drawing from research about equity directors' work to reconfigure their roles (Chapter 3), districts can prioritize organizational resources for their work, trust their expertise, and support their access to peer networks and professional development to continue to grow their own practice.

As Constance Daw and colleagues (Chapter 8) describe, Black and other racialized equity leaders can find or create humanizing spaces that both tend to their holistic well-being and support each other in doing the work, especially when it becomes risky. Leaders who identify as white and/or male can amplify their colleagues' insights and leadership, explicitly recognizing their knowledge and capacities while challenging racialized-gendered assessments and dismissals of their expertise. Regardless of identity, equity-focused leaders can move beyond zero-sum notions of power that infuse the everyday interactions in districts and reinforce dominant hierarchies and structures.

Finally, change in educational systems is never linear. Policies are rarely implemented at scale as intended. Ambitious equity plans often fall short in execution. Data disparities alone are insufficient for spurring action. Decision-makers and leaders routinely dismiss or blame those impacted by injustices. Rather than bemoaning these individual strategies as unsuccessful, we argue across the chapters for attention to how people coordinate and lead systems change through multiple strategies, relationships, and structures across time. Not every seed will grow to bear fruit. But equity leadership can proliferate and expand from multiple sources and efforts. We can stop expecting a singular policy, reform, or initiative issued from the top of the district hierarchy to trickle down to transform the system. Instead, leaders can undertake multiple strategies to build focused organizational capacity and routine activity toward more just systems.

An elder Black woman scholar and higher education leader recently suggested that this most recent "day" of work was an easy one—when the sun warmed the air, there was even a gentle breeze at our backs. She warned that the days ahead are of a different season. It will be a season of struggle. As we witness "our country moving closer to its own truth and dread, its own ways of making people disappear," as Adrienne Rich (2016) wrote, the experiences, insights, and lessons in this book illuminate practices, collective work, and change-making across systems. The chapters refuse the disappearance of the educators and leaders who carried these efforts from inside formal systems. As Patricia Hill Collins (2013) points out, leading change from the inside is no small task because "[c]hallenging power structures from the inside, and working cracks in the system, requires learning to speak multiple languages of power convincingly" (p. 38).

As educators, young people, families, and communities fight against violence, erasure, exclusion, and injustice, we must remember that night is also time to dream. Scholar activist and Combahee River Collective member

Dr. Margo Okazawa-Rey invites us to consider not simply what we are fighting against but what we are willing to struggle and live *for* (personal communication, March 6, 2025). Indigenous communities have long remembered and dreamed of sovereignty. Black feminists remind us that those enslaved once dared to dream of freedom; as Nikki Giovanni (Wang, 2020) famously said, "If the enslaved could believe, I know I can." And Langston Hughes warned about what happens to a dream deferred. As night falls, what might we dream as we yearn toward a new day?

How might dignity, belonging, connection, culture, identity, and well-being be woven into the fabric of learning in schools for every child? How might formal educational systems situate themselves in a broader ecosystem of education to partner across organizational boundaries? How might we engender learning opportunities in a wide range of contexts for a wide range of learners? How can we create the organizational conditions for educators to truly see and humanize their students—and for decisions to be shaped by those closest to historical injustices? How can we foster intergenerational learning to remember ancestral knowledges and co-construct sustainable futures?

As we work through the night, take turns to rest, and plan for a new day ahead, our strategies may need to evolve or transform to address the ever-changing context. But we will not be waiting for the next heroic leader to save the day. As Grace Lee Boggs reminds us (Boggs & Kurashige, 2012), *we* are the leaders we've been waiting for as we continue to do the work of equity leadership.

REFERENCES

Boggs, G. L., & Kurashige, S. (2012). *The next American revolution: Sustainable activism for the twenty-first century*. University of California Press.

Collins, P. H. (2013). Truth-telling and intellectual activism. *Contexts, 12*(1), 36–41. https://doi.org/10.1177/1536504213476244 (Original work published 2013)

Rich, A. (2016). *What kind of times are these. Collected poems: 1950–2012*. W. W. Norton.

Wang, J. (2020) *For Nikki Giovanni, finding purpose means "you cannot let the world change you."* University of Chicago News. https://news.uchicago.edu/story/nikki-giovanni-finding-purpose-means-you-cannot-let-world-change-you

Afterword

Firesticks for Fretful Nights

Keisha Scarlett

Recently, I faced one of the darkest moments in my career: a very public, contentious departure from my position as superintendent of St. Louis Public Schools, a mere year after I moved halfway across the country to take the position. Everything I stand for—educational equity, the brilliance of Black and Brown children, and the moral responsibility of systems to serve, not extract—came under attack. Throughout the ordeal, I experienced what felt like never-ending fretful nights. But each new morning, I woke up to simple things—like text messages from an elder—that provided me with just enough light to rise and keep going. Messages like: Look, you *survived.*

Nearly 10 years before I faced those fretful nights, I was serving as the human resources director for Seattle Public Schools—a district that was home. By then, I had spent 17 years in Seattle as a teacher, school leader, principal coach, and district administrator. I was the 2014 Washington State Principal of the Year, deeply rooted in instructional leadership.

In 2017, the superintendent of Seattle Public Schools contacted me with a request: to lead the district's Department of Equity and Race Relations (DERR). My initial response was an emphatic "no," despite the pioneering stature of DERR within the state and across the nation. In 2012, the department developed one of the first board-approved racial equity policies in the country. While I had been vocal about equity and racial justice throughout my career, I was reluctant to take on the responsibility and emotional labor that accompanied the role. I worried about being pigeonholed as a Black woman leading "equity," reduced to a symbol rather than recognized for my full leadership capacity. But after seeking counsel and advice from people I trust, I decided to push through my hesitations and accept the position.

A few days before I started the role, I attended a training during which I shared that I believed I had been asked to lead DERR not only because of my organizational leadership experience but also—undeniably—because I am a Black woman. A facilitator, whom I had only known for a few days, responded: "Keisha, you were chosen because of your humanity. I have only spent a few days with you, and I can already see that people are drawn to your humanity. Use this strength to make the education system more humanizing for its most dehumanized and marginalized students. Use this strength to bring healing." I emerged from that experience galvanized. How do we use education to humanize and to heal? That burning question became the guiding force in the work that lay ahead.

For the next several years, from 2017 to 2023, I served Seattle students and families in a series of senior leadership roles, including chief of equity and later chief academic officer. I led through the murder of George Floyd, the COVID-19 pandemic, the height of the Black Lives Matter movement, and intensifying political unrest. I focused on the lived experiences and voices of students. I worked to create places where youth—especially those marginalized by institutional and structural racism—could experience boundless possibilities in their learning and development. And the burning question that once galvanized me never faded: *How do we use education to humanize and to heal?*

Strides toward equity and justice have always been met with resistance. But the scope and intensity of today's full-on assault are deeply disorienting. Elected officials, corporate, university, and school leaders have retreated into silence, whitewashing prior equity commitments to avoid the wrath of the current administration. Our work and contributions are being erased from public records, curricula, and libraries. The path ahead is uncertain.

Throughout my life, my elders—many of whom are now ancestors—imparted countless sayings that I consider codes to live by: a collective playbook for resilience, discernment, and resistance. Their words were firesticks—small, potent truths that lit my path in moments of uncertainty. Their folk sayings carried generations of wisdom, shaping how we endure, organize, and rise in the face of adversity. And I wonder: *What might our elders say about these times?* About the silencing of equity leaders? About the dismantling of hard-won progress? What would they whisper to those of us carrying the torch?

The elders might say, *"Ole fyah stick easy fi ketch"—Old fire sticks catch fire easily.*

The Jamaican proverb reminds us that the wisdom, passion, and insight passed down through generations can quickly reignite movements for justice. Elders are the original firesticks, holding stories, struggles, and strategies. When their flame meets the energy and vision of rising generations, it creates an unstoppable blaze of change.

The elders might say, *"The devil is in the darkness."*

Night—its low visibility and the uncertainty it breeds—has often been used as a tool of domination. It is deployed to intensify policing, withdraw resources, manufacture economic scarcity, incite fear, surveil, exclude, and fragment communities. It breeds confusion, disrupts collective focus, and leaves people unsure of where—or how—to direct their energies toward liberation. But in moments of darkness, we must not despair. We must reorient, recalibrate, reposition, and reconnect with our senses to illuminate new pathways.

My elders might remind us that *"trouble don't last always."*

Indigenous ancestors and communities have shown us survivance (Vizenor, 2008)—not only through enduring oppression but through the intentional assertion of cultural identity, dignity, and sovereignty. My ancestors, enslaved Africans, were the original Afrofuturists. Though stripped of their freedom and severed from their homeland, they dreamed of freedom even while enduring the horrors of chattel slavery. They reclaimed the night, asserting their humanity through undaunted imagination, creativity, and resistance. Night, once weaponized, became a fugitive space and a protective covering from which to assert strategy, resilience, solidarity, and, ultimately, liberation.

In July 2024, just a year after I stepped into the role of superintendent of St. Louis Public Schools, I was placed on administrative leave under the cloud of an "investigation." It was one of the darkest professional moments of my life. During my administrative leave, I decided I needed to get away from the stress. One weekend, I traveled to Detroit for Afro Nation music festival with my daughter and close friends. When I arrived at the festival, it dawned on me that Afro Nation was not an escape. It was a return. A gathering of firesticks—young and brilliant—who know that joy is not the absence of struggle but the light that keeps us from being consumed by it. My presence there, in all my vulnerability, was a protest. It was healing. A month later, I was terminated from the job I had spent my career working to achieve.

Recently, a white woman asked me how I'm coping with the attacks on equity, education, and democracy. I told her about my recent Friday night line-dancing class, full of mostly middle-aged Black women, moving freely, laughing loudly, celebrating ourselves unapologetically. We danced to "Boots on the Ground (Where Dem Fans At?)" by 803Fresh, clacking fans and jazz boxes in sync. When I got off step, I looked down at the feet of the dancer in front of me, caught the rhythm, and kept going. When I looked back up, I saw smiling faces. Across the country, while many live in fretful nights, Black folks gather in fugitive spaces—on dance floors, at rodeos, in living rooms—moving together in joyful resistance.

So, what must we do with joy? Protect it. Share it. Organize with it. Move with it—boots on the ground, fans in hand. We mustn't wait for the storm to pass. We must dance together in the dark of the storm. Hold each other in rhythm. Build liberatory futures in the dark. This, too, is part of the playbook left by my ancestors. Joy is not a distraction from the work—it is the work. I say to our children and to those doing the work of equity leadership what gospel singer Shirley Ceasar taught us: *This joy that I have, the world didn't give it to me . . . and the world can't take it away.*

REFERENCE

Vizenor, G. (Ed.). (2008). *Survivance: Narratives of native presence*. University of Nebraska Press.

Index

Note: Page numbers followed by italic letters indicate: *t* for tables, *f* for figures

About the Editors and Contributors

Decoteau J. Irby is a professor of educational policy studies at the University of Illinois Chicago (UIC), codirector of UIC's Center for Urban Education Leadership, founding director of Brothers Teaching Initiative, and a member of Derute Consulting Cooperative. His research explores how leadership improves Black students' educational experiences and life outcomes. He is author of *Stuck Improving: Racial Equity and School Leadership* (2021) and a co-editor of *Dignity-Affirming Education: Cultivating the Somebodiness of Students and Educators* (2022) published by Teachers College Press. He holds a PhD in urban education from Temple University.

Ann M. Ishimaru seeks to foster joyful learning in educationally just schools and communities. She is a writer, researcher, and Killinger Endowed Chair and Professor of Educational Foundations, Leadership and Policy at the University of Washington College of Education, where she also directs the Just Educational Leadership Institute and is the faculty research director of the Leadership for Learning EdD program. She is the author of *Just Schools: Building Equitable Collaborations with Families and Communities* (2020) published by Teachers College Press. She holds an EdD from Harvard Graduate School of Education.

Shannon Paige Clark is an assistant professor of organizational studies at University of Maryland Eastern Shore. Shannon prioritizes research that is humanizing, participatory, and grounded in the premise that lived experiences are invaluable. She was an elementary school teacher who has been working in and with schools for over a decade, and she enjoys interacting with students and families. She holds a PhD from University of Illinois Chicago.

Constance Daw is a mother, daughter, sister, wife, Black Lady Principal, storyteller, musician, artist, and friend living free on the ancestral lands of the Puyallup Tribe of Indians. She is the principal of Grant Center for the Expressive Arts, an elementary school in Tacoma Public Schools, and a graduate of the Leadership for Learning EdD Program at the University of Washington Seattle.

Terrance L. Green is an educator, father, partner/husband, brother, son, the creator of the *Racially Just Schools* podcast, and an associate professor at the University of Texas at Austin (UT-Austin) in the College of Education. A former high school science teacher, his research focuses on antiracist and justice-centered systems leadership. Terrance has a PhD in educational leadership and policy analysis from the University of Wisconsin–Madison.

Ahreum Han is a postdoctoral research scholar at Rossier School of Education of the University of Southern California. Her primary research interests lie in mathematics teacher education to enhance students' mathematics learning experience through high-quality and equitable mathematics instruction. She holds a PhD in curriculum and instructions from the University of Illinois Chicago.

Teresa A. Lance currently serves as superintendent in a suburban school district outside Chicago, Illinois. Dr. Lance's leadership and research focus on how to integrate diversity, equity, and inclusion programs into educational organizations. She earned her EdD in educational leadership from the University of Phoenix, Arizona.

Fannie Martínez is a PhD candidate in educational policy, organizations, and leadership at the University of Washington Seattle. Her work examines how Latiné student perceptions and experiences of wellness influence wellness policies, curriculum, and practices in formal and informal educational spaces.

Andrew Matschiner is an assistant professor in the Attallah College of Educational Studies at Chapman University. His research examines how school districts as organizations attempt to address systemic racial inequality through activities such as professional development and new infrastructure like district equity directors and departments. A former high school teacher and instructional coach, he earned his PhD in education from the University of California San Diego.

Ishmael Miller is an assistant professor in the Division of Educational Leadership and Innovation at Arizona State University, Mary Lou Fulton Teachers College. Dr. Miller's research examines the intersection of educational leadership, anti-Blackness, and racial equity. He holds a PhD in educational policy, organizations, and leadership from the University of Washington Seattle.

Dayna Muñiz is the associate director of the Education Partnership at the University of Pennsylvania's Graduate School of Education. Her research interests center on equity-focused school leadership, the superintendency, organizational change, the experiences of minoritized educational leaders, and understanding schools as racialized organizations. She holds a PhD in educational leadership from Temple University.

Latish Reed is an author, educator, leadership consultant, and owner of Reed Consulting, LLC. Her book *Navigating the Complexities of Equity* helps leaders navigate organizational challenges and barriers to improved outcomes for marginalized populations. She has worked as a teacher, building- and district-level leader, and faculty member in principal preparation. She holds a PhD in educational leadership from the University of Wisconsin–Madison.

Keisha Scarlett is the founder and CEO of WOVΞN, LLC, an organization that empowers systems leaders through capacity-building, professional development, leadership coaching, and strategic support. Before founding WOVΞN, LLC, Dr. Scarlett spent 24 years in Seattle Public Schools as a middle school teacher, principal, chief equity officer, and chief academic officer, among other roles. She was most recently superintendent of St. Louis Public Schools. She earned her EdD in educational leadership and policy studies from the University of Washington.

Maurice Swinney is the chief innovation officer at Chicago Beyond. A nationally recognized equity leader in education, Dr. Swinney previously served as a Chicago Public Schools principal and first-ever chief equity officer before serving as interim chief education officer. He has been a classroom teacher and assistant principal. He holds an EdD in public school administration.